Mountain Biking Virginia

An Atlas of Virginia's Greatest Off-Road Bicycle Rides

Martín Fernández

FALCONGUIDES

GUILFORD, CONNECTICUT

An imprint of Globe Pequot
Falcon and FalconGuides are registered trademarks and Make Adventure Your Story is a trademark of
Rowman & Littlefield.

Distributed by NATIONAL BOOK NETWORK

Copyright © 2017 by Rowman & Littlefield

Photos by Martín Fernández unless otherwise noted.

Maps by Alena Pearce © Rowman & Littlefield

British Library Cataloguing in Publication Information Available

Library of Congress Cataloging-in-Publication data is available on file.

ISBN 978-1-4930-2549-7 (paperback)
ISBN 978-1-4930-2550-3 (electronic)

Printed in the United States of America

∞™ The paper used in this publication meets the minimum requirements of American National Standard
for Information Sciences—Permanence of Paper for Printed Library Materials, ANSI/NISO Z39.48-1992.

Contents

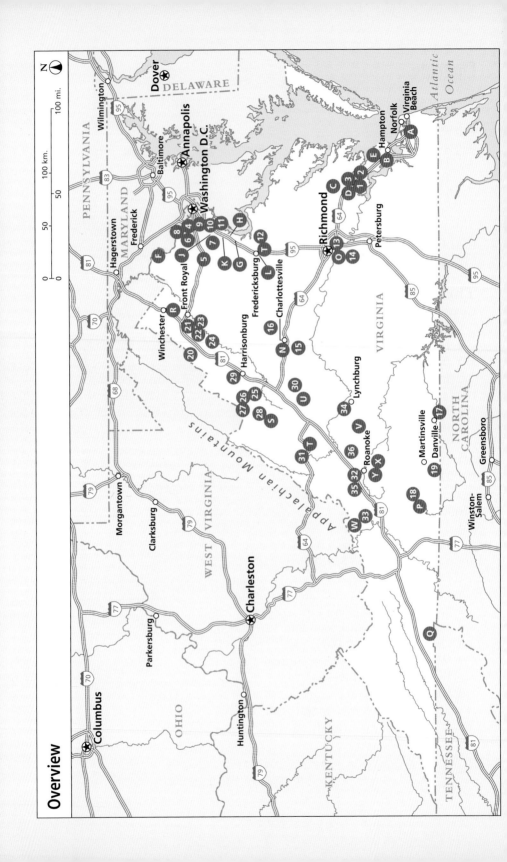

Overview

Acknowledgments

Without my wife, Courtney, this book would not be possible. Her encouragement and support has helped me every step of the way. To my parents, for all the love and support they have given me throughout the years. To my brother and sisters. To Ari, and all the rides ahead of us.

A special thanks to MORE, rvaMORE, FATMUG, FAMBE, EVMA, CAMBC, CAMBO, GLOC, SVBC, Roanoke IMBA, and all of the regional mountain bike groups, their volunteers, and individuals whose efforts ensure that we have places like these to enjoy our sport. JOIN them!

Special thanks to all the people who took some time from their busy schedules to show me their favorite rides—Evelyn Cooper and Mandy LaClair for their patience while I tagged along at Freedom Park and York River State Park. Greg Rollins and the crew at rvaMORE for hosting me and making me feel like one of their own. Thanks to Kristine McCormick and Carter Shumaker in Roanoke, Kelly Hazlegrove and Tim Miles in Lynchburg, Daniel Sheets in Danville, Bob Norris in Mountain Laurel, and Eric O'Connel in Woolwine.

A HUGE thanks to my good friend Mark Humbertson who not only shared his invaluable knowledge of the George Washington and Jefferson National Forests with me, but also kept me company along many of the miles that have been documented in this guide. His hospitality, patience, help, and willingness to share what he knows with me were critical in getting this book done; for that I will always be grateful.

And finally to you, the reader, for taking the plunge and getting this trail guide.

See you on the trail!
—Martín Fernández

Foreword

I appreciate the opportunity to encourage your readers to join a local organization such as The Mid Atlantic Off-Road Enthusiasts (MORE), The Fredericksburg Area Mountain Bike Enthusiasts (FAMBE), Richmond Virginia Mid Atlantic Off-Road Enthusiasts (rvaMORE), or any of the mountain biking groups listed in this guide. Joining them will help these organizations continue working to assure we are all able to ride our bikes on regional trails.

I would also encourage readers to work with other organizations such as hikers, runners, equestrians, and "friends of" to help establish and maintain positive and constructive relationships. We all value and respect public lands and their availability for recreation.

It is our responsibility to be good stewards of our natural resources and ensure recreational access for future generations.

Please consider how you can give back.

—Ernest "Ernie" Rodriguez, MORE President

Introduction

You'll find that this guide contains just about everything you'll ever need to choose, plan for, enjoy, and survive a ride in Virginia. Stuffed with useful Old Dominion-specific information, this book features thirty-eight mapped and cued rides and twenty-six honorable mentions, directions to regional lift-assisted mountain bike destinations, and advice on everything from getting into shape to mountain bike camping and getting the most out of cycling with your kids.

I've designed this FalconGuide to be highly visual—for quick reference and ease of use. This means that the most pertinent information rises quickly to the top, so you don't have to waste time poring through bulky ride descriptions to get mileage cues or elevation stats. They're highlighted for you. Yet a FalconGuide doesn't read like a laundry list. Take the time to dive into a ride description and you'll soon realize that this guide is not just a good source of information; it's a good read. In the end, you get the best of both worlds: a quick reference guide and an engaging look at a region.

How to Use This Guide

I've divided *Mountain Biking Virginia* into five sections, each representing one of the five major geographic regions of the Old Dominion. Within each section are the featured rides found in the region. Each ride is then subsequently divided into a variety of components.

The **Ride Specs** are fairly self-explanatory. Here you'll find the quick, nitty-gritty details of the ride: where the trailhead is located, the nearest town, ride length, approximate riding time, difficulty rating, type of trail terrain, elevation gain, and what other trail users you may encounter.

The **Getting There** section gives you dependable directions from a nearby city, right down to where you'll want to park.

The **Ride Description** is the meat of the chapter. Detailed and honest, it's my carefully researched impression of the trail(s). While it's impossible to cover everything, you can rest assured that I won't miss what's important.

In **Miles and Directions**, I provide mileage cues to identify all turns and trail name changes, as well as points of interest. Between this and the route map, you simply can't get lost. Where possible, I try to tell you how you can combine multiple rides to build your own "epic" outing.

Ride Information contains more useful information, including trail hotlines (for updates on trail conditions), park schedules and fees, and GPS coordinates to the ride's starting point. I'll also tell you where to eat after your ride, and what else to see while you're in the area.

The **Honorable Mentions** section details additional rides in each region that will inspire you to get out and explore on your own.

The State of Virginia has myriad places for mountain bikers to enjoy this sport. I've tried to select what I think are the most accessible and best destinations where you can put knobby tires to dirt. When I set out to write this book I found that I could probably write three volumes with the number of trails currently available in the region. I had to make some tough decisions as to what to exclude; where possible, I've added most destinations as honorable mentions. We're lucky that this region is a virtual mecca for mountain biking, coupled with the riding trails available in Maryland, bordering Pennsylvania and West Virginia; you could spend several years and not ride all of what is available. The George Washington National Forest alone would need a guidebook of its own to cover what is available within its borders. I've tried to select what I think are the best rides in the state, both from years of riding experience and from the advice of riders who call this area home. I've also included a feature that I originated in one of my other guides, *Best Bike Rides Washington, DC*, "You May Run Into" sidebars. I feel it is important to recognize many of the individuals who have tirelessly worked over the years to ensure we have these places to ride. Finally, I've built and continue to update a detailed website, www.mtbdc.com, to provide you with additional information, including changes to any of the routes in my books, and maps and details to other rides not included or detailed in this guide. Check the website regularly for updates as I'm out riding regularly and always document where I go to share with my friends and readers.

Regional Location Map

This map helps you find your way to the start of each ride from the nearest sizable town or city. Coupled with the detailed directions at the beginning of the cue, this map should visually lead you to where you need to be for each ride.

Profile Map

This helpful profile gives you a cross-sectional look at the ride's ups and downs. The elevation is labeled on the left, and the mileage is indicated on the top. Road and trail names are shown along the route, with towns and points of interest labeled in bold.

Route Map

This is your primary guide to each ride. It shows all the accessible roads and trails, points of interest, water, towns, landmarks, and geographical features. It also distinguishes trails from roads and paved roads from unpaved roads. The selected route is highlighted, and directional arrows point the way. Shaded topographic relief in the background gives you an accurate representation of the terrain and landscape in the ride area.

The Maps

I don't want anyone, by any means, to feel restricted to just the roads and trails that are mapped here. I hope you will have an adventurous spirit and use this guide as a platform to dive into Virginia's backcountry and discover new routes on your own. One of the simplest ways to begin this is to just turn the map upside down and ride the course in reverse (where allowed). The change in perspective is fantastic and the ride should feel quite different. With this in mind, it will be like getting two distinctly different rides on each map.

For your own purposes, you may wish to copy the directions for the course onto a small sheet to help you while riding, or photocopy the map and cue sheet to take with you. These pages can be folded into a bike bag, stuffed into a jersey pocket, or used with a map holder (Google: "BarMap of the Gods"). You can also take a snapshot of the book pages on your smart phone for quick and easy access. Just remember to slow or even stop when you want to read the map. I've also made most of the rides' GPS tracks available on my website, www.mtbdc.com, where you can download them to your preferred navigation device and follow turn-by-turn directions (where available).

Ride Finder

Best Rides for Sightseeing
1. Freedom Park
8. Great Falls National Park
12. James River Park System
22. Shenandoah River State Park
23. Kennedy Peak
29. Torry Ridge/Big Levels—Sherando Lake
30. Douthat State Park

Best Rides for Seeing Historic Landmarks
12. James River Park System
22. Shenandoah River State Park
23. Kennedy Peak
29. Torry Ridge/Big Levels—Sherando Lake
30. Douthat State Park

Best Rides for Kids and Families
5. Conway Robinson
6. Lake Fairfax
9. Wakefield Park
10. Laurel Hill
11. Meadowood
13. Pocahontas State Park—Morgan and Swift Creek Trails
15. Preddy Creek
18. Mountain Laurel Trails
22. Shenandoah River State Park (River Trails)
28. Rocktown Trails at Hillandale

Best Rides for Camping
13. Pocahontas State Park
22. Shenandoah River State Park
24. Lookout Mountain
25. Dowells Draft/Magic Moss
26. Narrowback Mountain
27. Reddish Knob
29. Torry Ridge/Big Levels—Sherando Lake
30. Douthat State Park

Best Rides with Technical Singletrack

7. Fountainhead Regional Park
19. Mill Mountain
20. Elizabeth Furnace
21. Mine Mountain
23. Kennedy Peak
24. Lookout Mountain
25. Dowells Draft/Magic Moss
26. Narrowback Mountain
27. Reddish Knob
29. Torry Ridge/Big Levels—Sherando Lake
30. Douthat State Park
31. Carvins Cove
32. Pandapas Pond (Poverty Creek, Brush Mountain)
34. Dragon's Back
35. Spec Mines/Dody Ridge

Best Rides with Flowy Singletrack

1. Freedom Park
3. York River State Park
7. Fountainhead Regional Park
11. Meadowood
13. Pocahontas State Park (Morgan and Swift Creek)
17. IC DeHart
18. Mountain Laurel Trails
25. Dowells Draft/Magic Moss
26. Narrowback Mountain (Tillman Trail)
27. Reddish Knob (Wolf Ridge Trail)
30. Douthat State Park
31. Carvins Cove
35. Spec Mines/Dody Ridge (Speck Mines)

Map Legend

81	Interstate Highway	1	Alternate Trailhead
50	US Highway		Bench
7	State Highway		Bridge
7	Featured State/Local Road		Building/Point of Interest
606	County/Forest Road	▲	Campground
	Local Road	○	City/Town
	Featured Bike Route	—	Dam
	Bike Route		Lodging
	Trail		Marina
	Featured Trail	17.1	Mileage Marker
	Railroad		Park Office
	State Line	P	Parking
	Small River or Creek	▲	Peak
	Body of Water		Picnic Area
	National Forest/Park/Wilderness		Restroom
	State Park/Forest		Scenic View/Viewpoint
		▲	Small Park
		1	Trailhead
		❓	Visitor/Information Center
			Waterfall

Coastal Virginia

Framed to the east by the Atlantic Ocean and Chesapeake Bay and the I-95 corridor and fall line to the west, Virginia's coastal region conjures images of our nation's and state's early history. In mid-May 1607, just a little over one hundred settlers landed on a site they named James City and established what would become the first permanent English settlement in North America, Jamestown. What would befall these brave colonists were several arduous years in which they suffered many maladies, including famine, attacks, and sieges by the local Indians and disease.

Among those first settlers was Captain John Smith, the fabled explorer who ventured into the Virginia wilderness and befriended Pocahontas, the eldest daughter of chief Powhatan. Their first meeting became legendary and has been often romanticized in many stories. Smith's and the colonist's relations with the local Indians were friendly but, by 1609, had turned sour. This ultimately led to the siege of Jamestown, where the settlers faced starvation that ultimately resulted in survival cannibalism.

By mid-1610, Jamestown was all but abandoned, but a resupply helped reestablish the Fort at Jamestown and revived the encampment. Today, all that remains are the ruins of the small settlement, but the region remains rich in its history. Colonial Williamsburg, along with Jamestown and Yorktown, celebrate the colonial days and our nation's early history with vivid re-creations of the past.

While the landscape lacks drastic elevation changes, Coastal Virginia riders have created several worthy mountain biking destinations. The Eastern Virginia Mountain Bike Association (EVMA) has spearheaded a stewardship effort that has resulted in the creation of multi-purpose trails that are bound to satisfy the most demanding riders. Where elevation is lacking, EVMA has provided riders with Technical Trail Features (TTFs) to spice up their rides. Beware though, several of the TTFs along the trails we'll visit are not for the faint of heart—or skill deprived. Elevated boardwalks, narrow skinnies, steep drops, and gap jumps abound in at least one of the detailed rides.

Although elevation is minimal, you will still climb. Several of the trails in the area make excellent use of the rolling terrain and provide riders with punchy ups and downs that will have your heart racing.

I've elected to document three of the most popular destinations in Coastal Virginia: Freedom Park, York River State Park, and New Quarter Park. Each will offer you a slightly different taste of what riding in this region is all about, and each will showcase the efforts placed by the volunteers of EVMA (evma.org) to provide local and visiting riders with a great mountain biking experience.

1 Freedom Park–The Alphabet Loop

With over 20 miles of singletrack trails for every level of rider, Freedom Park has become a favorite destination for riders from all over the eastern, central, and northern Virginia regions. The trail boasts five (A, B, C, D, and E) clearly marked loops and one easy to follow bunny trail for riders being introduced to the sport. Loop C is a destination trail for many daredevil riders in the region, since it boasts a myriad of TTFs to satisfy the most venturesome riders. Originally built in 2008 by EVMA, loop C has become a premier free ride destination.

Every TTF along the route varies considerably in difficulty, though each has an optional ride around. You can easily bypass all TTFs and still enjoy a challenging cross-country ride through this section of the park. However, if you do choose to challenge yourself on any of the TTFs, you should first check out all the angles before attempting to clear it.

Start: Start from the small parking lot adjacent to the Free Black Settlement Camp, the trailhead is clearly marked.
Length: 20.1 miles
Ride time: 3-4 hours
Difficulty: Novice to expert. Trails include sections of flat and twisty singletrack throughout all loops. Loop C contains some expert TTFs not suitable for beginners or intermediate riders. All TTFs have optional ride arounds.
Trail surface: Twisty singletrack; one section of paved path.

Lay of the land: Rolling wooded singletrack trails through old and new grown forests
Land status: Public
Nearest town: Williamsburg
Other trail users: Hikers
Trail contacts: Eastern Virginia Mountain Bike Association (EVMA), www.evma.org; James County Parks (757) 259-4022
Schedule: Daily 7:00 a.m. to dusk; trails closed due to wet conditions
Fees: Free to public; register at visitor center
Restrooms: Available in the visitor center

Getting there: From I-64, take exit 234 for VA 199 East. Continue for approximately 5 miles and turn right on Longhill Road, VA 612. Continue straight until you reach the entrance to Freedom Park, Hot Water Trail. Once in Freedom Park, continue following Hot Water Trail past the Williamsburg Botanical Gardens to the small parking area adjacent to the Free Black Settlement Camp. The trailhead is clearly marked. **GPS coordinates:** 37.31798, -76.79996.

The Ride

The Freedom Park trails are a result of a successful collaboration between EVMA and James City County.

Freedom Park is located in an area rich with history, and the grounds of this County Park are no different. Our ride starts close to the home of one of the nation's earliest Free Black Settlements. Dating back to the early to mid-1800s, three of the

Punchy climbs and descents are in abundance at Freedom Park.

settlement's cabins have been historically recreated to depict life during that period. The camp's buildings have been restored and furnished with items appropriate to the time, when this was a thriving community.

The park was also the site of the Revolutionary Battle of Spencer's Ordinary [Tavern], which took place on June 26, 1781. After learning that a detachment of Queen's Rangers were on the way to destroy supplies and boats along the Chickahominy River, local Militia leader Marquis de Lafayette ordered his troops to intercept the Rangers as they returned to Williamsburg. After an all-night march, the patriot militia made contact with the Rangers near the intersections of the Jamestown and Williamsburg Road, and fended off the attackers; subsequent skirmishes ensued, leading to twenty casualties from both sides, as well as several wounded and captured troops.

Our ride takes place within the Park's 600 acres and samples virtually all of the trails available for mountain biking in this eastern Virginia destination. The ride will start along trail A, the original and first mountain bike trail in the park. Originally

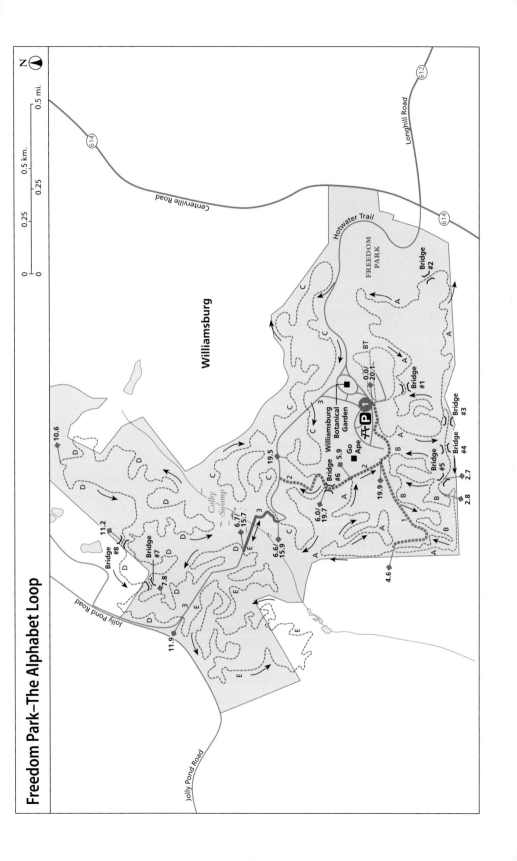

Freedom Park–The Alphabet Loop

built in 2002, the trail's 5 miles of intermediate hard packed and fast singletrack are perfect for introducing advanced beginners to the joys of singletrack riding. The trail has plenty of punchy climbs and descents that showcase many of the park's natural features, including several ravines. EVMA has done a great job of routing the trail to take advantage of the parks contours, and even though there is an absence of high elevation, the trail is challenging and fun. Since it was built in 2002, the trail has evolved and been rerouted several times to make it more sustainable; the result being a fast and fluid trail that is simply a joy to ride.

Loops B, C, D, and E are vastly similar to loop A, but each offers distinct challenges that will keep all riders satisfied. Loop C has had over a dozen TTFs added over the years to challenge advanced riders. The TTFs vary in difficulty, yet all offer ride arounds for riders not comfortable with man-made obstacles.

Miles and Directions

Start from the small parking area adjacent to the Free Black Settlement Camp and the Bunny Trail. We will begin measuring at the steel pylons and mailbox with trail maps at the entrance of Multi-use Trail 1. All of the Mountain Bike trails in Freedom Park are directional. Ride confidently knowing no one will be coming in the opposite direction. The trails are also clearly marked, so they are very easy to follow. Grab a map from the main Freedom Park Visitor Center.

0.0 Enter Multi-use Trail #1 and make an immediate left onto Loop A.

2.7 Stay to the left after the bridge, still on Loop A.

2.8 Continue on the B loop, the A loop continues to the left.

4.6 You reach the Multi-use Trail #1. Continue straight to finish out Loop B and then make a slight right to hop back onto Loop A. A right turn on Multi-use Trail #1 will take you back to the starting point.

5.9 You reach the end of Loop A and Multi-use Trail #2. Turn left. A right turn will take you back toward Multi-use Trail #1 and the starting point of the ride.

6.0 After a short downhill and bridge, make a sharp left onto Loop C.

6.6 Turn left onto the paved path (Multi-use Trail #3). Trail C continues straight across, we will come back and finish the ride along the other side of C, but not before we get some vitamin D and E.

6.7 Make a sharp right and enter Loop D. We will now ride the entire length of D, 5 miles. Multi-use Trail #3 continues on to Jolly Pond Road an alternate entrance point to Freedom Park.

7.8 You transition into a beautiful Pine Forest, one of my favorite parts of this ride.

10.6 As the trail curves to the left, you'll notice a blocked/seldom-used trail. This is an alternate access point from Lois Hornsby Middle School (Jolly Pond Road).

11.2 Continue following Trail D to the right. The visible trail to the left is actually a portion of Trail D we have just ridden.

11.9 Cross Multi-use Trail #3 and enter Loop E. A left turn along Multi-use Trail #3 will take you back toward the point where we entered Loop D. A right turn will take you to Jolly Pond Road.

15.7 Back on Multi-use Trail #3; the entrance to trail D is right across the paved path. Turn right to head back to Loop C.

15.9 Turn left onto Loop C.

16.1 You reach the first TTF; every TTF along C has an alternate easy line. We will continue following the alternate route, but feel free to hang out and sessions each obstacle. It's worth noting that you should ride within your ability, some of the Loop C TTFs are dangerous and could have dire consequences.

19.5 Stay left after the second teeter to remain on Loop C.

19.6 You reach the end of Loop C. Turn left onto the doubletrack, Multi-use trail #2.

19.7 Pass the entrance to Loop C on the right and head over the bridge back toward the starting point.

19.9 Continue following the doubletrack to the right around the playground, you are now on Multi-use Trail #1.

20.1 Pass the entrance to loop A, where we started the ride, to finish the loop.

20.1 The loop is complete.

Ride Information

Local Information

Visit the Williamsburg website for more information about local events and attractions—www.visitwilliamsburg.com

Bike Shops

Red Barn Bikes, Barhamsville, VA: www.redbarnbikes.com
Bikes Unlimited, Williamsburg, VA: www.bikewilliamsburg.com
Village Bicycles, Newport News, VA: villagebicyclesnewportnews.com

Local Events and Attractions

Go Ape Zip Line and Tree Top Adventure—goape.com
Busch Gardens Williamsburg—seaworldparks.com/en/buschgardens-williamsburg
Colonial Williamsburg—www.colonialwilliamsburg.com
Jamestown—www.visitwilliamsburg.com/topic/jamestown

Where to Eat

Pierce's Pitt Bar-B-Que—www.pierces.com
Two Drummers Smokehouse—www.twodrummerssmokehouse.com

Accommodations

There are myriad places to stay in the Williamsburg area. Camping is available at the Williamsburg KOA: www.williamsburgkoa.com

2 New Quarter Park–Redoubt Mountain Bike Trail

New Quarter Park in historic Williamsburg, VA, meanders through mature forests and offers intermediate riders a fun and challenging loop approximately 7.2 miles long. Meant to be ridden in a counterclockwise direction, the New Quarter Park trails take full advantage of the lay of the land. As you head out from the parking lot, the trail will follow the terrain's contours as it parallels a ravine and small creek that feeds into Queen Creek. The first half of the trail has several climbs that will keep your heart rate pounding. Several small TTFs, with alternate ride arounds, have been strategically placed to keep the ride interesting. The return leg toward the parking area parallels Lakeshead Drive, the park's entrance road, and offers less elevation change but remains fun and challenging nonetheless, as you head back to the car.

Start: Start from the clearly marked trailhead at the far lot of New Quarter Park.
Length: 7.1 miles
Ride time: 45 minutes–1 hour
Difficulty: Novice to intermediate. The trails are easy to follow; a few "punchy" climbs will test new riders.
Trail surface: Twisty hard packed singletrack with a few TTFs.
Lay of the land: Rolling wooded singletrack trails with ravine views.
Land status: Public

Nearest town: Williamsburg
Other trail users: Hikers
Trail contacts: Eastern Virginia Mountain Bike Association, www.evma.org
Schedule: May through Oct, daily 8 a.m. to dusk; Nov through Apr, Fri 10 a.m. to dusk, Sat, Sun 8 a.m. to dusk.
Fees: Free to public
Restrooms: Available adjacent to the parking area.

Getting there: From I-64, take exit 238 to VA 143. Continue on VA 143 for approximately 1 mile and turn left onto Parkway Drive. From Parkway Drive, exit onto Colonial Parkway. Take the second right to Hubbard Lane and then make an immediate right on Lakeshead Drive. Follow Lakeshead into New Quarter Park until you reach the parking area at the far end.
GPS coordinates: 37.293720, –76.645699.

The Ride

At 7.2 miles, the loop at New Quarter Park is perfect for intermediate riders and beginner riders looking to progress in their mountain biking skills.

Until recently, the trail had a series of elevated TTFs near its starting point, but safety concerns forced members of EVMA to remove them. Despite the lack of TTFs, the trails at New Quarter Park remain fun and challenging.

Like many of the sites in this region of Virginia, New Quarter Park is also rich in history. The parkland was originally surveyed shortly after it was acquired in the late 1970s. The survey yielded a list of more than 30 historic sites dating from prehistoric times to the Civil War. But it wasn't until around 2005, shortly after the land was converted into a County Park, that interest peaked throughout the surrounding community to rediscover what had once been on the grounds of the park's nearly 600 acres. With the help of the Virginia Department of Historic Resources, the Fairfield Foundation, the Tidewater Virginia Historical Society, and the Archaeological Society of Virginia, local residents have worked to conduct regular community digs to explore the area's past. Archaeologists selected an area high in the park that had great views toward the York River, reasoning that such a location would have been an ideal area for a settlement or home. The ensuing digs uncovered a myriad of valuable information and led to even more interest in the history of the area.

Among the finds were objects from Williamsburg's seventeenth century past. Today, community and public digs continue to be part of the regularly scheduled activities at New Quarter Park. The Fairfield Foundation continues to lead the archeological effort in the Park and is working to craft a model that other communities can use for public archaeology events.

In addition to the mountain bike trail, the park has ten picnic shelters, several hiking trails with scenic overlooks, a paved cycling trail suitable for family biking (children), an eighteen-hole disc-golf course, basketball and sand volleyball courts, a softball field, horseshoe pits, a large playground, and access to the waterways for canoes, kayaks, and fishing.

Miles and Directions

As you drive into the park, you'll notice several emergency access points along the tree line to the left—that is where you will be riding. Start from the parking lot at

The Redoubt Run Trail at New Quarter Park is clearly marked and easy to follow.

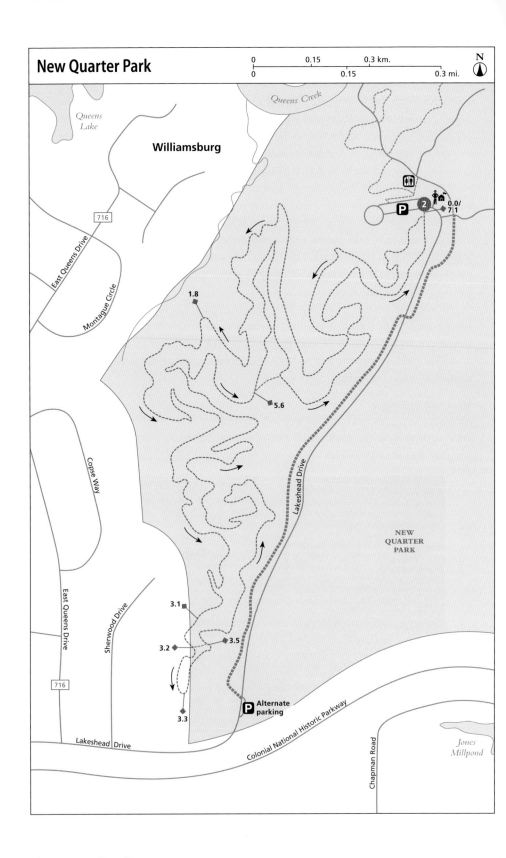

New Quarter Park

0   0.15   0.3 km.
0   0.15   0.3 mi.

N

Queens Creek

Queens Lake

Williamsburg

716

East Queens Drive

Montague Circle

P   2   0.0/7.1

1.8

5.6

Copse Way

Lakeshead Drive

NEW QUARTER PARK

East Queens Drive

Sherwood Drive

3.1

3.2   3.5

716

3.3

P   Alternate parking

Lakeshead Drive

Colonial National Historic Parkway

Chapman Road

Jones Millpond

the far end of the park. The trail entrance is clearly marked with a blue sign labeled Redoubt Mountain Bike Trail. The Mountain bike trail is directional and follows a counterclockwise direction. We'll begin marking right where the dirt meets the pavement. The trail is actually very easy to follow and clearly marked.

0.0 Head into the trail and follow it as it curves to the right and then to the left.

1.8 The trail will split here. There is a sign labeled TTF Option pointing to the left. This is the first of several similar forks you'll come across on the trail. Either fork will take you to the same spot, the TTF option simply offers an alternate, more difficult route, in this case a ramped log-over.

3.1 This fork in the trail is not signed, but just offers you with two alternate lines to tackle the short climb ahead. The left line is a little steeper, while the right lane is more gradual.

3.2 There is a short connector trail to the left that will allow you to connect to the return portion of the trail. Continue straight.

3.3 The trail will sweep to the left. At this point, you are heading back toward the starting point. You'll also begin noticing trails to the right; those are the emergency access points you noticed as you drove into the park.

3.5 The short connector trail mentioned at 3.2 will be to your left. Continue straight.

5.6 You reach a fork in the trail. Short loop to the right, long loop to the left. The long loop is a little over half a mile longer. We'll go left.

7.1 You're back at the starting point (6.6 if you chose the short loop).

Ride Information

Local Information

Visit Williamsburg has lots of information about local events and attractions—www.visitwilliamsburg.com

Bike Shops

Red Barn Bikes, Barhamsville, VA: www.redbarnbikes.com
Bikes Unlimited, Williamsburg, VA: www.bikewilliamsburg.com
Village Bicycles, Newport News, VA: villagebicyclesnewportnews.com

Local Events and Attractions

Go Ape Zip Line and Tree Top Adventure—goape.com
Busch Gardens Williamsburg—seaworldparks.com/en/buschgardens-williamsburg
Colonial Williamsburg—www.colonialwilliamsburg.com
Jamestown—www.visitwilliamsburg.com/topic/jamestown

Where to Eat

Pierce's Pitt Bar-B-Que—www.pierces.com
Two Drummers Smokehouse—www.twodrummerssmokehouse.com/

Accommodations

There are myriad places to stay in the Williamsburg area. Camping is available at the Williamsburg KOA: www.williamsburgkoa.com

3 York River State Park

York River State Park, just west of Williamsburg, is located on a fertile coastal plain and offers beginner to advanced cyclists over 20 miles of challenging singletrack trails. The trails are divided into two distinct loops, the Marl Ravine Trail (approximately 7 miles), and the newer John Blair trails (approximately 15 miles). Each loop can be ridden independently or combined to craft a much longer loop. The Marl Ravine Trail is the more challenging of the two loops, while the John Blair Trail is more "flowy" and offers riders multiple bailout points.

Start: Start from the first parking lot to the right immediately after the Contact Station. The doubletrack will be adjacent to the Contact Station.

Length: Up to 21.9 miles

Ride time: Depends on route chosen, up to 4 hours depending on ability

Difficulty: Novice to expert. The trails along the Marl Ravine offer more elevation and technical features than the trails along the John Blair Network. The John Blair trails can be split into "chunks" to allow beginner riders to ride as little or as much as they want.

Trail surface: Twisty singletrack with a few TTFs.

Lay of the land: Rolling Coastal Plain singletrack trails with a mixture of clay, sand, and limestone.

Land status: State Park, public.

Nearest town: Williamsburg

Other trail users: Hikers, equestrians

Trail contacts: EVMA, www.evma.org; York River State Park, www.dcr.virginia.gov/state-parks/york-river

Schedule: 8 a.m.–dusk.

Fees: VA State Park fees apply (depending on season and State License plates)

Restrooms: Available in the parking area and in the visitor center.

Getting there: From I-64, take the Croaker Exit 231B. Go north on Rte. 607 (Croaker Road) for 1 mile, then right on Rte. 606 (Riverview Road) about one and a half miles to the park entrance. Take a left turn into the park. **GPS coordinates:** 37.41293, -76.71375.

The Ride

York River State Park and the general Williamsburg area don't conjure images of mountain biking, but the members of EVMA have taken advantage of the coastal plains along the York River to craft two challenging and highly enjoyable loops that mountain bikers of all abilities can enjoy.

The park, named after the river it borders, was opened to the public in 1980 and includes historic Croaker Landing, an archaeological site listed in the National Register of Historic Places. During the seventeenth and eighteenth centuries, the area the park occupies was known as the Taskinas Creek Plantation and was the site of a public tobacco warehouse that local planters used to store their crops before they were shipped across the Atlantic to England.

Expertly built bridges allow for a smooth ride at York River State Park.

The Marl Ravine Trail is the "original" MTB loop in York River State Park. The trail was completed in the early 90s; built in cooperation between EVMA and the York River State Park. It is a directional (counterclockwise) mountain bike only trail. You can ride the trail confidently knowing that no other rider or trail user will greet you in the opposite direction.

The John Blair trail, named after one of the original signers of the Constitution and Williamsburg resident that once owned the Taskinas Creek Plantation, was officially opened to the public with great fanfare on June 7, 2014. The trail was initially flagged by then EVMA president Kirk Moore and built by volunteers from EVMA over the course of a little over two years. The trail is meant to flow through the coastal plain topography allowing beginner riders to focus on their skills, offering them several bailout points to make their rides as short or as long as desired. More advanced riders will love these trails because they have great "flow" and can be connected together to increase your ride's length.

Miles and Directions

Park in the lot to the right immediately after the Contact Station, we will start our ride from the gravel path that begins behind the Contact Station and parallels the road for a short period of time.

I've split York River State Park into two rides that can be very easily combined into one longer (20+ mile) loop. I do recommend that if you do decide to do both, that you do ride the Marl Ravine Trail first. Marl Ravine has fewer "exit" points, and since it is directional, bailing out is a little more difficult. The John Blair loop presents several opportunities to cut the ride short and make it back to the parking lot.

Both trails are incredibly easy to follow and are well marked with the familiar VA state parks trail posts.

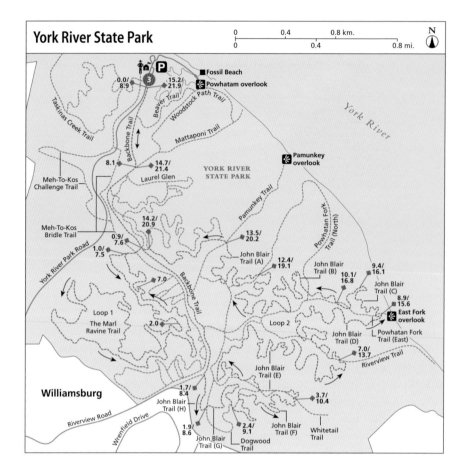

Loop 1—The Marl Ravine Trail

0.0 Start from behind the Contact Station where the gravel meets the pavement. Head down the gravel path; this is the Backbone Trail.

0.9 Turn right to access the Marl Ravine Trail; you'll cross over the equestrian Meh Te Kos Bridle Trail.

1.0 You reach the entrance to the Marl Ravine Trail. This is a directional loop. The exit to the trail is to the left where we will eventually come out.

2.0 After a short steep switchback climb, you'll reach an intersection marked Blue Jay Jump and Raccoon Run. Continue following the trail to the right to remain on the Main Marl Ravine loop. The offshoot to the left is a bailout/cut thru that allows you to cut the Marl Ravine in half.

7.0 The trail will split. The right branch is a little more technical than the left branch.

7.5 You reach the exit point of the Marl Ravine Trail. Turn right and double back toward the Backbone trail.

7.6 You're back at the Backbone Trail. Turn left to head back to the starting point. Otherwise, follow the markers in (parentheses) for loop 2.

8.1 Bear left and continue on the gravel road back to the parking area.

8.5 You're back at the starting point. This loop is complete.

Loop 2—The John Blair Trail

0.0 Start from behind the Contact Station where the gravel meets the pavement and head down the gravel path, this is the Backbone Trail.

1.7 (8.4) Turn left to enter the "H" section of the John Blair Trail. We will be riding each section, from H to A on our way back to the starting point.

1.9 (8.6) Cross over the Dogwood Trail and continue straight onto the G section of the John Blair Trail.

2.4 (9.1) Cross over the Dogwood Trail again and continue onto F section of the John Blair Trail. All the intersections are marked and present bailout points in case you need to cut the ride short.

3.7 (10.4) Cross the Whitetail Trail and continue onto the E section of the John Blair Trail.

7.0 (13.7) Cross the Riverview Trail and continue onto the D section of the John Blair Trail.

8.9 (15.6) Cross the Powhatan Trail (east Fork) and continue onto the C section of the John Blair Trail.

9.4 (16.1) Reach the commemorative bench for Margaritte Weyson McEver. You can get some glimpses of the river from this spot.

10.1 (16.8) Cross over the Powhatan Trail (north Fork) and continue onto the B section of the John Blair Trail.

12.4 (19.1) Cross over the Majestic Oak Trail and continue onto the A section of the John Blair Trail.

13.5 (20.2) Cross over the Pamunkey Trail and continue straight onto Bobcat Run.

14.2 (20.9) Veer to the left and then right to reach the Backbone trail. Turn right on Backbone. The entrance to the Marl Ravine Trail will be slightly ahead to the left.

14.7 (21.4) Bear left to stay on the Backbone trail.

15.2 (21.9) You're back at the Contact Station and the parking area, the loop is complete.

Ride Information

Local Information

Visit Williamsburg has lots of information about local events and attractions—www.visitwilliamsburg.com

Bike Shops

Red Barn Bikes, Barhamsville, VA: www.redbarnbikes.com

Bikes Unlimited, Williamsburg, VA: www.bikewilliamsburg.com

Village Bicycles, Newport News, VA: villagebicyclesnewportnews.com

Local Events and Attractions

Go Ape Zip Line and Tree Top Adventure—goape.com

Busch Gardens Williamsburg—seaworldparks.com/en/buschgardens-williamsburg

Colonial Williamsburg—www.colonialwilliamsburg.com

Jamestown—www.visitwilliamsburg.com/topic/jamestown

Where to Eat

Pierce's Pitt Bar-B-Que—www.pierces.com

Two Drummers Smokehouse—www.twodrummerssmokehouse.com

Accommodations

There are myriad places to stay in the Williamsburg area. Camping is available at the Williamsburg KOA: www.williamsburgkoa.com

In Addition

Chesapeake Bay

Certainly, one of the most prominent features in this region is the Chesapeake Bay—the largest inlet on the Atlantic coast of the United States. The unique character and identity of eastern Maryland and Virginia are woven inexplicably around the bay's coastal environment and economy, giving this region a flavor all its own.

The York River travels 35 miles to reach the bay and is one of the many broad, deep tidal rivers to pour into this vast waterway. Other major rivers feeding the bay are the Susquehanna, Severn, and Potomac in Maryland, and the Rappahannock and James in Virginia. The Chesapeake Bay is actually the "drowned" river valley of the lower part of the Susquehanna River, which pours into the bay at its head near the Maryland/Pennsylvania border.

In all, the bay measures nearly 195 miles long, ranges from 3 to 25 miles wide, and is deep enough to accommodate oceangoing vessels. It has about 27,000 miles of shoreline and covers 3,237 square miles of water. The Chesapeake Bay is considered one of the most important commercial and sport fishing grounds in the United States. It is famous for its oysters, crabs, and diamondback terrapins.

Another unique feature associated with the bay is the Chesapeake Bay Bridge-Tunnel, stretching between Cape Charles (the southern tip of Virginia's Eastern Shore) and a point east of Norfolk, Virginia. The bridge-tunnel carries motorists over and under 17.6 miles of uninterrupted ocean.

Honorable Mentions

Compiled here is an index of great rides in Virginia's coastal region that didn't make the A list this time around but deserve recognition. Check them out and let us know what you think. You may decide that one or more of these rides deserves higher status in future editions, or perhaps you may have a ride of your own that merits some attention. Some of these rides are documented on my website, www.mtbdc.com

A. **Indian River Park/Ipswich:** Indian River Park, aka Ipswich, located in the city of Chesapeake, is a small 90-acre urban forest park with about 6 miles of trails within the southeast side of route Rte. 13, Military Highway. You'll find a mix of trails, including singletrack and doubletrack paths and various BMX style obstacles. Several TTFs within the park will keep you entertained throughout your ride.
   GPS coordinates: 36.80256, −76.22379

B. **Lake Maury:** Located in Newport News, the Lake Maury trails offer riders approximately 10 miles of mostly flat urban singletrack and doubletrack trails along the west side of Lake Maury. Local riders have added several skinnies and a teeter to make the ride in this park a little more interesting. There are additional trails on the west side of Warwick Boulevard, but the majority of the fun is found along the Lake Maury natural area.
   GPS coordinates: 37.05775, −76.48261

C. **Wahrani Nature Trails:** Just 14 miles north of York River State Park (Ride 3), in New Kent County, are the Wahrani Nature Trails; a small park with a network of bi-directional singletrack trails with various TTFs added by EVMA. The trails are a little confusing to follow, but given the small area of the park, it's really not difficult to stay on track. Wahrani has a little more elevation than most of the Peninsula trails, so bring your climbing legs along for the ride. My recommendation is that you first ride the perimeter trails in a counterclockwise direction. From the main parking area along Rte. 33, follow the green blazed trail to the right and then continue making right turns to stay along the perimeter loop until you make it back to the starting point. If you do it right, you should ride a little over 4 miles. There are several internal trails you can explore along the way to increase your distance and add variety to your ride.
   GPS coordinates: 37.52766, −76.82179

D. Upper County Park: Just West of York River State Park (Ride 3) is a small county park with just under 4 miles of singletrack trails, which were built and are maintained by EVMA. The trails at Upper County Park, although short, do provide a fun alternative to riding in the area, and are great if you have a limited amount of time to ride. Although the trail was designed and built to be ridden in a clockwise direction, they are bidirectional, so they can be ridden either way. Much like the trails at York River State Park, the Upper County system offers riders several punchy climbs and descents that will keep your heart rate racing. The trail entrance, located at the far end of Leisure road, in a small cul-de-sac, is easy to find and is clearly marked. If you ride the system in the summer, plan for a visit to the park's pool. Do bring some cash though, because taking a swim requires a fee. **Note:** As of mid-August 2016, the trails at New Quarter Park were temporarily closed to all users while the county addressed a property lines dispute with a new landowner adjacent to the park. Please check in advance of your trip to make sure it has been reopened.

GPS coordinates: 37.4134, −76.8311

E. Harwood's Mill: Just east of Rte. 64 along Oriana Road and adjacent to the Harwood's Mill Reservoir are three directional loops built by EVMA that offer riders up to 6 miles of singletrack trails. The loops are labeled Beginner, Advanced, and Expert, but there is really nothing that makes them entirely too difficult. The trails are ideal for all levels of riders looking to increase their skills. More advanced riders will enjoy these trails at speed, making the numerous switchbacks and roots along the trails more challenging since there is very little elevation change and technical features.

GPS coordinates: 37.14875, −76.47795

Virginia Piedmont

Virginia's Piedmont is part of our nation's greater Piedmont region, which stretches from New Jersey to the north and Alabama in the south. In Virginia, the piedmont is characterized by the plateau that gently rolls from the base of the Blue Ridge Mountains and the Shenandoah Valley to the Eastern fall line and flat lands of Virginia's shore. The region is perfect for mountain biking since it offers rolling hills that vary in elevation from 200 to 800 feet above sea level. The Piedmont, which divides the state along its midsection, is also fertile and abundant with rich history. Early Virginia settlers traveled west along the region's rivers to the fall line, the westernmost navigable points of Virginia's main rivers, to deliver and collect goods. Several fall line communities, including Alexandria, Fredericksburg, Petersburg, and Richmond, the state's capital, prospered and became bustling centers for commerce. Today, these "gateways" to Virginia's piedmont will serve as our launching pad to mountain biking adventure.

As we explore the region, we will visit trails along the Potomac, Rappahannock, and James River watersheds, three of the main rivers for the state of Virginia. In the Northern portion, we'll get to experience some of the piedmont's riding at its finest. This includes Fountainhead Regional Park in Fairfax County, which has become a destination trail for all levels of riders, located along the rolling hills of the Occoquan Reservoir and the Bull Run Marina.

To the south, as we enter Virginia's central region, we'll ride along the demanding trails of the Rappahannock watershed and experience the urban riverside trails of Richmond's James River. Finally, as we reach Virginia's southern fringe, we'll hit the expertly built trails of Angler's Ridge along the Dan River Valley in the foothills of the Appalachian Mountains.

Northern Virginia

Traffic! Is there really anything more to say about Northern Virginia? Most of us in the Northern Virginia area are stuck in it going one direction, the other, or both, and it's only getting worse. (Do they really think building more roads will solve the problem?)

So what's the deal? Can you really find a good place to ride a bike in this overdeveloped suburb of DC? Absolutely!

Look no further than Wakefield Park and Lake Accotink, just a quarter mile off the Beltway. Here you'll find great off-road riding for a variety of skill levels, including everything from taxing singletrack to sluggish dirt paths. The ride is guaranteed to keep cyclists who are just leaving work, tired of rush hour and in need of a quick fix before heading home, in just the right mind-set.

But that isn't all. Northern Virginia is actually loaded with great places to pedal off-road. Some of the rides are in fairly standard places, such as Burke Lake Park with its meandering pathway around the lake, great for novices and families. Other mountain bike trails had to be built, such as the trails in Fountainhead Regional Park, planned by the Northern Virginia Regional Park Authority (now NOVA Parks) in close collaboration with the Mid-Atlantic Off-Road Enthusiasts (MORE). The stacked trail system at Fountainhead is a great circuit of tightly wound singletrack going up and down the hilly banks of the Occoquan Reservoir through a lush canopy of woods.

So even though it may take you a few nerve-racking hours to drive 10 miles through Northern Virginia traffic just to get to some of these rides, once you get out on the trails described in this book, all that frustration and energy will be well served on what is certainly some of the most fun riding in the region.

4 The Cross County Trail

This ride will take you on the Cross County Trail (CCT) from its northern terminus in Great Falls Virginia, to its southern end at Occoquan Regional Park. Along the 40 miles, we will travel past several other rides included in this book making it possible to create a "mega" epic ride, should you have the legs for it.

The CCT includes a combination of singletrack, dirt, bike paths, gravel roads, and on-road surfaces and is best completed on a mountain bike or reliable cross bike. I generally ride it on a rigid mountain bike with "slicks" (street tires). The trail is well marked with brown plastic pylons throughout its entirety, but there are certain intersections and points where it is not very obvious. Just follow the directions here and you should be fine. While on the trail, look for the distinguishable CCT markers. If you don't see one, chances are you've veered off course. For the most part, all branches out of the CCT are feeder trails into the CCT.

Start: Difficult Run Parking Area, Great Falls
Length: 39 miles one-way
Ride time: 3–5 hours
Difficulty: Difficult due to distance
Trail surface: Combination of singletrack, dirt, bike paths, gravel roads, and on-road surfaces.
Lay of the land: Wooded trails and roads of Fairfax County Virginia.

Land status: Public land
Nearest town: Great Falls at the starting point and Occoquan at the terminus.
Other trail users: Hikers, equestrians, and vehicle traffic in some sections.
Trail contacts: Fairfax County, Virginia, www.fairfaxcounty.gov/parks/cct
Schedule: Open year-round

Getting there: From Maryland, take I-495 South over the American Legion Bridge and take exit 44 onto Georgetown Pike (MD 193) toward Langley/Great Falls. The Difficult Run Parking Area will be to your left in approximately 3.7 miles. From Virginia, take I-495 North to exit 44 and follow the same directions as above. **GPS coordinates:** 38.978311, –77.249293.

The Ride

The Cross County Trail (CCT) is a unique achievement for Fairfax County. It is a trail nearly 40 miles in length that connects the county from one end to another. Along its path, it links hills and valleys, streams and meadows, and intersects urbanized landscapes and neighborhoods. Its very creation was a catalyst that united government agencies with citizen activists, environmental groups, trail enthusiasts, and private-sector organizations, and has been serving as an example of what can be achieved regionally when everyone puts differences aside and works together toward a common goal.

The trail was conceived in the mid-1990s when Fairfax resident and hiking enthusiast Bill Niedringhaus approached the county with an idea to connect existing trails in an effort to create one long corridor from Great Falls to Occoquan Regional Park. Park staff was extremely busy back then but they entertained Niedringhaus's idea. With support of the county, Niedringhaus and a few friends created the Fairfax Streams and Trails group and did considerable research on his proposal before presenting it to the County Board of Supervisors in 1998. Then-chairman Gerry Connolly realized that Niedringhaus was on to something great, so he presented a resolution to create the Cross County Trail, which the board unanimously approved. The county then sought and later received additional resources and Federal support for the project.

Shortly thereafter, other groups became involved. MORE and the group Fairfax for Horses jumped in, and by early 2000, construction to connect several portions of the trail began. By December of 2005, the entire route was mapped and completed, and today, the CCT is a jewel in Fairfax County.

Much of the trail follows the stream valleys of Difficult Run and Accotink Creek. The northern portion of the system begins near Great Falls and follows the Difficult Run into the heart of Fairfax. Because the county has banned construction in floodplains, the trail offers a linear park that stretches for nearly 15 miles. Most of the traffic here is via off-road singletrack trails. As you reach the southern portion of the system, you'll have to ride on a short section of road before rejoining the trail. At this point, the trails split between natural surface and paved paths, yet it does not lose its character as it continues to follow streams en route to Occoquan.

There are lots of stream crossings along the CCT.

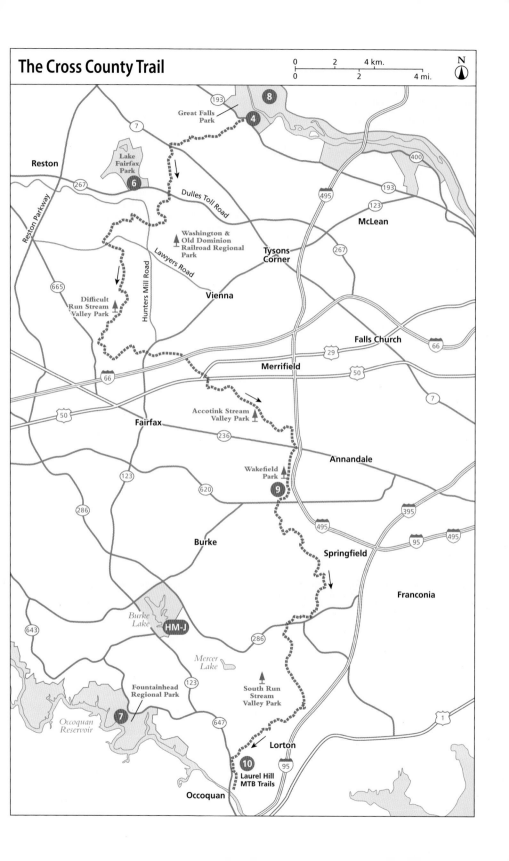

The Cross County Trail

0　　2　　4 km.
0　　2　　4 mi.

N

Reston

Lake Fairfax Park
6

Great Falls Park
8
4

McLean

Tysons Corner

Washington & Old Dominion Railroad Regional Park

Dulles Toll Road

Lawyers Road

Hunters Mill Road

Reston Parkway

Difficult Run Stream Valley Park

Vienna

Falls Church

Merrifield

Accotink Stream Valley Park

Fairfax

Annandale

Wakefield Park
9

Burke

Springfield

Franconia

Burke Lake
HM-J

Mercer Lake

Fountainhead Regional Park
7

South Run Stream Valley Park

Lorton

Occoquan Reservoir

Laurel Hill MTB Trails
10

Occoquan

Along the way, you can access several other parks and trail systems in the region. From the CCT, you can access Wakefield Park (Ride 9), Laurel Hill (Ride 10), the Washington & Old Dominion rail-trail (W&OD), Lake Accotink, and with a little extra effort, places like Fountainhead Regional Park (Ride 7), Burke Lake (HM-J), Holmes Run, and the Custis trail. This makes the CCT yet another valuable natural resource and a backbone trail from which to launch your very own cycling adventures.

Miles and Directions

0.0   Start from the Difficult Run Parking Area in Great Falls, Virginia. Look for the CCT sign to the right of the lot as you drive in. Head southwest on the CCT.

0.6   Reach the first of many stream crossings along the CCT.

1.0   Stay to the right at this intersection to continue on the CCT.

1.3   Come out onto Leigh Mill Road. The CCT continues to your right shortly before the bridge that crosses over Difficult Run.

1.7   You have a couple of options here. Stay on the bridle path as it circles to the right or climb up on the singletrack. For this ride, climb up over a series of short and steep switchbacks to the left. When you come up on the road, turn left, and as you reach the small court, look for the trailhead to the right.

1.9   Turn left into the doubletrack. If you had stayed to the right at the previous marker, this is where you would have ended up.

2.0   Stream crossing number two.

2.5   The trail comes out into a small parking area and continues on a paved road. Continue on the paved road until you reach Colvin Run Road.

2.7   Turn left and cross Leesburg Pike (VA 7) and then turn left into the clearly marked CCT shortly after you cross VA 7.

3.0   Stay to right to continue on the CCT.

3.8   Reach Browns Mill Road. You can cross Browns Mill and then turn immediately left to cross the Difficult Run River, or turn left and then pick up the CCT to the right. For now, skip the river crossing, and turn left and then right into the CCT. The CCT is now paved.

3.9   Turn right at this intersection to continue on the CCT.

4.3   Turn right into the gravel path to continue on the CCT. The left fork is a feeder trail.

4.4   Ride under the Dulles Toll Road.

4.7   Stay to the right to go over the bridge and continue on the CCT.

4.9   Turn left to go over another bridge, then turn right. Continue to follow the "worn" trail.

5.9   Continue to the left as you come out on the field.

6.0   After leaving the field and crossing a small bridge, turn left onto the gravel path and then into the singletrack.

6.1   Stay right at this T intersection. You are now on the W&OD, affectionately known as the WOD trail.

6.3   Use caution when crossing Hunter Mill Road.

6.9   Turn left into the CCT. This intersection is easy to miss since you will be heading down fast on the WOD. Don't hang out on the WOD at this intersection since riders from the opposite side of the WOD will be barreling down in your direction and could easily crash into you.

7.1 Turn right and head over the small wood bridge. (**Note:** At the time of this writing, this entire section was under significant construction and this area may be considerably different than what you are reading. It is safe to say, however, that the trail will be clearly marked and in better shape since the construction is a trail improvement project.)

7.5 Stay left and then right to continue on the CCT.

7.9 Reach Twin Branches Road. Cross the road and turn left to pick up the CCT on the other side. This section of the trail is called the Turquoise Trail. As you enter the trail, stay to the right.

8.5 After crossing the bridge, turn left at the T intersection.

8.6 Stay right at this intersection to continue on the CCT.

8.7 Cross Lawyers Road and continue on the CCT to the right. Then after a short, steep gully, continue to the left.

9.2 The trail continues to the right on the other side of the creek (Little Difficult Run).

9.5 The trail descends to the right and then switches back to the left. At the bottom, turn right to follow the CCT marker.

10.0 Cross this intersection and continue following the wood fence line to the right.

10.6 Cross Vale Road and turn left on the CCT as it parallels Vale Road.

10.9 Turn right to continue on the CCT.

11.0 Cross the Rocky Branch and continue straight.

11.1 Cross a small bridge and stay to the right.

12.2 Turn right at this and the next (12.9) T intersections to continue on the CCT.

13.0 Stay to the left after a short singletrack downhill and then cross the next intersection.

13.3 Power up a short, steep climb and come out onto Miller Heights Road. Turn right on Miller Heights Road.

13.6 The entrance to the CCT is clearly marked with a crosswalk and a trail marker. Turn left into the trail.

14.1 Follow the Oak Marr Golf Course fence line to the right.

14.7 Turn right onto the paved CCT and continue following the golf-course fence line. The CCT is paved again. At this point, all the singletrack portions of the ride are behind you. From now on, you ride on the road (3.2 miles on a combination of paved and doubletrack gravel paths).

14.9 Turn left on Jermantown Road and follow the trail along the sidewalk for a short distance. At the corner of Elmendorf Road, cross Jermantown and continue in the same direction on Jermantown Road.

16.2 Jermantown becomes Blake Road, and then Pickett after crossing Fairfax Boulevard.

15.3 Cross Chain Bridge Road.

16.6 Cross Rte. 66.

17.3 There's a 7/11 to the left—a perfect place to replenish and get some water.

17.6 Cross Fairfax/Arlington Boulevard.

17.9 Turn left into Pickett Park and then left into the parking lot. The CCT picks up at the far right corner on the backside of a small baseball field. Turn right into the CCT. You will now follow the trail as it parallels and crosses Accotink Creek for about 20 miles, along the way riding past Lake Accotink.

18.6 Turn right into the gravel doubletrack to continue on the CCT.

19.0 Cross Barkley Drive and enter into Sally Ormsby Park.

19.5 Cross Prosperity Avenue.

19.8 Stay to the right at this intersection. The path is now paved.

20.3 Cross Woodburn Road. Make a quick right into the CCT and then a quick left to continue on the CCT.

21.2 Stay right at this intersection.

21.4 The CCT curves to the right. You can start to hear the Capital Beltway traffic. This section of the CCT will run near the nation's busiest thoroughfare.

22.1 The trail comes out from the Little River Turnpike Beltway and underpasses under a set of power lines. Continue following the trail to the left as it curves around the outfield of the baseball field to left. When it reaches the pavement, turn left to head into the tree cover.

22.4 As the road curves to the right, the CCT picks up straight ahead.

22.6 Continue following the trail to the right to cross the creek and then immediately after crossing the creek, turn to the left.

22.8 Turn left to go over a bridge and then right immediately after you cross it. You are now in Wakefield Park and riding parts of the Wakefield Park ride (Ride 40).

22.9 You have the option of continuing straight at this intersection to remain on the CCT or following the path to the left toward the Audrey Moore RECenter. I'll take you that way since water and restrooms are available in case you need them.

23.1 After turning left, follow the trail to the right as it follows the edge of the tennis courts. Come out into the parking area and head straight to the rec center beyond the skate park to the right. When you reach the rec center, continue following the parking area to the left and pick up the CCT again at the far end. Turn right into the CCT at mile marker 23.6. After turning right, you'll go over a small bridge. To the left is the Wakefield area commonly known as "The Bowl," a small playground of intertwined singletrack trails. Continue on the doubletrack and come out into the athletic fields parking area. The trail picks up at the opposite far corner of the parking lot to the right.

23.9 Enter the CCT and go over the small arched bridge and continue following the paved path to the right.

24.1 Stay to the left and then to the right to go under Braddock Road.

24.6 Continue straight at this intersection and follow the signs to the Lake Accotink Marina. You are now on the Lake Accotink Trail.

25.7 Stay to the right at this intersection.

26.3 Pass the marina and turn right on the road and head toward the dam and the railroad overpass.

26.5 The road will curve to the left and head under the railroad viaduct. Follow it into the parking area to the right. The CCT continues at the far end to the right.

28.0 Continue following the CCT to the right. You'll pass several baseball fields to the left.

28.5 Ride under Old Keene Mill Road. The trail turns to gravel.

28.7 Continue following the trail to the left.

29.5 Continue straight past two intersections, and at the third one follow the path to the right up a steep climb to Hunter Village Drive. Cross Hunter Village and continue in the same general direction on the path along the road.

30.2 As Hunter Village Drive curves to the right, you'll reach a crosswalk. Use it to cross the road. Climb up the ramp and cross Rolling Road. Immediately after crossing, turn right and ride along the sidewalk that parallels Rolling Road for a short distance.

30.4 Turn left into the CCT. You'll be riding along the backside of some townhouses.

30.6 Turn right along the Fairfax County Parkway.

30.8 At the light, turn left to cross the Fairfax County Parkway and then right on Hooes Road immediately after you cross.

30.9 Turn left into the CCT—thankfully, it is right before the ominous climb you see up ahead.

31.1 The trail turns sharply to the right.

31.2 After crossing the creek, turn left and up to continue on the CCT.

31.3 After a steep climb, follow the trail to the left.

31.5 Stay left at this intersection, go over the small bridge, and continue following the Pohick Creek. You'll now ride parallel to and cross Pohick Creek several times before we finish.

32.8 After a short creek crossing, turn right and then go through the creek again. You'll see a house up high to the right as you ride under the power lines. Continue straight through the next intersection.

33.1 Cross the creek again. This crossing seems to be the deepest of all of the ones we've encountered thus far.

33.3 Continue straight following the creek.

33.9 Shortly before you reach the underpass for Pohick Road, turn left and shoot straight up to continue on the CCT. Once you reach Pohick Road, turn right to go over the overpass. The CCT will now parallel Pohick Road for a short distance.

34.1 Turn left to cross Pohick Road. Then, immediately after crossing, turn left again to stay on the CCT. The trail will actually follow the sidewalk as it heads toward Creekside View Lane.

34.2 Turn right to continue on the CCT.

34.4 Continue to the left.

35.1 Cross Bluebonnet Drive and then turn right at the T intersection to cross Laurel Crest Drive.

35.4 Cross Paper Birch Drive and hop on White Spruce Way to cross over Silverbrook Road. You can now see the old Lorton Penitentiary up ahead. After you cross Silverbrook Road, continue straight toward Lorton's other gated community, Spring Hill. The trail entrance is to the left as you reach the community gates.

35.5 Enter the CCT again and follow it as it circles the old penitentiary to the left.

36.0 Stay to the left and continue following the perimeter of the penitentiary. As you reach the last tower, veer right to continue on the CCT. The trail is marked with paint on the pavement and continues down the hill to the left. The Laurel Hill Ride (Ride 41) begins on the parking area to the left.

36.4 Continue straight and go over the bridge that spans Giles Run. After crossing the bridge, you'll see the Giles Run Meadow Trail trailhead to the left.

36.6 Stay left at this intersection.

36.8 The Barrett House parking area is to the right. Continue straight under the arched bridge.

37.0 Turn left on the road and head down to the stop sign to cross Lorton Road. Use caution at this intersection. The CCT continues on the other side of the road. Immediately after cross-ing the road, stay to the right. (To the left is the entrance to the Laurel Hill trails.) Continue following the trail southwest as it parallels Lorton Road until you reach Ox Road. (VA 123).

37.5 Turn left on VA 123. The Lorton Workhouse Arts Center will be to your left.

37.9 Turn left to enter the Occoquan Regional Park. The CCT will run parallel to the road shortly after you enter the park. Follow it to the bottom.

39.0 The ride is complete.

In Addition

Your Local Bike Shop

Some people will have you believe that your Local Bike Shop (LBS) is dead; or struggling to make it in a world where everything is ruled by online sales and marketing campaigns, but if you look throughout this book, you'll see that I list several local bike shops that are not only serving their communities, but thriving in them.

As I traveled the trails documented in this book, I was reminded of the importance that LBSs serve in our community. On more than one occasion I was "forced" to visit some of the shops I've listed. While in Roanoke, for example, I suffered a sidewall tear that would have otherwise ended my riding weekend had it not been for Black Dog bikes. A quick visit to the shop had me back on the trail. But beyond that, the guys at Black Dog armed me with additional information I did not have when I set out to visit this Southwestern Virginia destination.

I'm incredibly fortunate to live in an area of Virginia that is served by many excellent LBSs. Among them, The Bike Lane and Bikenetic.

The Bike Lane, located in both Springfield and Reston, have been a staple in the Northern Virginia cycling community for years. When not managing their business, owners Todd and Anne Mader are either riding or leading some community effort to make cycling better for the region. Anne, for example, was instrumental in helping MORE develop its sMOREs program, and most recently, helped secure the necessary funding for the new skills and pump track constructed at Lake Fairfax Park (Ride 6).

Jan Feuchtner and Helen Huley of Bikenetik run a bike shop in Falls Church, VA that has become a hub for not only cycling, but also for live music. Bikenetic has been voted "Best Bike Shop" in Falls Church and Northern Virginia for several years running, often besting national chains like REI for the honor. The shop is also rated as one of the best music venues in the small Northern Virginia urban center.

Bikenetic employees not only serve customers in the store, but are often out at local trails and roads leading rides and helping riders on the spot with anything they might need. Annually, Bikenetic also organizes two of the most popular cyclocross events in the region; events that not only highlight local destinations, but also help create an incredible sense of camaraderie between regional and visiting riders.

I try to ride with Jan and the Bikenetic team every Tuesday night at Wakefield Park (Ride 9) in Northern Virginia. The regular weekly rides are well attended and have become one of my favorites. During one of our recent rides, I asked Jan why he thought he, along with several other LBSs across our region have found a way to be successful, his answer was simple: "we're just a critical cog in the community. Our shop, and the events we promote, including these weekly rides, helps people identify with and get a sense of belonging to their community. We're more than a 'bike shop,'" he said, "we're a hub in the community and the connections we make with our customers are long-lasting and tangible."

Like Bikenetic, other LBSs around Northern Virginia and the rest of the Old Dominion have created ways to make those connections with their customers. Each of them have found a way to not only thrive in an often saturated market, but also develop a loyal group of customers that proudly act as ambassadors for their brand.

Take a moment and review the list of shops I list throughout the book and swing by to say hello. Chances are they'll have something to offer you beyond just a place to get a bike part or service your ride. In many cases you'll be making valuable like-minded friends for life. I know that I did...

Ride Information

The CCT bisects Fairfax County from north to south, beginning at Great Falls and ending in Occoquan Regional Park.

Great Falls Park—Falls Walk: A great way to learn about Great Falls from the Rangers at Great Falls Park: Visit www.nps.gov/grfa for additional information and event schedules.
Local Fairfax County events: www.fairfaxcounty.gov
Workhouse Arts Center, Lorton: www.workhousearts.org
Historic Occoquan: www.occoquan.org

Restaurants
Cock & Bowl: 302 Poplar Alley, Occoquan, VA 22125; (703) 494-1180; www.cockandbowl.com

Restrooms
Available at Occoquan Regional Park, Lake Accotink Park, Wakefield Park, Oak Marr Park, Colvin Run Mill Park, and Great Falls National Park. Portable restrooms are available seasonally at Byron Avenue Park, Eakin Community Park, and Thaiss Park.

This is a shuttle ride, unless you really want to make it an out-an-back and double the distance. A couple of things before you start: have plenty of water and make absolutely sure that each driver in the shuttle chain has their respective vehicle keys—trust me on this one.

5 Conway Robinson State Forest

Although short, the ride will certainly be a pleasing one. It has quickly become a favorite destination for my daughter and me to visit. The relatively flat trails and smooth surface make it a perfect destination for novice to intermediate riders. A short section of trail has been crafted to please more experienced riders and can easily be bypassed if you are not up to the challenge.

Start: Main Conway Robinson parking area

Length: 3.3 miles; additional if you ride the internal trails

Ride time: 0.5–1 hour

Difficulty: Easy

Trail surface: Doubletrack and singletrack trails

Lay of the land: Pine and old-growth hardwood stands

Land status: State forest

Nearest town: Gainesville and Manassas, VA

Other trail users: Hikers, equestrians, and hunters

Trail contacts: Virginia Department of Forestry, www.dof.virginia.gov

Schedule: Open year-round, sunrise to sunset

Getting there: Follow Route I-66W to exit 43B, US 29 N. Follow 29 North and make an immediate left on University Boulevard into the park's parking area. The trailhead is to the left of the main picnic area (as you face it). **GPS coordinates:** 38.803490, -77.587845.

The Ride

Conway Robinson State Forest is adjacent to the Manassas National Battlefield, and as such, has played an important role during the Civil War. Situated in Prince William County and near the junction of the Alexandria and Manassas Gap Railroads, it served as a key link to the South. Confederate generals recognized the geographic significance of the area and stationed their troops to protect and maintain possession of the railroad junction. Allowing the Union to control it would mean they could lose a key access point to the South's capital, Richmond, Virginia.

Only a few months had passed since the start of the Revolutionary War when northern citizens began clamoring for an advance on Richmond. They thought that by taking the South's capital city, they would quell the rebellion and hostilities would come to a quick end. Yielding to pressure from the public, and from political leadership, Brigadier General Irvin McDowell led his inexperienced army across Bull Run, and through much of the area where Conway Robinson State Forest is today, toward Manassas. Their aim was to capture Manassas Junction, the pivotal railroad town next to Brentsville that would give the North an overland route to the South's capital.

The southern army met the "surprise" attack planned by the North with determination and conviction on July 21, 1861. Led by a relatively unknown officer from

The trails at Conway Robinson State Forest are perfect for kids and novice riders.

theVirginia Military Institute (VMI), Thomas Jackson, the Southern forces held their ground and drove the northern forces back toward Washington, D.C. It was in that first battle that Jackson earned his nickname, "Stonewall." Jackson's brigade suffered considerable casualties that day, but they stopped the Union's assault and helped drive it back. It was another officer in the Southern forces, Brigadier General Barnard Elliott Bee Jr., who uttered the words that earned him and his brigade their nickname: "Look at Jackson standing there like a stonewall." It was also the first time that Union soldiers heard the RebelYell. It was Jackson who instructed his troops to "yell like furies" when they advanced and charged the enemy.

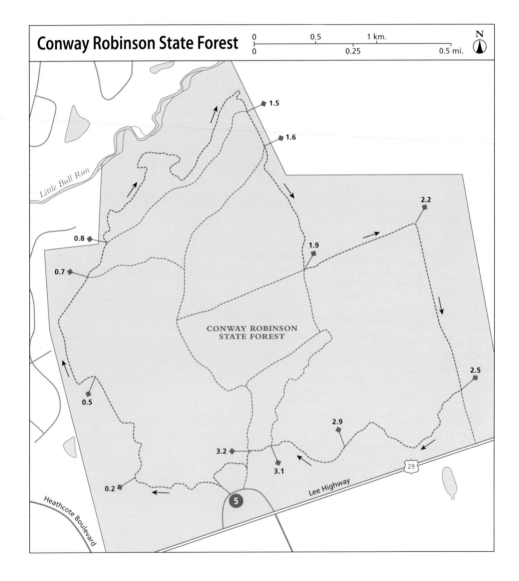

Conway Robinson State Forest

CONWAY ROBINSON
STATE FOREST

Both the South and North suffered great casualties in the First Manassas, and both armies came to the realization that the war would be longer, more arduous, and more brutal than they had ever anticipated. Nearly 5,000 men died in the battle, proving how difficult the war would be. Years later, more than half a million Union and Confederate soldiers would lose their lives in battle. The Second Battle of Manassas in late August of 1862 was of greater scale. More than 100,000 men fought in the fields of Prince William County, and more than 12,000 died, most from the Union. Ultimately, the North prevailed and today, Manassas and the areas adjacent to Conway Robinson State Forest are simple historic reminders of a painful past that has long been gone, but one that shaped the county, the state, and our nation as a whole.

Today, Conway Robinson State Forest offers us a glimpse in to the past. Acquired by the state in 1938, Conway Robinson State Forest is an urban oasis dedicated to the preservation of the natural woodland within it. Named after Conway Robinson, a nineteenth-century prominent Virginian, the 444-acre parcel remains one of the largest undeveloped parcels of land amid the suburban jungle of Northern Virginia. Hikers, cyclists, equestrians, and hunters can now enjoy an environment that has been carefully managed through passive silviculture techniques—the practice of controlling the growth, composition, and quality of forests.

We will ride the Conway trails in a clockwise loop. Although Conway has many intersecting trails, these tend to be very muddy, even long after rain has passed.

Miles and Directions

0.0 The trailhead is to the left of the pavilion as you look at the pavilion from the parking area. The trail is blazed with blue markings. Immediately upon entering the trail, stay to the left.

0.2 Cross the doubletrack to stay on the Blue Trail.

0.5 Stay to the right. The left branch is a neighborhood connector.

0.7 Stay to the left to continue to follow the blue loop.

0.8 Turn left onto the Orange Trail. The Orange Trail is the most technically difficult portion of this ride. You can bypass it and continue straight if you want.

1.5 Reach the blue loop again. Turn left to continue on the blue loop; right will simply take you back to the entry to the orange trail.

1.6 Continue following the Blue Trail as it curves to the left.

1.9 Turn left to continue following the blue blazes under the pines.

2.2 Turn right on the doubletrack. When I documented this ride, the Forest Service had done a controlled burn on the woods to the left.

2.5 Turn right to continue on the blue and the singletrack. Straight ahead will take you to VA 29.

2.9 Go over the bridge.

3.1 Stay to the left to stay on the Blue Trail. The Red Trail to the right is notoriously muddy and best avoided.

3.2 Turn left on the yellow trail. This doubletrack will lead you back to the parking area. We will immediately turn right to hop on the blue and ride behind the picnic pavilion. At the T intersection, turn left on the blue to complete the ride, or turn right and do the whole loop again.

3.3 The loop is complete.

Ride Information

Local Information

The city of Manassas is rich in history and there is a lot to do in the area year-round. Check out visitmanassas.org for regional attractions and the City of Manassas website for additional information—www.manassascity.org.

Bike Shops

Bull Run Bicycles, Manassas, VA, (703) 335-6131, www.bullrunbicycles.com
A-1 Manassas Cycling, Manassas, VA, (703) 361-6101, www.a1cycling.com

Local Events and Attractions

Manassas National Battlefield Park: www.nps.gov/mana/index.htm

Where to Eat

Okra's Cajun Creole Restaurant
Manassas, VA
(703) 368-3427
www.okras.com

Zandra's Taqueria
Manassas, VA
(571) 359-6767
zandrastacos.com

In Addition

Biking with Kids

Shortly after my daughter was born I could not wait to take her out on the trail with me. Now that she's older, we head out regularly to ride both on and off-road. Here are a few simple tips to remember when riding with young kids:

- Start Early; I've found that my daughter will ride further when we go out in the morning; In the afternoon she generally tires quickly

- Invite a friend; if you have a friend who is also trying to get his daughter (or son) out on the bike, ask them to tag along. Kids often tend to have more fun when there is someone of their same age with them; Check out MORE's "sMOREs program"; their calendar at http://www.more-mtb.org has regularly scheduled rides suitable for children. All of the clubs mentioned in the book have some kind of kids program to get lots of children riding together.

- Take your time. When out with kids, a 4 mile ride may take up to 2 hours. This is all about them getting to know their bikes and having fun.

- Take breaks; Plan your route, if you know there is a playground or other interesting kid friendly landmark along the way fit it into your ride to add a little variety and to give your child a break. It will keep them interested and entertained, plus they'll get a rest.

- Bring snacks and plenty of water; and make sure you eat and drink them. When I ride with my daughter one of our rituals is to find a nice spot to sit down and have our snacks.

- Be prepared; bring whatever tools you may need. Always carry your phone and some cash in case of an emergency and always let someone else know exactly where you'll be and how long you plan to be away. This tip applies to riding with adults as well, and especially when riding on your own.

- Have Fun; Be enthusiastic and encouraging. Always praise whatever little accomplishment your child makes on the bike and express pride in what they do—it will want them to come back and ride with you again and again.

- Be Safe; don't ride above your ability or allow your child to take unnecessary risks. We, after all want to ride again tomorrow…

6 Lake Fairfax

The trails at Lake Fairfax have seen a considerable transformation over the last few years. What were once soggy and boggy unsustainable tracts have been converted to a network of sustainable ribbons across this Fairfax County destination.

Start: Michael Faraday Court parking area adjacent to and behind the Skate Quest Ice Rink
Length: Up to 12 miles
Ride time: 1.5-3 hours
Difficulty: Easy/intermediate
Trail surface: Mostly singletrack, some doubletrack

Lay of the land: Rolling trails through the dense forest of Lake Fairfax Park
Land status: County park
Nearest town: Reston, VA
Other trail users: Hikers
Trail contacts: Fairfax County Virginia, www .fairfaxcounty.gov/parks/lakefairfax; Mid-Atlantic Off-Road Enthusiasts, www.more-mtb.org
Schedule: Open year-round sunrise to sunset

Getting there: From I-495, take VA 267 (tolls) west for approximately 6 miles and exit onto Hunter Mill Road (exit 14). Make an immediate left onto Sunset Hills Road to continue west toward Reston. Continue on Sunset Mills Road for approximately 1.2 miles and turn right onto Michael Faraday Court. Cross the Washington & Old Dominion Trail (W&OD) and continue straight to the far end of the parking area. The trailhead will be to your left as you drive in. **GPS coordinates:** 38.950733, -77.331256.

The Ride

When I first documented the trails in the vicinity of Lake Fairfax, there was very little to talk about. Initially I had set out this destination as a point-to-point ride, taking riders from the southeast of VA 7 to the Difficult Run parking area, where Ride 4 of this edition begins. Along the way, riders would pass what's now the starting point of this loop.

Back then, there were very few trails to choose from, and the best alternative was to send riders along Colvin Run along the water's edge. That route, historically, was often soggy, muddy, and otherwise susceptible to damage from heavy use.

MORE set out to change the landscape of the area, and in collaboration with Fairfax County worked to develop new sustainable trails along Lake Fairfax, repair unsustainable ones, and work on maintaining and improving the trails along Colvin Run to offer all users additional opportunities in the park. Today, there are more than 10 miles of easy to intermediate trails around Lake Fairfax that can be tied together with the W&OD, a paved bike path, and the CCT (Ride 4) to craft a longer loop. In fact, in 2014, MORE held the NoVa Epic and used most of the trails in this Northern Virginia destination to piece together a 25-mile loop through mostly singletrack trails.

Lake Fairfax is compact, and there are a lot of trails to the south of the lake that crisscross each other to create a maze of trails. Much like the trails at Lake Accotink

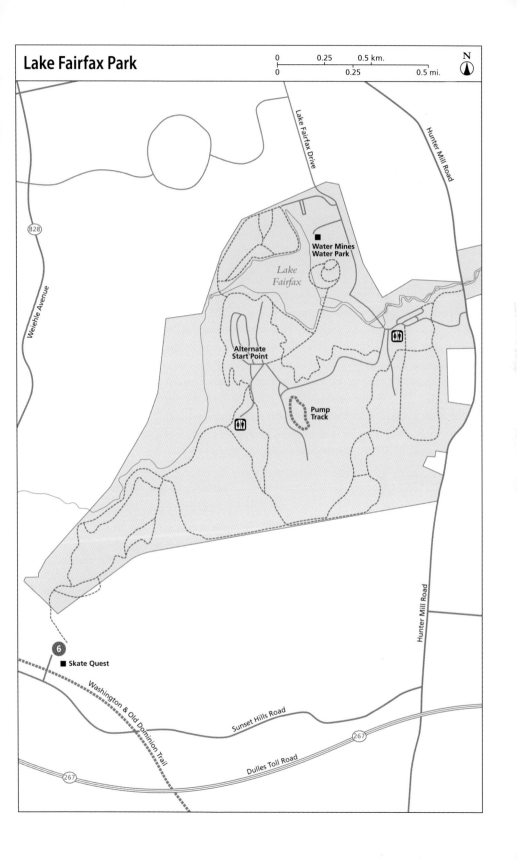

Park in Annandale, Virginia, it is difficult to piece together and give you directions for an actual loop. For that reason, I'm only providing you with a starting point and general guidance on where to head. It's hard to get lost within the park, and once you've ridden the network of trails that meander under its canopied forests, you'll be able to craft a loop of your very own.

MORE holds regularly scheduled rides in this park for riders of all levels. Check their events calendar regularly for upcoming rides at Lake Fairfax, including a spring/summer kids ride series The best way to learn the system is to follow along on one of their guided rides.

Despite all the progress made by MORE to build and maintain these tails to be sustainable, they are still susceptible and easily damaged after extended periods of rain. Please do not ride them when wet, especially after heavy rains.

MILES AND DIRECTIONS

Start your ride from the parking area at the end of Michael Faraday Court and behind the Ice Skating Rink. As you drive into the parking lot, you'll see the trailhead to the left. Chances are there will be lots of other riders in the vicinity as well, so getting someone to point you in the right direction should not be a problem. Once you enter the park, the trail splits into three branches, all of which will take you northwest toward the lake. My personal preference is to follow the furthermost right trail and take that in a counterclockwise direction to the lake, returning then along the banks of Colvin Run. Doing so will provide you with a sense of the system's perimeter. There are lots of other trails within these boundaries to play in.

Ride Information

Local Information

Visit the Fairfax County website for information on events and things to do in Reston Virginia—www.fxva.com/our-community/herndon-reston/things-to-do-va

Bike Shops

The Bike Lane, Reston Town Center, Reston, VA, (703) 689-2671, thebikelane.com
Bikenetic, Falls Church, VA, (703) 534-7433, bikenetic.com

Where to Eat

Pollo Peru
Reston, VA
(703) 707-8484
www.facebook.com/polloperu

7 Fountainhead Regional Park

This ride will take you through one of the region's most successful off-road cycling projects. Originally conceived by a band of riders from MORE in early 1994, and redesigned with the International Mountain Biking Organization (IMBA) in 2010–2012, the new Fountainhead Trail is challenging, fun, and an incredibly rewarding system of trails. The once straight and steep climbs and downhills that crossed the park have been replaced with challenging switchbacks and screaming berms. Fountainhead is a glorious playground in which to take your mountain-biking skills to the next level.

Start: Fountainhead Park
Length: 14.8 miles (green 2.2 miles, blue 4.7 miles, black 3.9 miles)
Ride time: 1.5–3 hours
Difficulty: Moderate to difficult
Trail surface: Technical singletrack and doubletrack
Lay of the land: Wooded and hilly
Land status: Northern Virginia Regional Park
Nearest town: Springfield, VA

Other trail users: None; this loop is mountain-bike specific
Trail contacts: Northern Virginia Regional Park Authority, (703) 352-5900; Fountainhead Regional Park, (703) 250-9124, www.fountainheadproject.org; Mid-Atlantic Off-Road Enthusiasts (MORE), (703) 502-0359
Schedule: Open daily from dawn to dusk, Mar to Nov

Getting there: From the Capital Beltway (I-495), take exit 5 west onto Braddock Road. Head south on VA 123. Continue past Burke Lake Park to the Fountainhead Regional Park sign on the right side of the road. Turn right at this sign on Hampton Road. Follow Hampton Road to the park entrance on the left. Park in the first parking lot on the right. The trailhead is to your left. **GPS coordinates:** 38.724367, –77.330382.

The Ride

When I first included Fountainhead Regional Park in *Mountain Biking the Washington D.C./Baltimore Area*, I wrote, "the Fountainhead Regional Park Mountain Bike Trail was opened in the spring of 1997. Before then, bicycles were not permitted on any of the trails within the park. The Fountainhead Regional Park Mountain Bike Trail represents an important opportunity and major breakthrough in the Washington Metropolitan area. It was planned by the Northern Virginia Regional Park Authority (NVRPA) in close collaboration with MORE and initially funded, in large part, by Recreational Equipment, Incorporated (REI). This flagship mountain bike trail project was designed specifically for mountain bikers and will serve as a real litmus test for other park officials who are interested in constructing and maintaining mountain-bike-specific trail ways at their parks."

Suffice it to say, I think the litmus test proved to be a success. Since it was opened, the trails at Fountainhead have evolved considerably, and after a period of transformation are better than ever. The original loop, which was roughly 4.5 miles, has more than doubled in length, and the trails are far better than what was originally laid out. Today, with the help of IMBA and careful planning, the trails are an off-road cyclist's dream. Tight switchbacks, rock outcroppings, banked turns, technical drops, and fast descents are but a few of the features that have recently been incorporated into the improved trail design. Drainage issues and a variety of troublesome erosion problems have been addressed, and the entrance and exit to the trail have been divided so that there is no longer a two-way-traffic trail. The entire loop continues to be a directional loop, which ensures that you'll never run into a rider going in the opposite direction. This makes riding the new downhill and banked turns extremely fun.

Additional improvements have also been made at key intersections. Additionally, a new boardwalk and bridge leads riders to a new exit trail, and midway through the ride, you can hang out and play around in a technical section that was designed to improve your handling skills.

Initially there was a little bit of an uproar when announcements were made that Fountainhead would receive a facelift. Some riders felt that the goal of the New Fountainhead Project was to "dumb down" the trails and take away its challenging sections. On the contrary, the new Fountainhead continues to be a challenging trail that has been made longer.

Of particular pride to me is that the original name of Shockabilly Hill has been retained. Back during the first Fountainhead Project, one of the sponsors for the trail was FAT City Cycles, a custom frame builder from Massachusetts and makers of one of my first "real" mountain bikes. My relationship with FAT helped us secure a Shockabilly frame set to raffle off during one of several events promoted by MORE in support of the project. Having that prize helped MORE to raise the funds necessary for the project. In exchange, my friend Valerie Dosland, a MORE board member, suggested to FAT that we would name one of the trails after their bike. They agreed to the deal, so we coined the steepest part of the trail (at the time) Shockabilly Hill (SOB). As you close out the ride, you'll come to an intersection giving you the option of riding old Shockabilly or the new, improved version (SAB).

Fountainhead is a closely monitored trail. When conditions are not favorable for riding, the trail gates are closed and access is denied to the system. Do not bypass the gates. If the trail is closed, please respect the closure and come back another day. Bypassing the gates only threatens access for other users. Before heading out to Fountainhead, I highly suggest you check the trail's status. Park managers and project leads have set up a Facebook page (www.facebook.com/thefountainheadproject) where they promptly post trail conditions, and a ride line (703-250-9124) is also available to obtain more information.

Fountainhead continues to be a showpiece for the mid-Atlantic region. From its early ambitious beginning, to its successful redesign, Fountainhead is certainly bound to bring a smile to your face.

The entrance to the new black diamond loop at Fountainhead is particularly hard . . . for a reason.

Fountainhead Regional Park

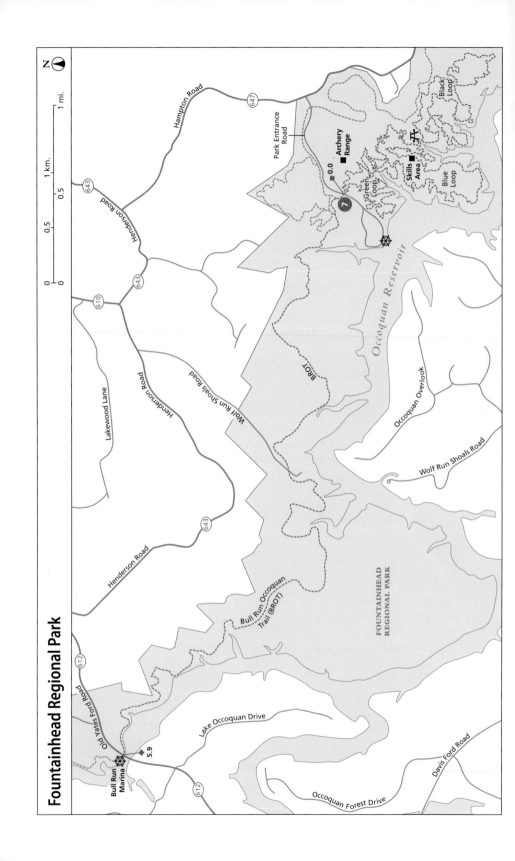

The Bull Run Occoquan Trail

A recent addition to Fountainhead's riding inventory is the Bull Run Occoquan trail commonly known as the BROT. Although the BROT has been a staple in the park for quite some time, it was only recently opened to mountain bikes. The trail is an out-and-back from the main parking area at Fountainhead to the Bull Run Marina. Beyond the Marina, the trail remains off limits to bikes. The opening of the BROT to bikes is the result of a strong collaborative relationship between NOVA Parks and MORE. MORE's successful completion of the Fountainhead Project, combined with the clubs continued support of other trails users helped the trail's opening happen.

The trail is rugged and at times severe; it is a classic example of what riders had available in the region in the early 90s, before MORE became heavily involved in advocacy. NOVA Parks and MORE intend to transform the BROT into a more sustainable and enjoyable trail for hikers and cyclists by rerouting several troublesome sections. The ultimate goal is to transform the BROT into a multi-use sustainable trail with additional loop options along its length.

The entrance to the BROT is directly opposite the mountain bike specific trail at Fountainhead. The BROT can also be accessed along the Bull Run Marina from the large parking area along Old Yates Ford Road.

Miles and Directions

Fountainhead Regional Park is an easy trail to follow. As part of the new design, the trail has been adequately marked, and all intersections are clear and easy to understand. The trail is unidirectional to avoid any collisions, and it is mountain-bike specific, so you will be unlikely to run into any other trail users. Do watch your speed, though, and ride within your abilities.

Fountainhead is a "stacked" system. The first, green loop is the easiest and closest to the parking area. If you have difficulty riding that, I suggest you skip the blue and black loops. If you enjoy the green loop, then continue on to the blue loop, which offers additional challenges. The blue loop will take you farther away from the parking area. Finally, if you have no troubles with the green or blue loops, then hammer away at the black. Be warned, though, the entrance to this loop has been made hard for a reason, because you will most definitely encounter lots of challenging and technical sections beyond what you experienced in the green or blue loops. And the black loop will take you farther away from the lot.

Ride Information

Local Information

Occoquan's website for local information—historicoccoquan.com

Fairfax County Convention and Visitors Bureau: (800) 7FAIRFAX—www.visitfairfax.org

Bike Shops

The Bike Lane, Springfield, VA, (703) 440-8701, thebikelane.com
Olde Towne Bicycles, Woodbridge, VA, (703) 491-5700, oldetownebicycles.com
Village Skis & Bikes, Woodbridge, VA, (703) 730-0303, vsbsports.com

Local Events and Attractions

Historic town of Occoquan
www.occoquan.com

Harbor River Cruises in Occoquan
(703) 385-9433

Historic Occoquan Spring Arts & Crafts Show
(703) 491-2168

Accommodations

Bennett House Bed & Breakfast
9252 Bennett Dr.
Manassas, VA
(703) 368-6121

Sunrise Hill Farm B&B
5590 Old Farm Inn
Manassas, VA
(703) 754-8309

In Addition

You May Run Into: Larry Cautilli

Larry's quest for fitness led him to buy a bike in early 1985. Then, a few years later he added another, a Mountain Bike. It was with that mountain bike that Larry began racking up the miles. "It became an addiction," Larry said. "The more I rode, the more I wanted to ride. I really can't pinpoint what one thing I love about cycling, but if I had to, it is just being on the bike."

That fix to just "be on the bike" has become our benefit. In early 1996 when MORE was beginning to work on the first loops at Fountainhead, Larry used most of his 200 hours of "use or lose" leave to manually work on the trails. Over the years he has seen the loops evolve. Most recently, due in large part to Larry's dedication, the trails at Fountainhead have been transformed into a regional mountain biking destination.

Larry loves to ride Gambrill State Park in Frederick and the Frederick Watershed, but you'll undoubtedly find him spinning the trails at Wakefield and now, more than ever, over the fruits of his efforts at Fountainhead. If you see him, say hello and make sure you thank him for a job well done, he certainly deserves it.

8 Great Falls National Park

Great Falls National Park is a natural haven for thousands of Washingtonians seeking solitude from the daily grind of gridlock and government. Trails abound throughout this park on the river, offering cyclists, hikers, and equestrians alike rugged terrain. Some portions of the park's trails are wide, dirt carriage roads dating back through history and meandering through the scenery, while others are steep, rocky, and narrow, keeping even agile cyclists on the tips of their seats. Come one and all to this park of presidents, dignitaries, and commoners and enjoy what folks throughout time have been enjoying along the rapids of the Potomac.

Start: Great Falls National Park visitor center

Length: 6.8 miles

Ride time: 1–1.5 hours

Difficulty: Moderate due to occasional steep, rocky singletrack

Trail surface: Rocky, dirt trails and carriage roads.

Lay of the land: Wooded, rocky, and hilly terrain along the banks of the Potomac River.

Land status: National park

Nearest town: McLean, VA

Other trail users: Hikers, equestrians, climbers, kayakers, and tourists.

Trail contacts: National Park Service, (703) 759-2915

Schedule: Open 7 a.m. to sunset

Fees: Small entrance fee

Getting there: From the Capital Beltway (I-495): From exit 13 northwest of McLean, take VA 193 (Georgetown Pike) west toward Great Falls. Go about 4 miles, then turn right on Old Dominion Road, which becomes the park entrance road. Go 1 mile to the end of this road and park at the visitor center. Telephones, water, food, restrooms, and information available inside the visitor center. **GPS coordinates:** 39.003029, -77.256459.

The Ride

Great Falls is one of the nation's most popular national parks. How appropriate then for it to be located just 14 miles from our nation's capital. And what a thrill for cyclists to know that mountain biking is not only allowed at the park—it's welcome. Along with hikers, historians, rock climbers, and kayakers, off-road cyclists come in droves to enjoy the park's public resources. There are more than 5 miles of designated trails to enjoy in this park, all of which conveniently intersect to create hours of off-road adventure. The trails vary in intensity, ranging from rolling forest roads beneath tall oaks and maples to steep, rocky singletrack overlooking the dramatic Mather Gorge. The park's unequaled beauty, proximity to Washington, and accessible trails combine to make Great Falls National Park Northern Virginia's most popular off-road cycling haven.

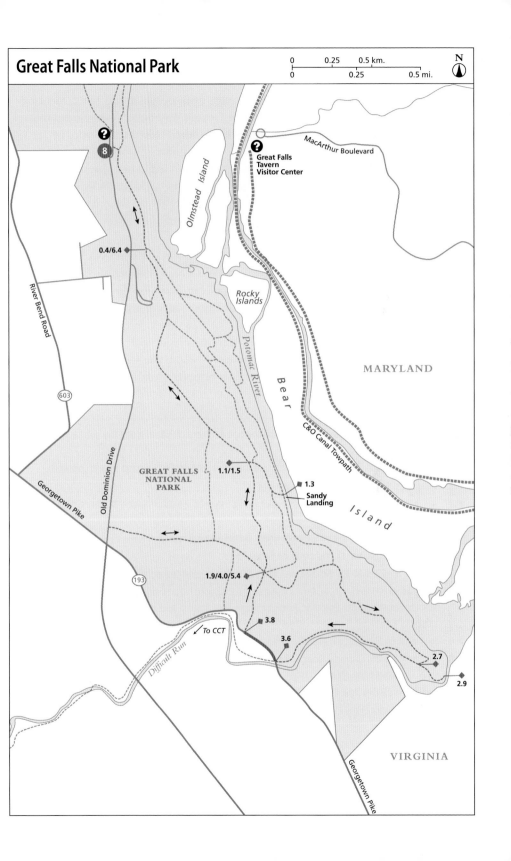

Great Falls National Park

0   0.25   0.5 km.
0   0.25   0.5 mi.

N

❓

8

❓ Great Falls Tavern Visitor Center

MacArthur Boulevard

Olmstead Island

0.4/6.4 ◆

Rocky Islands

River Bend Road

Potomac River

B e a r

MARYLAND

603

C&O Canal Towpath

Old Dominion Drive

GREAT FALLS NATIONAL PARK

1.1/1.5 ◆

■ 1.3

Sandy Landing

Georgetown Pike

I s l a n d

193

1.9/4.0/5.4 ◆

■ 3.8

To CCT

3.6 ■

Difficult Run

◆ 2.7

◆ 2.9

VIRGINIA

Georgetown Pike

The ride begins at the visitor center parking lot and travels south along Old Carriage Road through the middle of the park. Old Carriage was used in the 1700s to carry settlers to their dwellings at Matildaville, ruins of which still stand. Henry Lee, a Revolutionary War hero and a friend of George Washington's, developed this small town. Named after Lee's first wife, Matildaville lasted only three decades before fading into history.

The route bends deep into the park and travels up and down the rocky pass along Ridge Trail. During the winter months, breathtaking views of the gorge show through deciduous trees. The trail then descends quickly to the Potomac (another great view) and follows along Difficult Run before heading north again back toward the start.

Great Falls has always been a popular place to visit for locals and world tourists alike. Some have come to survey the river's rapids. George Washington formed the Patowmack Company in 1784 to build a series of canals around the falls. Theodore Roosevelt came to Great Falls to hike and ride horses during his presidency. Today, thousands come to enjoy Great Falls as well. But they don't come to build canals, develop towns, make trade, or seek solitude from the presidential office. They come only to ride the park's great trails, kayak the rapids, climb the steep cliffs, and bear witness to the magnificent scenery at Great Falls National Park.

Miles and Directions

0.0 Start at Great Falls Visitor Center. Follow the horse/biker trail south along the entrance road.

0.4 Bear right at the restrooms and go around the steel gate on Old Carriage Road (unpaved).

1.1 Bear left down the trail to Sandy Landing.

1.3 Arrive at Sandy Landing, a beautiful spot along the river, great for viewing Mather Gorge. Return to Old Carriage Road.

1.5 Turn left, continuing on Old Carriage Road. Begin a steady uphill.

1.9 Turn left near the top of this climb on Ridge Trail.

2.7 Turn left after the steep descent on Difficult Run Trail. Head toward the Potomac.

2.9 Arrive at the Potomac River. This is another great spot to view Sherwin Island, where Mather Gorge and the Potomac River converge. Turn around and follow Difficult Run Trail west along Difficult Run Creek toward Georgetown Pike.

3.6 Turn right on Georgetown Pike. Be careful with traffic and ride on the dirt shoulder.

3.8 Turn right on Old Carriage Road. This is the first dirt road you come to along Georgetown Pike. Go around the gate and begin climbing.

4.0 Turn left on Ridge Trail. Follow this toward the entrance road.

4.7 Reach the park entrance road (Old Dominion Road). Turn around and continue back on Ridge Trail.

5.4 Turn left on Old Carriage Road.

6.4 Go through the gate at the beginning of Old Carriage Road and head back to the parking lot at the visitor center.

6.8 Arrive back at the visitor center and parking lot.

Ride Information

Local Information

Fairfax County Convention and Visitors Bureau, (800) 7FAIRFAX—www .visitfairfax.org

Local Events and Attractions

Colvin Run Mill, (703) 759-2771
Wolf Trap Farm Park for the Performing Arts, (703) 255-1800

Where to Eat

Great Falls Village Centre
Great Falls, VA
(703) 759-2485
www.greatfallsvillagecentre.com/restaurants/

9 Wakefield Park/Accotink Trail

Wakefield Park is quite possibly the most popular mountain-bike destination in the Metro Washington, D.C. area. Its close proximity to the Capital Beltway makes it a popular destination for all the northern Virginia suburbanites who live and/or work inside the Beltway. On any given afternoon, the parking lots of Wakefield Park are brimming with activity from people using the soccer fields, Audrey Moore RECenter, skate park, tennis courts, and the extensive network of bike trails that run parallel to Accotink Creek and the nearby power lines.

Start: Aubrey Moore Recreation Center parking area

Length: 5.5 miles

Ride time: About 1 hour

Difficulty: Moderate

Trail surface: Singletrack and dirt trails

Lay of the land: Wooded and relatively flat, next to the Capital Beltway

Land status: County parks

Nearest cities: Annandale, VA; Alexandria, VA

Other trail users: Hikers

Trail contacts: Fairfax County Park Authority, (703) 324-8700; Lake Accotink Park, (703) 569-7120; Wakefield Park, (703) 321-7081

Schedule: Open daylight to dark year-round; night riding allowed only on designated MORE rides Tues and Thur

Getting there: The park is less than 0.5 mile from the Capital Beltway off Braddock Road in northern Virginia. Exit west on exit 54A, Braddock Road, and turn right in less than 2 miles into Wakefield. Drive straight for approximately 0.5 mile and then turn left where the tarmac ends into the main Audrey Moore RECenter parking area. Park adjacent to the recycling bins to the right. **GPS coordinates:** 38.817901, -77.223256. **GPS coordinates (Accotink Trails):** 38.801682, -77.234768.

The Ride

Sometimes it's interesting to see where you will find challenging trails. More often than not, Washingtonians and nearby DC suburbanites have to venture far out to the west or north of the city to find natural-surface trails that crisscross the forested spaces of Frederick County in Maryland and the George Washington National Forest in Virginia. But, as it turns out, there are surprising opportunities closer to home for dirt lovers to enjoy. One such location is the network of trails that exists only minutes from the Capital Beltway in Wakefield Park. For those nature enthusiasts who can't afford to venture out and drive over an hour to distant trail networks, Fairfax County's Wakefield Park has become an oasis for indoor and outdoor recreational activities.

Wakefield Park is the home of the Audrey Moore RECenter, a facility that includes a multitude of activities for Fairfax County residents and visitors alike. The rec center—dedicated to longtime Fairfax County politician Audrey

Wakefield is home to the Wednesdays at Wakefield summer races.

Moore—measures in at nearly 76,000 square feet, houses a 50-meter pool with various diving boards and spectator seating, a spacious sundeck, locker rooms, saunas, and showers. There is also a large gym with multiple basketball hoops and volleyball nets. The rec center also includes a cycle studio, should you feel compelled to cycle indoors. If you want to mix in a strength workout before or after your ride, there is also a spacious fitness center with a multitude of cardio equipment, free weights, and a stretching area.

On the outside, you'll find seven well-maintained athletic fields, including five softball fields, a football field, and a soccer field. You'll also see a basketball court, a skate park, and eleven lighted tennis courts to go along with the more than 6 miles of natural-surface singletrack mountain-biking trails.

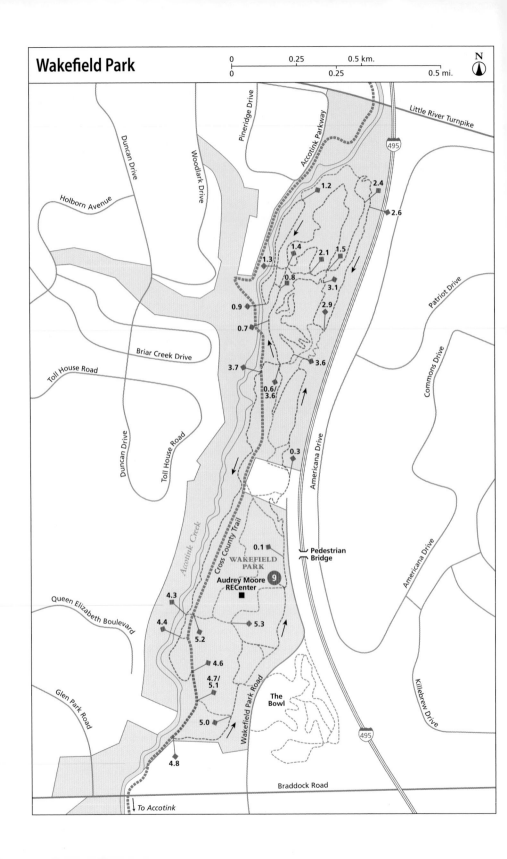

Wakefield Park

Little River Turnpike

Pineridge Drive

Accotink Parkway

Duncan Drive

Woodlark Drive

Holborn Avenue

495

2.4
2.6

1.2

1.4   2.1   1.5
1.3
0.8
3.1
0.9

2.9
0.7

3.6
3.7

0.6/
3.6

Briar Creek Drive

Toll House Road

Duncan Drive

Toll House Road

Patriot Drive

Commons Drive

0.3

Americana Drive

Acotink Creek

Cross County Trail

0.1   Pedestrian
          Bridge

WAKEFIELD
PARK   9
Audrey Moore
RECenter

Americana Drive

4.3

4.4   5.3

5.2

4.6

4.7/
5.1

Queen Elizabeth Boulevard

Glen Park Road

Wakefield Park Road

The
Bowl

5.0

Killebrew Drive

495

4.8

Braddock Road

↓ To Accotink

The trails at Wakefield have been through a drastic transformation over the past decade. The early popularity of mountain biking in the mid-1990s and subsequent 2000s brought a tremendous number of riders into the park. Unfortunately, the original power line and wooded trails that existed within its boundaries were not designed for off-road cycling, thus they suffered considerably with the number of riders that used them on a daily basis. Park managers and MORE recognized the problem and took action to improve and preserve the network of trails.

With the help of IMBA's trail crew, the muscle of local area volunteers, and the support of the Fairfax County government, regional riders set out to improve the trails of this Beltway destination. Thanks to the efforts and dedication of those biking advocates, today the park in Wakefield houses more than 6 miles of sustainable, enjoyable, and challenging trails, all within 0.5 mile from the Capital Beltway.

Our loop will take you through those renovated trails and partially through part of the popular Wednesdays at Wakefield (W@W) summer series of mountain-bike races. While challenging, it is a ride that can be easily conquered by beginner riders and enjoyed by accomplished dirt lovers alike. I highly recommend you change directions on this loop or change it around to make it your own. To add a little distance to your ride, also venture out and include sections of "The Bowl," a small area of the park that lies between the Beltway and the park entrance road that offers a couple of extra miles of singletrack. You may also want to give the trails a shot at night. Thanks to a well-crafted partnership between Fairfax County and MORE, night riding is allowed in the park on Monday, Tuesday, and Thursday nights from dusk to 10:30 p.m. Bear in mind that night riding is allowed in some Fairfax County Parks, and, to ensure this privilege remains, please don't ride the trails during any non-designated nights.

The ride outlined below is a suggested route. My advice is just to go out and explore all the trails around the power lines to find the loop that you like best. I have not included The Bowl in this write up, but you can easily add 3 more miles to your ride by riding it.

Miles and Directions

0.0 Start immediately adjacent to the recycling bins and turn left on the gravel road toward the pedestrian bridge that spans over the Capital Beltway.

0.1 As you reach the pedestrian bridge, take the narrow singletrack trail that shoots up to the left. Follow this trail as it zigzags through this small section of woods.

0.3 Cross the dirt road and ride on the singletrack that runs parallel to I-495. When the trail splits, take the fork to the left along the perimeter of the power station.

0.4 Continue on the singletrack trail toward the left after crossing the small creek. The trail will then veer to the right slightly before reaching the CCT. Continue on it over the short boardwalk and rock section, and then immediately head into the woods to continue on the trail that runs parallel to the power lines.

0.6 Cross over the creek and continue straight across this intersection. Get ready for a short burst.

0.7 Continue straight past this intersection and continue the short climb.

0.8 After a short downhill, turn left and then immediately left again into the main trail (basically, a big U-turn).

0.9 Turn immediately right into the creek trail.

1.2 Continue bearing to the right (follow the yellow arrows) to return to the main trail.

1.3 Turn left at the first intersection. There is a yellow arrow marker clearly visible here. Follow the trail to the right for a short climb until it ends at the next intersection.

1.4 Turn left and pass one intersection, the exit of Phase 4. We'll be back at this point shortly.

1.5 Turn left. This is the second intersection and the entrance to Phase 4. Remain on Phase 4 and go over eight small wood bridges.

2.1 Turn left onto the trail we were just on. This time, continue straight past the entrance to Phase 4 and out into the power lines. The trail will veer to the left under the power lines. At this point, you'll ride toward and around the back of the second set of towers visible from where you are.

2.4 The trail veers to the left as you reach the second tower and then back to the right and behind the tower. After a short switchback, climb, you'll emerge on the top adjacent to the two towers.

2.6 You are now at the base of the two towers. Follow the trail as it runs parallel to the Beltway back in the direction you came from. This time ride back toward the second set of two towers from which you originally came from.

2.9 Turn right to ride the trail on the inside of the two towers. Immediately after passing the second tower (single pylon), turn right to head back down a series of jumps that end with a sweeping left-hand berm turn into the woods at 3.0.

3.1 Continue following the trail to the left for approximately 0.5 mile. The right fork takes you back to the entrance of Phase 4. This trail will gradually climb and then descend via a series of switchback berm turns along the power lines.

3.6 Turn right before the trail shoots out into the open and then immediately right again. You'll see the creek, which we crossed at mile marker 0.6. Continue straight until you reach the CCT and turn left at 3.7.

3.7 After turning left on the CCT, go over a small bridge and immediately turn right onto the Creek Trail. You will now remain on the Creek Trail for nearly a mile.

4.3 Stay to the right to remain on the Creek Trail.

4.4 Stay to the right to remain on the Creek Trail.

4.6 The Creek Trail comes out of the power lines and veers to the left and back and intersects the CCT. Make a sharp right. Our return trip will bring us back to this intersection shortly.

4.7 Continue to the right and cross the creek.

4.8 Turn left on the CCT. A right turn will take you to Lake Accotink.

5.0 Immediately before reaching the parking area, turn left to follow the trail along the outfield fence line.

5.1 Turn right to return to the trail you were just on a few minutes ago, and then right again when the trail comes out into the power lines.

5.2 Go over the bridge and turn right to remain under the power lines. As soon as you reach the two large towers, turn right to head up to the soccer fields and the Audrey Moore RECenter.

5.3 Turn right on the paved trail that runs around the perimeter of the soccer field and then right again to head up between the skate park and the rec center to reach the parking area.

5.5 You're back at the lot and the starting point of the ride.

Ride Information

Local Information

Fairfax County Convention and Visitors Bureau, (800) 7FAIRFAX—www .visitfairfax.org

Bike Shops

The Bike Lane, 8416 Old Keene Mill Rd., Springfield, VA, (703) 440-8701, thebikelane.com

Bikenetic, 201 W. Jefferson St., Falls Church, VA, (703) 534-7433, www.bikenetic.com

Local Events and Attractions

Wakefield Farmers' Market: Wednesday, May 2 through October 31, 2–6 p.m.

Mountain-bike races are conducted throughout the summer, including the Wednesdays at Wakefield (W@W) Mountain Bike Race series. potomacvelo.com

Trail-running races are conducted within Wakefield Park as a part of the Backyard Burn race series coordinated by Ex2Adventures in the spring and fall. www.ex2 adventures.com

In Addition

Night Riding

Absence of light does not mean we have to stop riding. Equipping yourself with one (or two) of the many powerful lights available on the market today will allow you to extend your riding season, and hit your local trails at night.

Riding a trail you're familiar with at night is like riding a completely different destination. I love hitting my local singletrack in the dark of night, because it provides me with a completely "new" riding experience. Riding at night heightens the senses and it really reveals how much attention you are paying to the trail during the daylight hours. At night, you notice things that simply don't manifest themselves during the day. You'll experience a completely new world and in the process bring your riding to the next level.

So, how do you make that dark outing successful? For starters, you need to make sure you pick the right light for the job. Stay away from anything powered by AA or AAA batteries; those lights WILL NOT provide you with enough coverage for what is needed to safely operate a bike on trails in the dark. Begin your search for lights that produce at the very least 500–700 lumens.

Being "visible" to others is not as critical off-road as it is on the road; instead, what's ahead of you is what it's all about. Having a small taillight helps other riders in a group gauge where you are, but knowing what's ahead of you is critical for safety. I highly recommend you opt for a single handlebar light and a helmet-mounted light. Having both will allow you to gauge depth more accurately. In addition, it will help you see what's going on along your periphery. As you turn your head, the beam on your helmet will provide you with a better view of the surroundings, while the bar mounted light will stay on the trail, where your bike is rolling.

Additional tips

Know your run time: Don't ride longer than your battery lasts—trust me—if you can, bring an extra battery.

Wear glasses: Most sport glasses come with the option to swap dark shades with clear lenses. I highly recommend you use those clear lenses to protect your eyes.

Think about the future: When selecting a lighting system think about future upgrades. Light & Motion lights, for example, have stayed true to their battery configuration so you can use their older batteries on newer systems.

Carry a spare light in your pocket: A cheap portable flashlight is fine, but if you can afford an all-in-one system even better; this light is for "emergencies." If you ride with only a bar mounted light, the spare light can help you change a flat, or fix a mechanical without having to take your light off the bars.

Ride open destinations only: Most jurisdictions and local parks are closed from sundown to sunrise and poaching trails at night is just as bad for access as riding illegal trails. Check with your local area club, they generally do the legwork to get permission for organized night rides. My local club (MORE), for example, has organized night rides virtually every night of the week.

Have fun!

10 Laurel Hill

The ride through the hills and meadows of Laurel Hill will take you through a parcel of land that was once home to a Revolutionary War hero, thousands of reformatory inmates, and a magazine of intercontinental ballistic missiles.

Start: Giles Run Meadow Trailhead parking lot by the playground; alternate start points: Barrett House, Lorton Workhouse Arts Center Parking Area
Length: 10.9 miles; optional 2-mile reformatory loop (good for kids)
Ride time: 1–2 hours
Difficulty: Easy/moderate
Trail surface: Mostly doubletrack and singletrack trails with a short section of hard surface on the CCT trail

Lay of the land: Rolling, open fields with some wooded section; former site of DC Penitentiary
Land status: County park
Nearest town: Occoquan, VA
Other trail users: Hikers, equestrians
Trail contacts: Fairfax County, www.fairfaxcounty.gov/parks/laurelhill
Schedule: Open year-round, dawn to dusk

Getting there: Laurel Hill is in Lorton, Virginia, approximately 20 miles south of Washington, D.C. From I-95, take the Lorton Road exit. Head west at bottom of ramp (a right turn whether coming north- or southbound on I-95). The Giles Run entrance is on the right in about 0.25 mile down Lorton Road. Follow the driveway up until you see the prison complex. The parking lot is on the left, next to the playground. **GPS coordinates:** 38.709430, -77.239068.

The Ride

Laurel Hill, located in Lorton, Virginia, is a relatively new addition to a growing list of off-road cycling trails in Fairfax County. Named after the original hometown of one of the area's first settlers, Joseph Plaskett, Lorton has a very colorful history. And Laurel Hill, the geographic area where this ride takes place, is no different. The ride will take you through what was once the home of a Revolutionary War hero, thousands of the most hardened criminals, and a magazine of six Nike intercontinental ballistic missiles aimed toward the Soviet Union.

Lorton's history starts well before the arrival of Joseph Plaskett in the mid-1800s. The area had been home to the Powhatan people, a confederation of tribes that farmed and hunted the lands of the coastal plains and tidewater region. Like in so many regions in the east, it didn't take long for the Native Americans to be displaced by the arriving settlers. Yet, it really wasn't until Joseph Plaskett added a post office to his popular country store that Lorton was finally placed on the map.

Roughly around the same time that Lorton gained postal recognition, another prominent American and contemporary to both George Mason and George Washington settled in the area, giving it prominence. William Lindsay, a major in one of

Virginia's militias during the Revolutionary War and a presumed aide to George Washington himself, built a home for his family on a hilltop overlooking his 1,000-acre plantation and named it Laurel Hill after what is believed to have been the original Lindsay family estate in Ireland. In 1871, Lindsay suffered severe wounds in the battle of Guilford Courthouse and returned home, where he spent his last decade alongside his wife and sixteen children. Upon his death, the major was buried in the estate, where his grave remains visible to this day. Over the years his home was renovated and expanded, and was even once occupied by the superintendent of the Lorton prison. Today, unfortunately, it stands in disrepair.

The area remained in the shadows until the early twentieth century, when then-President Theodore Roosevelt commissioned the building of a progressive penitentiary and reformatory for the District of Columbia in the meadows of Laurel Hill. Roosevelt firmly believed that the natural surroundings of the area and exposure to nature and hard work provided an ideal environment suitable for the rehabilitation of prisoners. With that in mind, the Lorton Reformatory and Penitentiary was built, and at its peak, grew to accommodate more than 7,000 inmates within nearly 3,000 acres of land. The prison's dwindling popularity, changing attitudes, and the sprawl of the late twentieth century toward the Virginia suburbs forced its closure and transference from the Federal government to Fairfax County by the beginning of the twenty-first century.

Lorton's proximity to Washington, D.C., also made Lorton the perfect location for a Nike missile site. During the peak of the Cold War, when the arms race between the United States and the Soviet Union was at its height, the army acquired 30 acres from the Federal government on the grounds of the penitentiary and built a double pad with six Nike missile magazines. The site maintained operations until the early 1970s when Secretary of Defense James R. Schlesinger ordered its closure. As a result, most of the missile structures were razed and today very little evidence of their existence remains.

Prior to acquiring the land from the Federal government, Fairfax County was mandated to develop a "Reuse Plan that would maximize use of land for open space, parkland or recreation." In 1999, a citizen task force was appointed to develop the plan, which was later adopted by the County's Board of Supervisors and presented to Congress. Then, by November 2001, with the transfer of the last of the prisoners from the penitentiary complete, the Lorton prison was officially closed. By July 2002, after an extensive survey, more than 2,000 acres of land in the facility were transferred to Fairfax County at a cost of $4.2 million and thus began the renovation of the Lorton facilities.

Today the area is most commonly referred to as Laurel Hill to honor the legacy of William Lindsay and to preserve its historical significance. The phased approach toward development outlined in the Reuse Plan is well under way and over the past decade, the facilities have seen a dramatic change. Several of the old penitentiary buildings have been restored and now house a thriving community of artists and craftsmen that host cultural and community events. An environmentally oriented eighteen-hole golf course is up and running, and, luckily for cyclists, an extensive system of trails has been built and is now open for the enjoyment of the community. Future plans include the restoration of the original eighteenth-century Lindsay home and additional work to the penitentiary and reformatory buildings to include residential units, restaurants, retail shops, and educational facilities.

Brisk winter days are the best time to visit the trails at Laurel Hill.

At its peak, the Lorton Penitentiary and Reformatory held more than 7,000 prisoners. On November 19, 2001, amid little fanfare, the last handful of prisoners left the correctional facility for transfer to other Federal facilities across the country.

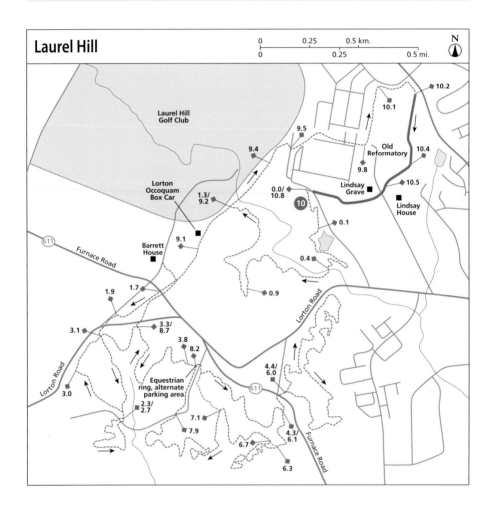

Miles and Directions

0.0 Start the ride from the far end of the parking area where the paved path begins by the small playground with the climbing apparatus. Head down the path and turn left to enter the singletrack. The trail will then turn right and head toward the Meadow Pond.

0.1 Pass the Meadow Pond. The trail is easy to follow and well-marked from here on.

0.4 Cross the creek and continue on the other side to the right. The trail will curve left and then right as it climbs to the wood line.

0.9 Stay right at this intersection to continue on the Giles Run Meadow Trail.

1.3 Turn left on the doubletrack. You are now on the Cross County Trail (CCT).

1.5 Stay left to continue on the CCT.

1.7 Right before the Barrel Arch Bridge, there is a trail to the right. This is a short connector that will take you to the Barrett House and an alternate starting point for this ride. Continue straight under the barrel bridge and past the trail intersection to the left.

1.9 Turn left on the pavement and cross Lorton Road. Use Caution. The trail is clearly visible on the other side of the road. Follow it and turn left at the first intersection, then follow the trail to the right.

2.2 Turn left at this intersection and then immediately right at the bottom and left again to enter the Slaughterhouse loop.

2.3 Pass the Slaughterhouse and turn right to follow the trail as it climbs to the top of the hill via a series of switchbacks.

2.7 You're back where you started the Slaughterhouse loop. Exit and head back up the way you came in. Upon exiting, turn right and then immediately left to climb back up to the Workhouse loop.

2.8 Turn left. Follow the arrow labeled "To CCT."

3.0 Turn right on the CCT and continue back to the point where you started this first loop. If you turn left on the CCT, it will take you to the Lorton Workhouse, an alternate starting point for the ride.

3.1 Turn right and then immediately left to head down into the other side of the Workhouse loop.

3.3 Continue straight. You will take the trail to the left on your way out.

3.8 Stay to the left at this intersection to head toward the yellow (Pasture loop). Cross the road, pick up the trail, and then turn left to follow the yellow loop.

4.3 Turn left at this intersection to head up toward Furnace Road and the Apple Orchard loop. After the Apple Orchard loop, you'll return to this spot.

4.4 After crossing the road, you'll be in the Apple Orchard loop. You can go either direction. For now, go left and follow the loop in the clockwise direction. There are a couple of well-marked intersections on the loop; just make sure to stay to the right on both (left if you're heading counterclockwise).

6.0 You're back at the entry point of the Apple Orchard loop. Turn left to head back to the Pasture loop.

6.1 Turn left on the Pasture loop (yellow trail) and head south toward the incinerator.

6.3 Veer left at this intersection to enter the Power Station loop.

6.7 Turn left to continue on the Pasture loop.

7.1 Continue following the trail to the left to enter the Dairy Barn loop. If you were to turn left and head back up, you would reach the Workhouse loop.

7.9 Cross the dirt road and pick up the Workhouse loop directly across the road to the left. If you head down the road to the left, you would reach the Slaughterhouse loop. To the right is the entrance to the Pasture loop (mile marker 3.8 above).

8.2 Stay left at this intersection. You'll double back on the Workhouse loop for a short distance before making your way back to the Giles Run Area.

8.7 Turn right at this intersection to cross Lorton Road and head back toward the CCT.

8.8 Turn right on the CCT and head back the way you initially came in. The Barrel Arch Bridge will be to your immediate right.

9.1 Stay to the right to continue on the CCT. The old Lorton Occoquan Boxcar will come up on your left.

9.2 To the right is the intersection of the Giles Run Meadow Trail. Continue straight over the bridge. (Or you can head back up and ride it in the opposite direction to your vehicle if you wish.)

9.3 Immediately after crossing the bridge, stay to the left to go on a quick sightseeing loop around the perimeter of the penitentiary. (The short hill to the right will take you back to the parking area.)

9.4 Continue to the left and circle the pond in a clockwise direction, heading up to the path you see along the side of the reformatory.

9.5 Turn right and then immediately left to go around the reformatory. If you continue straight after turning right, you'll end up in the parking area.

9.8 Continue following the path to the left. The main prison wall will be to your right.

10.1 The blacktop ends. Turn right on the sidewalk and follow it to the stop sign. At the stop sign turn right and follow the dirt path around the next watchtower.

10.2 Turn left on the road when the dirt path ends. The prison wall will now be immediately to your right.

10.4 The wall ends. Continue following the fence line along the perimeter of the road.

10.5 You'll get a good glimpse of the Lindsay house to the left and his grave immediately to the right by the prison gates. Continue straight on the road.

10.8 Turn left into the parking lot and head back toward the playground and the starting point of the ride.

10.9 The loop is complete.

Optional Maximum Security Prison Loop

This loop is excellent for kids or if you're looking to do a quick run after or before your ride.

0.0 Start at the Giles Run parking area by the playground. Start measuring from the first access point to the parking lot, by the yellow pylons. Exit the lot by turning right and then follow the left fork along the perimeter of the reformatory. You'll now be on the CCT.

0.3 After a short down and up, you'll reach the first watchtower. To the right is the Lindsay house, to the left his grave.

0.5 Reach the second watchtower. There is a gap in the fence that allows access to the athletic fields. You can get a closer look at the facilities around here. Continue following the road that runs along the reformatory wall.

0.6 At the time of this writing, there was a chain-link fence blocking the road. Turn right as you reach the fence and then follow the dirt path to the left to continue riding along the perimeter of the reformatory.

0.7 Turn left on White Spruce Road. Stay on the near sidewalk, which will put you on the paved blacktop trail. Turn left on the path to follow the perimeter of the reformatory. If you're lucky, you'll get a glimpse of the new prison residents. Virtually every time I ride through here, I have seen gophers, groundhogs, and red foxes running around.

1.0 Turn right on the brick path.

1.3 You have three options here. Turn left to head back to the parking lot. Follow the middle path to head down to the CCT. Or turn right and quickly left to take a slightly longer route to the CCT. For now, turn right and then immediately left and follow the path around the pond.

1.4 Turn right.

1.5 Don't cross the bridge. Make a sharp left and head back up toward the parking lot.

1.6 Follow the path toward the right between the watchtower and the guard house to complete the loop; or, turn left and do the loop in the opposite direction. I'd opt for the latter.

Ride Information

Local Information

Town of Occoquan—www.occoquanva.gov
Lorton, VA—www.virginia.org/Cities/Lorton

Bike Shops

The Bike Lane, Springfield, VA, (703) 440-8701, thebikelane.com
Olde Towne Bicycles, Woodbridge, VA, (703) 491-5700, oldetownebicycles.com
Village Skis & Bikes, Woodbridge, VA, (703) 730-0303, vsbsports.com

Local Events and Attractions

Lorton Workhouse Arts Center, www.lortonarts.org/calendar.php
Historic Occoquan, historicoccoquan.com

Where to Eat

Antonelli's
Lorton, VA
(703) 690-4500
antonellis-pizza.com

Cock and Bowl
Occoquan, VA
(703) 494-1180
cockandbowl.com

11 Meadowood Recreation Area

The Meadowood mountain bike trails are a hit with riders of all skill levels. In addition to an easy-to-navigate perimeter loop, the Meadowood mountain bike trails include three internal trails (The Boss Trail, Stinger, and Yard Sale) that offer intermediate to advanced mountain bikers several man-made features to test their skills on, including a set of high wooden berms, several rock obstacles, and multiple opportunities to take your bike airborne.

Start: Old Colchester Road parking area
Length: 6.9 miles
Ride time: 1-1.5 hours, longer if you do multiple loops
Difficulty: Easy/intermediate
Trail surface: Mostly singletrack, with elevated boardwalks and berms
Lay of the land: Mature hardwood forest of the Mason Neck Peninsula

Land status: Beaureau of Land Management (BLM) park
Nearest town: Occoquan, VA
Other trail users: Hikers and equestrians
Trail contacts: BLM, www.blm.gov/es/st/en/fo/lpfo_html/recreation.html
Schedule: Open year-round

Getting there: Take the Capital Beltway (I-495) toward northern Virginia and follow the signs for I-95 South. Take exit 163 for VA 642 toward Lorton and turn left onto Lorton Road. Continue for approximately 0.5 miles and turn right onto Lorton Market St (600). Follow Lorton Market Street will become Gunston Cove Road as it curves left, continue to the intersection with US-1. Cross US-1, you are now on Gunston Road, the Meadowood parking area will be approximately 1 mile to the right immediately after Gunston Elementary School. **GPS coordinates:** 38.680545, -77.219717.

The Ride

The Meadowood trails and recreation area are a relatively new leisure destination operated by the BLM. The nearly 800 acres of meadows, ponds, and hardwood forests where the trails currently lie were transferred in a land swap between Pulte Home Builders, Fairfax County, and the Federal government in 2001. In late October of the same year, the land was assigned to BLM, which currently manages it to ensure an open space for recreation and environmental education.

Before the land was acquired and transferred to the BLM, it had been a working farm with horse stables. It also included a series of wooded trails that were in varying states of disrepair. Many of the trails were along steep lines, causing erosion and posing safety and water issues. Once the BLM took over the day-to-day management of the location, they fixed some immediate problems and developed an integrated activity plan in which they outlined their vision for the area and identified the potential use scenarios. These included hiking, fishing, horseback riding, and cycling (mountain biking). The plan also identified and recognized that the legacy all-terrain vehicles and old farm equestrian trails should be abandoned and replaced with new sustainable routes.

Meadowood is physically divided into two distinct areas by Belmont Boulevard. The east side of the system, and closest to the Meadowood Field Station (management offices) and adjacent to the existing horse boarding stables, is primarily an equestrian destination; bikes are not allowed there. The west side had remained undeveloped, and since mountain biking would be one of the allowed activities in the system, the BLM worked with IMBA representative and trail specialist Dan Hudson to lay out a potential biking and hiking loop. The area surveyed included some of the old farm trails, and it was recommended that many of these be rerouted or rebuilt.

In 2009, the BLM, using American Recovery and Reinvestment Act (ARRA) funds, hired two term staff members, Doug Vinson and David Lyster, with trail-building experience to oversee the recommendations made by Dan Hudson and IMBA. After a period of additional planning, Vinson and Leyster began building the recommended loop in early 2011. By January 2012, they had completed the South Branch Trail.

The wood features of the Boss Trail are an absolute blast to ride.

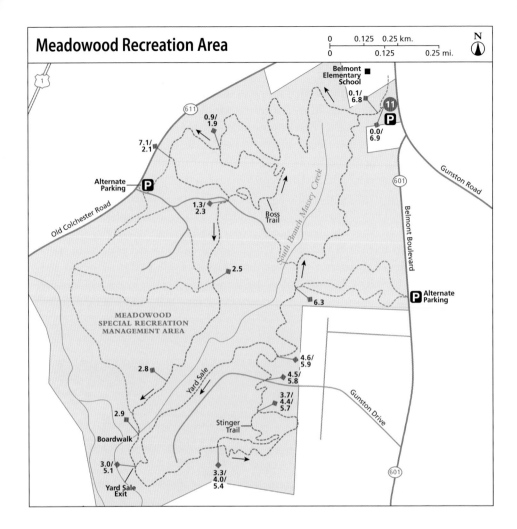

Meadowood Recreation Area

Not satisfied with their effort, Doug and David set out to begin Phase 2 of the Meadowood project. Enlisting the help of volunteers and MORE, they began to solicit and raise funds for several extensions to the loop. Again, with the help of IMBA, they crafted a design that added three additional trails, accessible from the South Branch trail. The new trails, Boss Trail, Stinger, and Yard Sale have more advanced trail features, including banked turns, rock outcroppings, narrow log crossings, jumps, and steep climbing turns.

Miles and Directions

0.0 Start from the new lot along Gunston Road and enter the trail.

0.1 Immediately turn right to follow the loop in a counterclockwise direction. The loop I document here includes all three internal trails, Boss, Stinger and Yard Sale (in that order). You can bypass all three and still get a good ride along the main perimeter loop.

0.9 Continue past the exit for Boss Trail. We will revisit this intersection shortly.

1.1 Continue following the main loop to the left. The fork to the right will take you to the Old Colchester Road Parking area. An alternate starting point.

1.3 The main loop continues straight. We'll turn left and enjoy the Boss Trail. Boss contains several Technical Trail Features (TTFs). All TTFs along Boss have an alternate path except for the two berms at the beginning of the ride. The berms, however, are technically easy to ride.

1.9 You're back on the main loop. Turn left and back track along the next section of trail. This is the same intersection we visited at mile marker .9.

2.1 Continue following the main loop to the left. This is the same intersection we visited at mile marker 1.1.

2.3 You're back at the intersection with the Boss Trail. This time we will continue straight and past the next doubletrack intersection. If you want to cut the ride short, turn left on the doubletrack until you hit the perimeter loop, then turn left again to finish it. The next section of trail is a super fun downhill. The Mountain Bike trail will intersect the Meadowood hiking trails at least twice in the next 1/2 mile (2.5 & 2.8). Just continue staying to the left as you head down to the elevated deck.

2.9 You reach the elevated deck, continue straight until you hit the next section of singletrack.

3.0 Continue past the exit point for Yard Sale. We will revisit this intersection shortly.

3.3 Continue past the exit point for Stinger. We will revisit this intersection shortly.

3.7 Turn left into Stinger. Immediately after the left turn there is a small TTF, a log drop as the trail turns to the left. Most riders have made a path around it.

4.0 Back on the main loop. Turn left to double back along the next section of trail. We'll ride this section one more time on the way back from Yard Sale.

4.4 Continue straight along the main loop past the entrance to Stinger.

4.5 Continue straight over the doubletrack.

4.6 Turn left to hit Yard Sale, Meadowood's Jump Line. Only the first part of Yard Sale contains a series of jumps (that can be rolled). The second half is a great section of twisty singletrack.

5.1 You reach the main loop, turn left and double back past the exit and entrance to Stinger and past the entrance to Yard Sale.

5.4 Continue past the Stinger Exit.

5.7 Continue past the entrance to Stinger.

5.8 Continue straight over the doubletrack.

5.9 Continue straight past the entrance to Yard Sale.

6.3 Continue past the next three intersections. A right turn on either of the first two will take you back toward the Belmont Boulevard parking area. A left along the third intersection will take you back toward the entrance to the Boss Trail, mile marker 1.3.

6.8 Follow the trail to the right and away form the main loop, this is the exit point to the Gunston Road Parking Area.

6.9 The loop is complete.

Ride Information

Local Information

Town of Occoquan—www.occoquanva.gov
Lorton, VA—www.virginia.org/Cities/Lorton

Bike Shops

Olde Towne Bicycles, Inc., Woodbridge, VA, (703) 491-5700, oldetownebicycles.com
Village Skis & Bikes, Woodbridge, VA, (703) 730-0303, vsbsports.com

Where to Eat

Vinny's Italian Grill
Lorton, VA
(703) 339-7447
www.vinnysitaliangrill.net

Honorable Mentions

Compiled here is an index of great rides in Northern Virginia that didn't make the A list this time around but deserve recognition. Check them out and let us know what you think. You may decide that one or more of these rides deserves higher status in future editions, or perhaps you may have a ride of your own that merits some attention. Some of these rides are documented on our website, www.mtbdc.com

F. Freedom Center: Home of the popular mountain-bike races Snotcycle and Hotcycle. Located in Loudoun County, and on private property, the Freedom Center was conceived and built by the guys from Mountain Bike Loudoun County (MTB LoCo, www.mtbloco.org). The trail offers intermediate riders a mixture of tough climbs, flowy singletrack, and fast downhills within the Freedom Center's property. A small pond provides a perfect spot to take a break and enjoy the rural setting of the facility. MTB LoCo maintains the trails and a short pump track on the property and often schedules organized rides to show you around. Check MTB LoCo's website for additional information, including their plans to design, build, and maintain a new multi-use system of trails in Loudoun's Evergreen Mills Park.
GPS coordinates: 39.228722, –77.550227

G. Locust Shade Park: Located just outside the gates of Quantico is a small county park with a series of short singletrack trails perfect for novice mountain bikers. If you are ever headed south along I-95 and are stuck in the dreaded corridor's evening traffic, and have your bike with you, take a quick detour to kill some time while the traffic dies down. The trail currently totals no more than 3 miles, but it is a perfect place to take young kids who are getting their mountain-biking skills into shape. A couple of short climbs might prove difficult for some, but the rest of the system is easy to navigate and negotiate. Plans are currently under way by the Prince William County Department of Parks and Recreation to revitalize the trails in this small county park and make them more like the trails just a little further north at the Meadowood Recreation Area in Lorton (Ride 11).
GPS coordinates: 38.531300, –77.351904

H. Marine Corps Base Quantico: The trails at Marine Corps Base Quantico have been around for several years and have seen a dramatic transformation. The primary reason I do not detail this network of singletrack goodness is because of its location, an active military installation. Quantico's access could very well go away in the blink of an eye, but because of the efforts of an active mountain-biking community within the base—primarily the Quantico Mountain Bike Club (QMTB Club)—the chances of that happening are very slim. For years, the trails were accessible to the general public, but a couple of incidents involving cyclists and training marines changed that, and the trails remained closed for

A small pond provides a perfect spot to take a break and enjoy the rural setting of the facility, Honorable Mention F, the Freedom Center.

nearly a decade until they were opened again a few years ago. To access the trails, you will need a valid QMTB membership card, easy to obtain from the club, or a valid Department of Defense ID. Once in, you will be able to enjoy a great, challenging system of trails that will test all of your abilities. The trails at Quantico are clearly marked and easy to follow. The QMTB club has placed directional arrows at key intersections to guide you on one of three loops, an easy, intermediate, and difficult course. To learn more about the trails at Quantico, or to join the QMTB club, please visit them on the web at www.qmtb.org.

GPS coordinates: 38.533711, −77.332655

I. The Fredericksburg Quarry: The trails at the Fredericksburg Quarry have been around since the late 1980s, but it wasn't until the mid-1990s that the mountain-biking community began to lay claim to the network of trails and take interest in their development and maintenance. Unfortunately, that interest resulted in several uncoordinated efforts that did more damage than good to the trail system. Shortly after Hurricane Isabelle cut through Virginia in 2003, a small group of dedicated volunteers set out to transform the area and coordinate various efforts in an attempt to reclaim the trails, help sustain them, and protect the environment around them, and in the process worked to ensure continued access to mountain bikes.

That group organized and formed the Fredericksburg Area Trail Management and User Group (FATMUG). Today, FATMUG's organization and over-all efforts have resulted in a system of well-designed environmentally sustainable trails. Today, the focus at the Quarry is to improve and maintain the trails for maximum sustainability. The primary reason I do not document this system of trails in the book is because a vast majority of them cut through private property. I do,

The USGS trail along the Rappahannock River comes to life in spring with a myriad of wild flowers, including these colorful bluebells.

however, provide additional details on my website (www.mtbdc.com) including a detailed cue sheet, GPS download, and map you can use for your own outings. For additional information on this regional Northern Virginia destination, visit fambe.org or fatmug.org.

GPS coordinates: 38.316643, −77.485698

J. Burke Lake and Mercer Lake: This ride isn't designed for thrill seekers or singletrack lovers. Instead, it reveals the lighter side of off-road bicycle riding, leading cyclists on a pleasant trip past flower gardens and lakeside vistas. The route is mostly flat and smooth. You will travel along well-maintained dirt paths that go around Burke Lake or you can meander along South Run on a paved bicycle path. There's plenty for off-road cyclists to do along this easy route to and from Burke Lake, so bring the family and enjoy the ride.

GPS coordinates: 38.747708, −77.275922.

K. Prince William Forest Park: In Prince William County lies a relatively large park, preserved as one of the few remaining piedmont forest ecosystems in the National Park Service. Within its 18,000 acres are 35 miles of hiking trails, hundreds of acres open to primitive camping, a scenic paved road looping through the park (incidentally named Scenic Drive Road), and a plethora of wildlife and plant life for city folks to enjoy. Four miles of the Scenic Drive have a dedicated bike lane providing a paved, relatively flat surface ideal for beginning bicyclists. More experienced cyclists have the option of off-road biking on any of the ten fire roads in the park, or a short section of trail designated as multi use, the Muchette Trail. The landscape at Prince William Forest Park is also great for "Gravel Grinding," or taking an easy spin through a great natural resource. Efforts are currently under

The beginner loop at Motts Run Reservoir is perfect for beginners and kids of all ages.

way to open some of the trails at Prince William Forest Park to bikes, however, unless otherwise noted, all singletrack in the park are closed to mountain bikes. **GPS coordinates:** 38.6086716, −77.3604226.

L. Motts Run Reservoir: On April 11, 2015, The Fredericksburg Area Trail Management User Group (FATMUG) celebrated the grand opening of the first 2 miles of what will eventually be a 12-mile stacked system of trails at Motts Run Reservoir. The first section is made up of twisty singletrack aimed at beginner riders. The trail offers a sampling of what's to come in the future, and chances are, by the time you read this, several more miles will have been added to the system.

The additional 10 miles will cater to more intermediate and advanced riders, and will be structured as a stacked loop, progressively increasing in difficulty. The park is closed on Tuesday and Wednesday, as well as November through March. In addition, parking is available outside the gate. Between April and October, the park gates are closed at 7 p.m.

GPS coordinates: 38.319200, −77.554033

M. Mount Vernon: Tucked away in a small corner of Alexandria, in the Mount Vernon neighborhood, sits a small track (95 acres) of land that is undergoing a serious transformation. Thanks, in part to the local residents, and in cooperation with the Fairfax County Park Authority and MORE, legacy trails are being rerouted and rebuilt to create a system of sustainable trails in an otherwise underutilized portion of wooded land. Years of advocacy efforts finally paid off, and a band of volunteers from MORE—along with IMBA's Trail Care Crew—finally began work to "formalize" the existing network of trails. When all is said and done, there will be a little over 3 miles of singletrack trails in this urban destination. The trails can easily be accessed from the Mount Vernon Recreation Center, or from the bike path along Fort Hunt Road.

GPS coordinates: 38.77309, −77.06465

N. Lodi Farms: The trails at Lodi Farm have been around for quite some time. They used to be known as Hollywood Farm, but it really wasn't until the Frederick Area Mountain Bike Enthusiasts (FAMBE) got involved that the trails took the shape they hold today. Lodi Farm is a private property and requires a daily use/ride pass of $5 or an annual membership pass of $30. Access is controlled by FAMBE. Before heading out to Lodi check their website (fambe.org) to ensure the trails are open and accessible. Lodi Farms is detailed in full in my other book, *Mountain Biking the Washington D.C./Baltimore Area*, available at mtbdc.com.

GPS coordinates: 38.4327117, −77.4171381.

Central Virginia

I f there is anything to be said about the Old Dominion, it's that it is a state rich in history. From the arrival of settlers in 1607, the creation of the first permanent settlement in Jamestown, the birthplace of our founding fathers, and the battles of the savage Civil War, Virginia has played an important role in the history of the United States.

No other location captures that history better than Virginia's Central region, where the nation's first settlers built bustling commerce centers along the Piedmont's fall line. It's where the State's Capital, Richmond, was built and where Thomas Jefferson helped draft the Declaration of Independence. It is also where some of the deadliest battles of the Civil War were fought.

It is often said that the region between our Nation's Capital, Richmond, and Petersburg contains the most blood-soaked ground in the country. In 1864, after taking command of the Union Army, General Grant drove his troops relentlessly south heeding the battle cry of northern citizens: "on to Richmond." Grant's Overland Campaign began in May of that year in Spotsylvania. Lee's Army, over the course of three battles, inflicted more casualties against the Union than he had soldiers in his Army. More than 60,000 Union men perished that May, but Grant's relentless push south continued. Grant's campaign eventually led to the siege of Petersburg, which held the central Virginia City at bay for 10 months from June 1864 through April of the next year, ultimately culminating in the fall of the Confederacy. That defeat solidified Lincoln's Emancipation proclamation and set free more than 3 million enslaved people in the South.

Geographically, Central Virginia is full of hills that are not only perfect for our sport, but that are incredibly beautiful to look at. It is no wonder that prominent historical figures such as Thomas Jefferson, James Monroe, and James Madison, chose this region for their homes. Jefferson's Monticello, nearby our Walnut Creek ride, and the University of Virginia, are must see sites for any visitor to the region. Along the "little Mountain," Jefferson built his architectural masterpiece (his home) and showcase gardens. It is here that Jefferson began drafting the Declaration of Independence and where he ultimately retired and died 50 years to the day after its signing.

The trails we'll visit in Virginia's Piedmont and along its central region are the perfect preparation for what lies further ahead to the West along the Shenandoah Valley and the South West along the Blue Ridge Mountains.

Richmond Regional Ride Center

IMBA has been working on a program that recognizes the efforts of regional destinations when it comes to their mountain bike offerings. The Ride Center designation is basically recognition that a specific region has facilities to accommodate all levels of riders, from families looking for a mellow ride in the woods, to experts seeking the thrills of the sport.

Richmond's Ride Center designation is a result of a collaborative effort between rvaMORE, the state Department of Conservation and Recreation, the city of Richmond, the Paralyzed Veterans of America's Mid-Atlantic chapter, and the Friends of Pocahontas State Park. Led by volunteers from rvaMORE (rvamore.org), the coalition raised over $320,000 to rehabilitate over 20 miles of existing trails at Pocahontas State Park (Ride 13), and construct an additional 22 miles. Together, with the excellent trails already in existence along the banks of the James River at James River Park System (Ride 12), Richmond residents and visitors will have access to nearly 70 miles of off-road cycling trails.

Richmond's Ride Center is unique in that it also includes a trail specifically built for cyclists with disabilities. Working in conjunction with the Paralyzed Veterans of America, Mid Atlantic Chapter, and rvaMORE, the Richmond Ride Center seeks to raise awareness to adaptive sports, especially hand cycling. The purpose-built trails in the Swift Creek area of Pocahontas State Park provide disabled athletes with a safe environment where they can increase their skills and continue to live an active and healthy life.

12 James River Park System

Urban. The James River Park System of trails are a perfect example of a well-crafted urban system of trails. Although our ride specifically starts at the Pumphouse parking area, you can feasibly access this loop from a myriad of locations throughout the north and south banks of the James River without ever getting in your car. The James River Park System is composed of five distinct downtown trails, Dogwood Dell, the North Bank, Belle Isle, Buttermilk, and Forest Hill Park. Our ride samples all of these trails to piece together an 11-mile loop that will leave you highly satisfied. Each of the trails offers a different challenge. Young riders will love the trails and Skills Area at Belle Isle.

Start: Start from the Pump House parking area along Pump House Road adjacent to Baker Field and the north side of the Boulevard Bridge.
Length: 11 miles
Ride time: 1.5-3 hours
Difficulty: Intermediate to expert. Belle Isle is suitable for riders of all levels. The Buttermilk, North Shore, and Forest Hill Park trails contain technical and advanced features.
Trail surface: Mostly singletrack. Expect sections of doubletrack and portions of pavement through Richmond's streets.
Lay of the land: Rolling technical singletrack along the shores of the James River within the city of Richmond.

Land status: Public
Nearest town: Richmond
Other trail users: Hikers, runners
Trail contacts: rvaMORE, www.rvamore.org; Richmond Department of Parks, Recreation and Community Facilities, www.richmondgov.com/parks/; Friends of the James River Park, www.jamesriverpark.org/
Schedule: Closed from sundown to sunup and for 24 hours following rain of 1 inch or more.
Fees: Free to public
Restrooms: Limited availability while on the trail. Portable toilets are generally available at the Pumphouse.

Getting there: From I-95 through Downtown Richmond: Take I-95 S to exit 74A, I-195N/Powhite Parkway (toll). Take the exit for VA 161 toward Idlewood Avenue and turn left on S Boulevard. Continue for approximately 0.25 miles and turn left onto VA 161 S. Pump House Drive. Will be to your right shortly before the toll booths, turn right. The parking area will be to your left as Pump House Drive curves right. **GPS coordinates:** 37.53045, -77.4497.

The Ride

One cannot talk about Richmond without first addressing the city's significance in our Nation's history. Richmond's history dates back to the late 1600s when prominent Indian trader William Byrd I was granted the lands along the James River Falls that would eventually become the city. William Byrd II inherited the lands from his father and by 1742, when the area had been sufficiently developed and become a major tobacco-growing center, the town of Richmond was chartered, receiving its name from a suburban town in southwest London.

By this time, civil engineer and city founder William Mayo, had subdivided the area around the James River into thirty-two squares and laid the foundation of what would eventually become the neighborhood of Church Hill and the city we know today. It is from Church Hill that revolutionary patriot Patrick Henry delivered his famous "Give me Liberty or Give me Death" speech in 1775. The speech, from one of Virginia's most gifted orators, was the catalyst that ensured Virginia contributed troops to the Revolutionary effort. Soon after, Richmond became the State's capital, and in May 1782, it was incorporated as a city.

Richmond continued to play an important role in the state's and Nation's history. The City was the Capital of the Confederacy and suffered vastly as a result of the Civil War. In early April of 1865, when the fall of neighboring Petersburg was imminent, Confederate President Jefferson Davis, along with his cabinet and soldiers, began to flee the city to avoid capture. Davis ordered retreating Confederate troops to destroy all bridges, warehouses, and the armory as they left. The ensuing fires burned out of control and destroyed large portions of the city. Occupying Union troops eventually quenched the unchecked fires before then President, Abraham Lincoln, toured the Confederate Capital.

Shortly thereafter, during the battle of Appomattox Courthouse, General Robert E. Lee surrendered to Union General Ulysses S. Grant putting an end to one of our Nation's bloodiest chapters. Richmond then began the long process of reconstruction and renewal. Over the years, the city has grown considerably, and it continues to be Virginia's commerce capital, much as it was 300 years ago.

Today, the James River Park system is a result of the city's effort to serve the varying recreational interests of Richmond's diverse population. From the trails along the river's banks walkers, runners, and cyclists can see firsthand Richmond's history on display, and many of the sites are without a doubt worth seeing.

Miles and Directions

0.0 Park at the Pumphouse Trail parking area along Pumphouse Drive. We will begin measuring our ride at the parking area gate. From the gate, head west along Pumphouse Road toward Pumphouse park. You'll see small directional signs along the right directing you to the Dogwood Dell mountain bike and hiking trails.

0.2 Turn right into the Dogwood Dell mountain bike trail. The entrance is clearly marked with a trail kiosk and map. Immediately after entering the trail you'll reach a T intersection, turn left. We will ride Dogwood Dell in a clockwise direction.

0.7 After a short climb you'll reach a "y" intersection (marked DD8) continue to the right. The left fork is a short multi-use connector to Byrd Park.

1.14 You're back at the entrance of the Dogwood Dell trail. Turn left and then left again onto Pumphouse Road and head back to the parking lot.

1.4 After entering the parking area, head to the trail kiosk at the far end. Take the right fork down and under the Boulevard Bridge to ride east along the North Bank Trail. Get ready for some great Richmond singletrack.

The James River Park trail system is heavily used but well maintained.

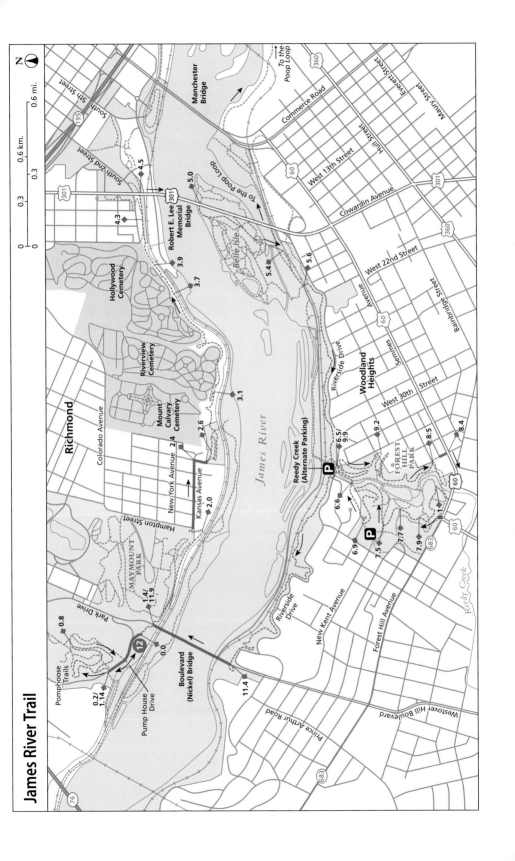

James River Trail

1.8 The trail will turn to doubletrack gravel. Kanawha Canal and the railroad tracks will be to your right.

2.0 Make a sharp left to climb up to Kansas Avenue. The climb is steep, but definitely doable. Be in the right gear and before you know, it you'll be at the top. Continue east along Kansas Avenue. Continue following the brown directional signs to the North Bank Trail.

2.4 Turn right onto Texas Avenue. Texas Avenue dead ends on a parking area (alternate starting point). Go through the parking area to the traffic circle and hop back onto the North Bank Trail.

2.6 Stay to the right at this intersection and continue following the North Bank Trail. The trail to the left takes you down to Texas Beach Park. The next section of trail is super fun.

3.1 Follow the left fork along the biker only path. The trail will curve left and then right along a couple of switchbacks and follow the boundary of Riverview and Hollywood Cemeteries. If you have time, I urge you to take a side trip and visit Hollywood Cemetery, one of the most beautiful garden cemeteries in the country. Hollywood Cemetery contains the resting place of the only president of the Confederate States of America, Jefferson Davis, the Monument of the Confederate War Dead, and James Monroe.

3.7 Go over a short bridge and then left to continue following the singletrack as it parallels the railroad tracks and the river.

3.9 A steep, punchy, and rocky climb will deliver you to "Bubba's Bench," continue following the North Bank Trail toward the entrance to Belle Isle, or, pause and take a break to admire the view of the James River from this spot.

4.3 Stay to the right and continue on the gravel to the underpasses. The paved fork to the left will take you toward Oregon Hill.

4.5 You've reached the underpasses, turn right over a short wood bridge and then immediately left and down to the parking area along Tredegar Street. Turn right onto Tredegar and follow the pedestrian bridge to Belle Isle. The bridge was opened to the public in 1988.

5.0 You are now on Belle Isle. The small island, rich in history, was once home to a fishery, an ironworks, and power plant, and during the Civil War served as a Prisoners of War (POW) camp. The island was turned into a park in 1973 and now has several trails you can ride along including a designated bike skills park. Hang around if you wish. We will continue along the Belle Isle Connector as it parallels the Robert E. Lee Bridge toward the footbridge that connects with the Buttermilk trail.

5.4 After crossing the footbridge, you'll reach a "T" intersection. Follow the Low Water Trail to the right toward Buttermilk and Reedy Creek. The left, east trail can extend your ride toward the Poop Loop.

5.6 Climb the steps to go over the railroad track. Immediately after crossing, turn right to continue along the Buttermilk Trail. Buttermilk east continues to the left and ends at West Commerce and Semmes Avenue.

6.5 You reach a Y intersection marked "BMT7." At this point, you can continue straight and to the right to remain on Buttermilk. We will head up and to the left toward Riverside Drive and Forest Hill Park. Cross the road and head down and to the right along the doubletrack to enter into Forest Hill Park. The trail to the left will be our exit point. We will ride this loop in a counterclockwise direction.

6.6 Make a sharp right and go over the "rail less" concrete bridge. It's much easier than it looks.

6.9 Stay to the left.

7.5 Cross the brick walkway.

7.7 Continue following the stone wall, the maintenance area will be to your right.

7.9 Stay right.

8.1 There's a sign that points down to the left. Unfortunately, the bridge that used to span the creek below had washed out at the time I documented this. We'll follow the trail up to Forest Hill Avenue and turn left and then left again along Semmes Avenue. Crossroads Coffee will be to your right and Coqui's Cyclery at the corner of Forest Hill and Semmes.

8.4 Turn left on West 34th St.

8.5 Turn left immediately after the small baseball diamond and before the metal railing along the intersection of West 34th St. and Spring Hill Avenue. Turn right at the bottom of the short hill to continue on the Forest Hill Park trail.

9.1 After a series of great downhill switchbacks, you'll go over a small bridge, make a sharp right turn to continue up the trail.

9.2 Stay to the left. The trail to the right is a neighborhood connector. The next section of trail will deliver you back to Riverside Avenue.

9.9 You're back at the entrance point of the Forest Hill Park Trails. Turn left on Riverside Drive and then immediately right onto the entrance road to the Reedy Creek Parking area. The Buttermilk trailhead will be to your left. This will be the final section of the Buttermilk trail, and likely the most challenging; pick your lines accordingly and be careful.

11.4 You reach the terminus of the Buttermilk trail; ride under Westover Hills Boulevard and follow the trail to the left. The trail will then switch back and get you to the top of Westover Hills Boulevard. Turn left and follow the bike path over the Boulevard (Nickel) Bridge.

11.9 Turn left onto the dirt path and onto the Pumphouse parking area, the loop is complete.

Ride Information

Bike Shops

Coqui Cyclery: www.coquicyclery.com
3Sports: www.threesports.com
Agee's Bicycles: agees.com
Conte's Bike Shop: contebikes.com
Carytown Bicycle Company: www.carytownbikes.com

Local Events and Attractions

Take a Kid Mountain Biking—Annually (October), check rvamore.org for additional info
Hollywood Cemetery—www.hollywoodcemetery.org/

Restaurants

Asado: asadorva.com
City Dogs: www.citydogsrva.com
Crossroads Coffee: crossroadsrva.com
Brew: www.brewgastropub.com (near Pocahontas State Park)
Capital Ale House: capitalalehouse.com
Legend Brewing Company: www.legendbrewing.com
Triple Crossing Brewing Company: www.triplecrossingbeer.com

You May Run Into: Greg Rollins

I had heard of Greg for many years. Having been involved with MORE up in the Northern Virginia/Maryland regions we often collaborated and shared info with our neighbors to the south in Richmond, and Greg's name was often one that came up in our discussion—"we'll talk to Greg to get the word out," or "Greg down in Richmond will know who to reach out to..."

But it wasn't until I actually set out to write the new edition of Mountain Biking Virginia that I began to converse with and ultimately meet and work with Greg, and city employees on a small project along Buttermilk Trail. That's when I began to understand the full impact he's had on the Mountain Biking Community in this Central Virginia destination.

Part of my research is often asking regional riders if they know someone who they think I should highlight in my books, someone who has made a difference in the cycling community, and whose efforts are critical in ensuring that we have access to trails such as the ones I feature here. Time and time again, Greg's name came up from riders in the Richmond area. When I ultimately reached out to him, he was reluctant to be featured in the book, and told me "it wasn't just about one person, it's bigger than me…there are so many people that give their time and effort to our trails that it would be unfair to focus on just one of us."

It's precisely for statements like that, that he should be featured. Greg is absolutely right; it's not just about one person. However, ultimately one person's leadership and example is what guarantees others to jump in and help out. He's provided just that for his community.

Greg has been the president of rvaMORE from 2006–2007 and 2009–2016, and in that position has helped lead Richmond's volunteers to earn IMBA's coveted Ride Center designation. He most certainly didn't do it alone, but his efforts, along with those of former rvaMORE trail boss Wayne Goodman, and a coalition of other regional groups helped raise over $320,000 in just two years to build several new trails, including a skills and dirt jump park, a 7-mile purpose-built off-road hand cycle-trail and mountain bike trail, as well as Bell and Blueberry, two of the finest flow trails in the area.

He's quick to say that "access is not guaranteed," and continually works to foster relationships with local land managers to ensure it is. He understands that in order for us to have great places to ride, you must be involved. He leads by example so that others follow along to ensure that all of us—and future generations of riders—continue to have safe, challenging, and enjoyable places where to practice our sport.

13 Pocahontas State Park—The Playful One

Pocahontas, meaning the "playful one," is an aptly chosen name for this park located just southwest of Richmond. The name is familiar and often associated with the Central Virginia region and the colonial history of the region. Legend states that Pocahontas, daughter of Algonquian Chief Powhatan, was instrumental in saving the life of Captain John Smith, the leader of Jamestown's first settlers. Her deeds toward Smith fostered a friendship with the early settlers that ultimately culminated in Pocahontas converting to Christianity, being baptized with the name Rebecca, and marrying one of, if not, the first of Virginia's tobacco growers, John Rolfe.

Shortly after marrying Rolfe in 1614, Pocahontas gave birth to a son, Thomas, and traveled to England with her husband and a dozen other Native Americans. In England, "Rebecca" became somewhat of a celebrity, and was the source of much scrutiny. She was presented to King James' court not only as the "first Christian of the Virginian nation" but also as an example of a "civilized savage," in the hopes that more investments would be sent to the Jamestown settlement.

During the trip, however, Pocahontas fell ill and ultimately succumbed to tuberculosis, never to return to her native Virginia again.

Her name is legendary, and her story has been romanticized. She became the subject of art and literature, and in our case, a State Park. Unlike other state parks around Virginia, whose land is deeded to the state, Pocahontas State Park's forestland has been deeded to the park itself. As such, recreational opportunities take precedence over other land uses such as timber production. This is why at Pocahontas you'll find a myriad of recreational activities to choose from, including camping, hiking, swimming, horseback riding, and last but not least cycling; both on and off-road.

The park has seen a burst of mountain biking development of the past several years. Starting in 2013, rvaMORE spearheaded an effort to revitalize many of the park's trails and build multiple more trails to help the Richmond Area earn IMBA's coveted Ride Center designation. Richmond formally earned the distinction in early August 2015, just in time to boast the achievement at the Richmond 2015 UCI Road World Championships.

Within the park's 7,604 acres, you will find three distinct trail systems, the Swift Creek Trails, the Morgan Loops, and the Lakeview loops. Each can be ridden individually or combined to piece together an epic ride.

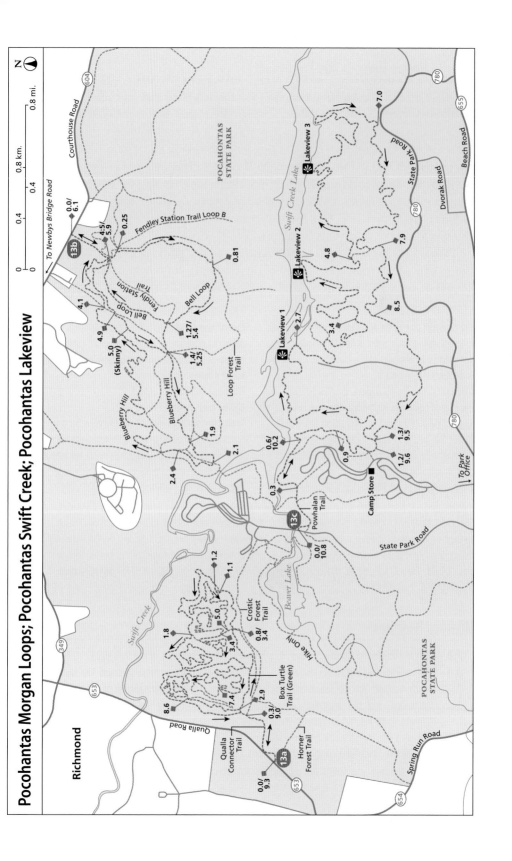

Pocohantas Morgan Loops; Pocohantas Swift Creek; Pocohantas Lakeview

The trails around the Morgan section of Pocahontas State Park just south of Richmond are incredibly easy to follow. Strategically placed trail maps with "You Are Here" indicators will let you know where you are at all times, and the relatively compact area makes it ideal for a quick outing into the woods. The system is made up of several trails, all within the confines of the Box Turtle Trail, an easy to ride singletrack loop suitable for even young children, yet challenging enough for the most experienced mountain bikers. This ride will sample virtually all the trails in the system, including Box Turtle, Tall Oaks, Morel Ravine, and Little West Virginia. This ride will give you a good sense of what Pocahontas has to offer.

Park at the Qualla Road Trail parking area. You can pay your fees at the small pay station opposite the trailhead. We will begin measuring our ride from the entrance to the Qualla connector trail that is to the right of the trail kiosk.

Start: Start at the Qualla Connector trail, it is immediately to the right of the trail kiosk.
Length: 9.3 miles
Ride time: 1–2 hours
Difficulty: Novice to expert. Box Turtle, the perimeter trail is suitable for riders of all skill levels. The internal trails, including Tall Oaks, Morel Ravine, and Little West Virginia offer more experienced riders more technically difficult and demanding trails.
Trail surface: Hard packed singletrack trails.

Lay of the land: Easy rolling singletrack trails along the perimeter loop with more difficult sections within. All trails are directional.
Land status: State Park
Nearest town: Richmond
Other trail users: Hikers
Trail contacts: rvaMORE, www.rvamore.org; Friends of Pocahontas State Park, www.fopsp .org; text POCA to (804) 292-2939 for status
Schedule: 7 a.m.–dusk.
Fees: VA State Park fees apply.

Getting there: From I-95 through Downtown Richmond. Take I-95 S to exit 62 for VA-288 N toward Chesterfield. Take the State Rte. 604/Courthouse Road exit and turn left on Courthouse Road. Turn right onto Newbys Road (Rte. 649) and continue for approximately 2 miles. Turn left onto Qualla Road (Rte. 653), the parking area will be 1.2 miles to the left. **GPS coordinates:** 37.386078, –77.601171.

Miles and Directions

0.0   Start at the Qualla Connector trail, it is immediately to the right of the trail kiosk.

0.3   Cross the fire road (Crostic Forest Trail) and continue following the singletrack. The trail is clearly marked. You will reach the Box Turtle Trail shortly after, turn right. All of the trails in this system, with the exception of a couple of connectors are directional. Ride confidently knowing there will not be any traffic in the opposite direction.

0.8   Cross the doubletrack toward the trail kiosk. We'll come back to this intersection a little later. This is one of the connector trails and a bailout point.

1.1   Fork in the trail. The trail to the right offers a more challenging line, albeit shorter route. Continue left following the easier line.

1.2 This is the merge point for the alternate "expert" line. Continue straight following Box Turtle.

1.8 Continue on Box Turtle to the right. The trail to the left is an exit point that will take you to previous marker 0.8.

2.9 Back to the point where we started to ride Box Turtle, continue to the left and backtrack so we can sample the internal trails.

3.4 Turn left at this intersection (we crossed this at marker 0.8) and head down toward the entrance of the Morel Ravine Trail (second right). You'll be on the Morel Ravine Trail for a little over 2 miles.

5.0 You reach the exit of the Morel Ravine Trail. Turn right and ride past the Morel Ravine entrance, unless you want to ride it again! A left turn will take you back up to the exit point.

5.2 Continue to the left to enter the Tall Oaks Mountain Bike Trail. The trail to the right is the bailout point from the Box Turtle Trail (marker 1.9).

7.4 Continue straight into Little West Virginia. The Tall Oaks Mountain Bike Trail continues to the left. Little West Virginia is slightly more difficult than what we've ridden thus far, but definitely fun. You'll encounter more log overs, skinnies, and other obstacles to make the ride a little more challenging.

8.6 You've reached the intersection of the Tall Oaks Mountain Bike Trail. Continue to the right (straight) along Tall Oaks to finish out the loop.

8.9 Back on Box Turtle. Make a right and then an immediate left to hop on the Qualia Connector Trail to close out the ride.

9.0 Cross the fire road (Crostic Forest Trail). A left will take you back toward the Swift Creek (Ride 13b) and Lakeview (Ride 13c) should you wish to extend your ride further.

9.3 Arrive back at the Qualia Parking area, your ride is complete.

13b   Swift Creek Trails

The Swift Creek Trail System includes the Gateway trails, Bell Lap, and Blueberry Hill trail. These trails can be quickly accessed from the Loop Forest parking area off Courthouse Road. The Swift Creek Trails are the newest trails in Pocahontas State Park.

Park at the Courthouse parking area and enter the park via the gravel road. We will start measuring from the gate just past the trail kiosk.

These trails are relatively easy to follow and can be easily combined in several ways to craft different loops. The track I recommend below is the one I found the most fun and which I think, takes advantage of most of the area trails. You can combine this loop with the Morgan loop and the Lakeview Loop to further extend your ride.

Also, located within this portion of the park are purpose-built trails for disabled riders. Former rvaMORE president and Marine Corps Veteran, Wayne Goodman deserves much of the credit for the implementation of the purpose-built trails, and the effort to make Richmond a designated Ride Center. Goodman—also responsible for leading much of the development along the trails in the James River Park (Rides 13a–c)—suffered a spinal cord injury in 2010 and was forced off the bike. Thanks to recreational therapy services offered at McGuire Veterans Affairs Medical

Center, he was able to return to cycling, albeit on three wheels. The purpose-built trails at Pocahontas are a legacy to his outstanding efforts in the region. You'll likely see Wayne and other disabled cyclists ripping through the trails, including the more challenging Blueberry.

Start: Start from the parking area along Courthouse Road.
Length: 6.2 miles
Ride time: 45 minutes–1 hour
Difficulty: Novice to expert. The loop highlighted here is suitable for all levels of riders.
Trail surface: Hard packed singletrack trails.
Lay of the land: Rolling singletrack trails. One section of Bell Grant built flow trail. All trails are directional.

Land status: State Park
Nearest town: Richmond
Other trail users: Hikers
Trail contacts: rvaMORE, www.rvamore.org; Friends of Pocahontas State Park, www.fopsp .org; text POCA to (804) 292-2939 for status
Schedule: 7 a.m.–dusk.
Fees: VA State Park fees apply.

Getting there: From Richmond: Take 95 South to exit 62 for VA-288 N toward Chesterfield/Powhite Parkway. Continue for approximately 15 miles to the Courthouse Road Exit (604) and turn left. The parking area will be 1 mile on your right. **GPS coordinates:** 37.400650, –77.554911.

The trails at Pocahontas State Park Swift Creek area have several log skinnies to test your balance.

Miles and Directions

0.0 Enter the park and follow the doubletrack/gravel road past the entrance/exit to Blueberry Hill on your right and past the trail kiosk. The gravel road you are on is the Fendley Station Trail loop. Do pause at the trail kiosk to take a look at the map so you get your bearings. We'll come back to this spot several times.

0.25 Turn right from Fendley Station/Loop Forest Trail onto the starting point of the Bell Built Trail and get ready for some serious fun. The next 0.5-mile will bring a serious grin to your face.

0.81 Turn right onto the gravel road (Loop Forest Trail) and then immediately right again to hop on the Bell Lap Trail. It is clearly marked.

1.27 Bell Lap continues straight, turn left onto the doubletrack (Fendley Station). A right turn will take you back up to the trail kiosk.

1.4 Continue following the doubletrack to the left, you should see the entrance to Blueberry Hill up ahead to the right. Enter Blueberry Hill.

1.9 Turn right on the doubletrack and then left again to continue on Blueberry Hill.

2.1 Continue through this intersection. A left turn will take you over the lake toward the Lakeview and Morgan loops.

2.4 Continue straight–keep following the signs for Blueberry Hill.

4.1 Continue straight on Blueberry Hill.

4.5 You're back at the main kiosk area. As soon as you exit Blueberry Hill, make a sharp right (almost "U" turn) and go into the actual "entrance" for Blueberry Hill trail.

4.9 Continue straight on Blueberry Hill.

5.0 The trail forks here and meets up again within 100 yards. The right trail will take you over a fun and long skinny, the left fork simply bypasses this feature.

5.25 You're back on the doubletrack and the point where we first entered Blueberry Hill. This time, turn left on the doubletrack and follow it as it curves to the right.

5.4 Turn left on Bell Lap. This is the point where we veered left at mile marker 1.27. This time around, we will complete the Bell Lap Trail.

5.9 Arrive back at the main trail kiosk; your ride is basically complete at this point. Turn left and head back toward the parking area on Courthouse Road.

6.1 The loop is complete.

13c   Lakeview Loops

Like all of the trails in Pocahontas State Park, the Lakeview Mountain Bike Trail System (loops 1–3) is really easy to follow and very well marked and maintained. And, like the rest of the trails in the system, they are unidirectional, so you can be confident that you will not encounter a rider coming toward you in the opposite direction. Adding the Lakeview loops to the Swift Creek Trails or the Morgan trails is also simple, so you can easily extend your rides further. You can spend pretty much an entire day just in Pocahontas, and ride nearly 40 miles without doubletracking on very many portions of trail.

There are several options for parking at Pocahontas to access the Lakeview Mountain Bike Trail System. For this ride, we will start at the main parking area immediately above the lakeshore. Drive approximately 2 miles into the park and pick a spot in the parking area to the right. Pay close attention as you drive in, around 1.7 miles in you'll go over a small bridge over the Third Branch, a creek that connects the Swift Creek Lake with Beaver Lake. Our trailhead will be immediately before you cross the bridge to the right (to the left when you ride back down the road).

Start: Start at the main parking area immediately above the lakeshore and ride along State Park Road as if leaving the park. We'll actually begin measuring from the Powhatan trailhead along State Park Road where it crosses the Third Branch that connects Swift Creek Lake with Beaver Lake.

Length: 11.1 miles

Ride time: 1.5–3.5 hours.

Difficulty: Intermediate to expert. The Lakeview trails offer advanced riders a great system of intermediate to advanced singletrack trails.

Trail surface: Singletrack trails; one short section of doubletrack at the beginning of the ride.

Lay of the land: Rolling singletrack with great views of Swift Creek Lake. All trails, with the exception of the Powhatan access trail are directional.

Land status: State Park

Nearest town: Richmond

Other trail users: Hikers

Trail contacts: rvaMORE, www.rvamore.org; Friends of Pocahontas State Park, www.fopsp .org; text POCA to (804) 292-2939 for status

Schedule: 7 a.m.–dusk.

Fees: VA State Park fees apply (depending on season and State license plates)

Getting there: Take I-95 S to exit 62 for VA-288 N toward Chesterfield/Powhite Parkway. Continue on VA-288 N for 6 miles and take the exit for VA-10 E/Iron Bridge Road toward Chesterfield. Continue on Iron Bridge Road for 5 miles and turn right onto Beach Road (Rte. 655). Continue on Beach Road for 4 miles and turn right onto State Park Road. The Powhite trailhead will be 1.7 miles to your right immediately before crossing the bridge over the Third Branch. Continue straight and park in one of the lots to the right. **GPS coordinates:** 37.384429, -77.580950.

Miles and Directions

0.0 We will actually start measuring from that trailhead. After you park, head down State Park Road back toward the exit. Immediately after crossing the bridge over the Swift Creek, the trailhead will be to your left and clearly marked. Enter here and follow the signs to the Lakeview Mountain Bike Loop Trails (approximately 0.6 miles). Immediately after entering the trail, veer to the left.

0.3 Follow the trail to the left, you are now on the Powhatan Trail (doubletrack).

0.6 As Powhatan curves to the right you'll notice a spur to the left heading up to a trail kiosk follow it. This is the entrance to the Lakeview Spur. The Spur is two-way traffic and will get you to Lakeview 1.

0.9 The trail will split offering you the option to follow a more difficult line. We will stick to the "easier" route. You'll come across several of these "forks" in the trail as you venture further in. We will continue to follow the easier lines.

The loops along the lake get their name from the various "lake views" you'll encounter along the way.

1.2 Continue following the trail straight and to the left. To the right and immediately off the trail is a pump and bike repair station.

1.3 After a small creek crossing, you'll reach a "T" intersection. Continue to the left, this is the entrance to Lakeview 1. The trail to the left is the exit of Lakeview 1.

2.2 Turn right on the fire road and then immediately left to continue on Lakeview 1.

2.7 A bench along the side of the trail offers a nice view of the lake below.

3.4 You reach the entrance to Lakeview 2. Continue to the left to follow Lakeview 2, a right turn will basically take you back along Lakeview 1 to complete the loop.

4.8 You reach the entrance of Lakeview 3, continue to the left to continue onto Lakeview. 3. A right turn will take you back to close out Lakeview 2 toward Lakeview 1.

7.0 Continue straight through this intersection.

7.9 Continue following the trail to the left to hop back on Lakeview 2. The trail to the right will take you back toward marker 4.8, the entrance to Lakeview 3.

8.5 Continue following the trail to the left to hop back on Lakeview 1. The trail to the right will take you back toward marker 3.4, the entrance to Lakeview 2.

9.5 You're at the starting point of Lakeview 1. Turn left to hop on the Lakeview Connector trail. You are now backtracking toward the starting point.

9.6 The pump will be to your left, continue to the right.

10.2 You've reached the end of the Lakeview Connector, turn right to follow the Powhatan Trail back to the starting point along the same route we rode in.

10.8 You're back at the State Park Road. The loop is complete. Turn right and head back up to where you parked your vehicle.

Ride Information

Bike Shops

Coqui Cyclery: www.coquicyclery.com
3Sports: www.threesports.com
Agee's Bicycles: agees.com
Conte's Bike Shop: contebikes.com
Carytown Bicycle Company: www.carytownbikes.com

Local Events and Attractions

Take a Kid Mountain Biking—Annually (October), check rvamore.org for additional info

Hollywood Cemetery—www.hollywoodcemetery.org/

Restaurants

Asado: asadorva.com
City Dogs: www.citydogsrva.com
Crossroads Coffee: crossroadsrva.com
Brew: www.brewgastropub.com (near Pocahontas State Park)
Capital Ale House: capitalalehouse.com
Legend Brewing Company: www.legendbrewing.com
Triple Crossing Brewing Company: www.triplecrossingbeer.com

14 Walnut Creek

The trails at Walnut Creek are the result of years of hard work by volunteers from Charlottesville's cycling, hiking, and trail running community. The efforts from all these groups have yielded over 12 miles of multi-use trail that are incredibly challenging and fun to ride. At Walnut Creek, you'll find a network of technical, steep, and highly demanding trails that will continuously challenge you. Additional amenities, including a refreshing beach where to take a swim after a hot ride, have made this Albemarle park a go to destination in Central Virginia.

Start: Start form the main bike staging/parking area located to the right of Walnut Creek Park Road.
Length: 9.8 miles
Ride time: 1.5-3 hours
Difficulty: Intermediate to expert due to difficult climbs and technical singletrack.
Trail surface: Rocky and rooty singletrack with occasional creek crossings.
Lay of the land: Singletrack trails through dense forest around a lake setting with steep climbs and descents.
Land status: Public County Park
Nearest town: Charlottesville

Other trail users: Hikers, trail runners, and anglers.
Trail contacts: Charlottesville Area Mountain Bike Club, cambc.org; Albemarle County, www.albemarle.org/department .asp?department=parks
Schedule: Open for daylight hours year-round. Daily 11:00 a.m.-7:00 p.m. (from Memorial Day weekend through Labor Day)
Fees: Admission charged from Memorial Day to Labor Day, discount for Albemarle County residents.
Restrooms: Available in the lake area. A portable toilet is generally available in the bike staging area.

Getting there: From Charlottesville: Take Rte. 29 South; turn left onto Rte. 708 (Red Hill Road). Turn right onto Rte. 631 (Old Lynchburg Road). The park is 0.5 mile on the left. **GPS coordinates:** 37.926929, -78.589070.

The Ride

Bring your legs, and lungs. Walnut Creek is not really known for "gently" rolling terrain, but instead for its lung busting and thigh crushing hills. They're not long hills, just punchy and steep, and frequent enough to keep you honest. But all is not pain at the lake just outside.

The trails were originally flagged and built in the early 2000s by volunteers from the Charlottesville Area Mountain Bike Club (CAMBC). Most of the trails are named after local area bike shops, and local cycling volunteers who donated their time and effort to make things happen. Wilkins Way, for example, is named after one of the original volunteers, Doug Wilkins, who helped flag and build the first 5 miles of trails around the 23-acre lake within the 525-acre park.

Over time, additional miles were added to the system and today it boasts nearly 13 miles of singletrack. The folks at the CAMBC continue to do a phenomenal job when it comes to maintaining these trails, and are often out in force ensuring that they remain a viable destination, not only for Charlottesville riders, but also for mountain bikers across the region.

The most common loop around Walnut Creek takes riders in a counterclockwise direction along the Orange "C'ville Bike & Tri Just Climb It" Trail to the blue Bike Factory trail, before merging onto the red Wilkins Way trail. Once on Wilkins, you'll begin to find the myriad of options available in the park. Trying to guide you through this section would be virtually impossible. The yellow trail, for example, forks at least three times within a 300-yard span. The loop I've chosen to highlight will take you in a clockwise direction so that you can descend what I think is one of the best downhills in the park, along the orange blazed "Charlottesville Bike & Tri Just Climb It" trail.

You'll encounter several ruins along the ride at Walnut Creek, remnants of the area's past.

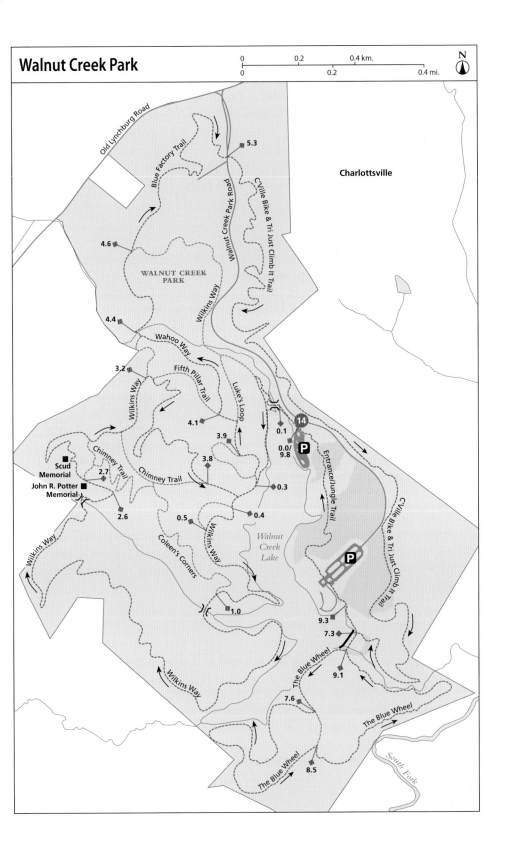

Walnut Creek Park

N

| 0 | 0.2 | 0.4 km. |
| 0 | 0.2 | 0.4 mi. |

Charlottsville

Old Lynchburg Road

Blue Factory Trail

5.3

Walnut Creek Park Road

C'ville Bike & Tri Just Climb It Trail

4.6

WALNUT CREEK
PARK

Wilkins Way

4.4

Wahoo Way

3.2

Fifth Pillar Trail

Wilkins Way

Luke's Loop

4.1

3.9

0.1

14

0.0/
9.8

P

Entrance/Jungle Trail

C'ville Bike & Tri Just Climb It Trail

3.8

Scud
Memorial

Chimney Trail

2.7

John R. Potter
Memorial

Chimney Trail

0.3

2.6

0.5

0.4

Wilkins Way

Coleen's Corners

Walnut
Creek
Lake

P

Wilkins Way

1.0

9.3

7.3

Wilkins Way

The Blue Wheel

9.1

7.6

The Blue Wheel

The Blue Wheel

South Fork

The Blue Wheel

8.5

Although mountain bikers built the trails with cyclists in mind, the trails at Walnut Creek are multiuse. Walnut Creek has become a regular stop for the XTERRA Regional Series. The race itself has been a local favorite for over a decade. The XTERRA brings triathletes from across the region to compete in what are considered some of the most technical trails, not only for cycling, but for running as well.

If you want to just sample some of the "easier" trails in the system, then I suggest you park closer to the lake and do a loop around The Blue Wheel, a 2-mile loop that will give you a sense of what Walnut Creek has to offer.

Miles and Directions

0.0 Drop into the trail and follow it as it skirts the lake.

0.1 Make an immediate left over the bridge. Once over the bridge, turn left again to follow the green trail. Basically, a U turn. The lake will be on your left.

0.3 Continue on the Red Trail to the left past the next two intersections (green first, yellow second). We will revisit this section a little later in the opposite direction.

0.4 The Red Trail will split. Either branch will take you to the same place. The left branch is a more technical "expert" line.

0.5 The red branches merge again.

1.0 Continue following the Red Trail past the purple trail.

2.6 Continue straight past this intersection. This is a "shortcut" to the yellow trail. We are actually skipping the Yellow Trail on this loop.

2.7 Continue to the left along the red trail. One of two old homesites and the Yellow Trail will be to your right. You'll also pass the John R. Potter Memorial, a small spot dedicated to a local area rider who perished in a cycling accident. You can't miss it. A series of flags and small cairn mark the spot. Be on the lookout for another memorial for Scott "Scud" Scudamore. A local rider (and very close friend) who worked on and rerouted part of this trail. Continue past this spot following the Red Trail to the left.

This is where things can get a bit confusing. The red trail follows the perimeter of the park, all other trails to the right meander through each other to create a confusing maze that even local riders sometimes have a hard time following. Pay close attention to the blazes on the trees.

3.2 You reach the intersection of the Red and Brown Trails. Make a sharp right onto the brown trail. You'll basically head back in the direction you were riding along the red trail. This marks the beginning of a super fun descent.

3.8 The Brown Trail will end and merge with the yellow trail. Continue straight and down and turn left on the Red trail. At this point, you are backtracking along the red trail, but only for a short distance. You're at marker 0.3 mentioned a little earlier.

3.9 Turn left onto the Green Trail and then immediately right again to hop on the white trail.

4.1 Stay right on white. Brown continues up to the left toward marker 3.2.

4.4 You reach the creek and the red trail. A left turn up the steep grade will take you back toward marker 3.2. We'll continue right over the creek and along the Red Trail.

4.6 Continue straight, the trail is now blazed with blue markings. A right turn will keep you on the Red Trail and a shorter route back to the starting point.

5.3 Cross the road and hop on the Orange Trail. Get ready for some fun. The Orange Trail will now descend toward the dam as it parallels the road. There are a couple of opportunities to exit the trail and cut the ride short should you wish to.

7.3 You reach the dam. Turn left to go over the dam and access the Dam Trails. Once you enter the Dam trails, head up on to the right to ride them in a counterclockwise direction. Or, if you prefer, continue straight up the gravel road and across the parking area to finish out the ride.

7.6 Continue following the trail to the right. The left fork is a shortcut to shorten the dam loop.

8.5 Continue straight past the old homesite and the connector trail to the left. A left turn will take you back to marker 7.6.

9.1 You reach the exit of the Dam Trails, turn right to go over the dam and then left and up along the gravel road. You can choose to ride the short section of singletrack that starts along the right of the gravel, or straight up to the beach parking area. Cross the back parking area toward the paved trail on the other side.

9.3 Enter the singletrack and follow it to the right as it weaves down and through the disc golf holes.

9.8 Cross over a small bridge and the grassy area to hop back onto the bike staging and parking area. The loop is complete.

If you ride during a hot summer day, I highly recommend you venture down to the beach and take a dip in the lake's cool waters; it will be a refreshing end to your ride.

Ride Information

Bike Shops

Blue Ridge Cyclery: blueridgecyclery.com
Bike Factory: bikefactory.com
Blue Wheel: www.bluewheel.com

Local Events and Attractions

Visit Charlottesville has a comprehensive list of events and attraction in downtown Charlottesville and Albemarle County: www.visitcharlottesville.org
Charlottesville is home to the University of Virginia (UVA), check out UVA's calendar for a myriad of events from arts to athletics: calendar.virginia.edu
Thomas Jefferson's Monticello: www.monticello.org
Walnut Creek has a 23-acre lake with a beach; if hit the trails during a hot and muggy Virginia Summer, a dip in the lake is a welcome end to any ride.

Restaurants

Beer Run: beerrun.com
Sticks Kebob Shop: www.stickskebobshop.com
Jack Brown's Beer & Burger Joint: www.jackbrownsjoint.com
Three Notch'd Brewing Company: threenotchdbrewing.com (bring your own food)

15 Preddy Creek

Preddy Creek is a small park on the outskirts of Charlottesville that has a well-groomed perimeter loop ideal for beginner mountain bikers and kids. Don't let that dissuade you from visiting though. Preddy's trail builders have expertly crafted a trail that takes advantage of the rolling terrain, making it super fun to ride. The trail also has an "expert" extension that allows more advanced riders to enjoy narrower technical singletrack, with "unavoidable" obstacles.

Start: Start form the trail kiosk adjacent to the bathrooms in the main trail parking area.
Length: 7.1 miles
Ride time: 45 minutes–1.5 hours
Difficulty: Novice to expert. The main perimeter loop is fairly easy. The internal trails and Advanced Mountain Bike Loop are more challenging.
Trail surface: Doubletrack and singletrack hard packed trails.
Lay of the land: Rolling doubletrack and singletrack trails. Along Preddy Creek

Land status: Public
Nearest town: Charlottesville
Other trail users: Hikers, dog walkers, trail runners
Trail contacts: Charlottesville Area Mountain Bike Club, cambc.org; Albemarle County, www.albemarle.org/department .asp?department=parks
Schedule: 7:00 a.m. to dark year-round
Fees: Free to public
Restrooms: Available at the trailhead next to the park kiosk.

Getting there: From 29 North, 4 miles beyond Airport Road turn right on Burnley Station Road, travel 2.6 miles and park entrance is on the left. **GPS coordinates:** 38.174470, -78.367927.

The Ride

Preddy Creek is a small County park located northeast of Charlottesville. The 571-acre park, dedicated in May of 2011, has approximately 8 miles of multipurpose use trails enjoyed by hikers, equestrians, and mountain bikers.

The main Preddy Creek loop is approximately 4 miles in length. However, if you add the Advanced Mountain Bike Loop and the internal trails to your ride, you can easily accumulate 10 miles and ride away satisfied. The loop I document here uses nearly all the trails in the system with little doubletracking. Use it as a starting point to craft your own route around this easy to follow trail system.

All the trails in Preddy Creek Park are well marked and easy to follow. Not documented in this loop are the "Meadow Loops." The Meadow Loops are simply "mowed" trails around the adjacent meadows that are neither technical nor much fun for mountain biking. If you chose to try them out, they are easily accessible from the parking area and adjacent to the entrance to our ride. Be alert for other trail users. Hikers with dogs are usually present as well as equestrian enthusiasts. Share the trail!

The Charlottesville Area Mountain Bike Club has been working with the county to add a professionally built skills park adjacent to the parking area, between the road and parking area. The space is a little over half an acre, so it should provide plenty of room for an adequate track.

CAMBC is also working in partnership with the county to build a new bridge across Preddy Creek, in order to gain access to up to 8 additional miles of trail. Hopefully, by the time you read this, Preddy Creek will have been expanded and offer many more riding opportunities.

The trails at Preddy Creek Park are well marked and easy to follow.

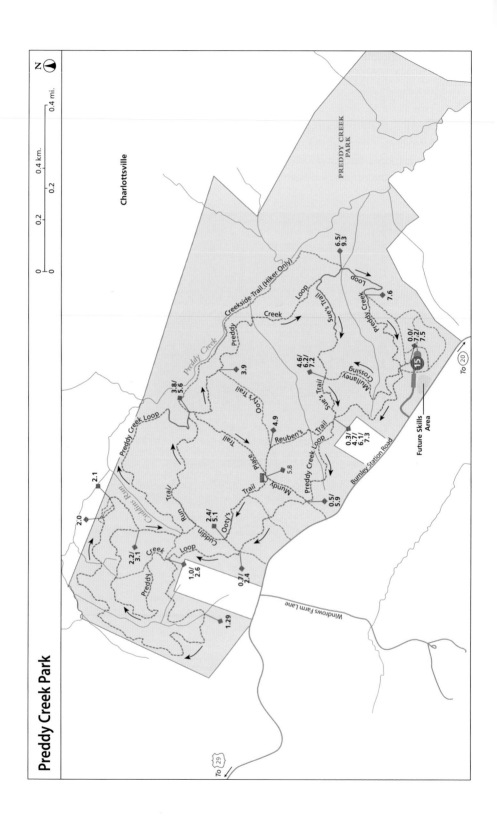

Preddy Creek Park

Charlottsville

PREDDY CREEK PARK

To 20

To 29

Future Skills Area

Burnley Station Road

Windrows Farm Lane

Preddy Creek Loop

Cuddin Run

Preddy Creek Loop

Creekside Trail (Hiker Only)

Preddy Creek

Ooty's Trail

Reuben's Place

Mundy Trail

Ooty's

Cuddin Run Loop

Snet's Trail

Sker's Trail

Mullaney Crossing

Preddy Creek Loop

Preddy Creek

0   0.2   0.4 km.

0   0.2   0.4 mi.

N

3.8/5.6

2.1

2.0

2.2/3.1

2.4/5.1

1.0/2.6

0.3/2.4

1.29

3.9

4.9

5.8

0.5/5.9

0.3/4.1/6.1/7.3

4.6/6.2/7.2

6.5/9.3

7.6

0.0/7.2/7.5

15

0.0 Start where the dirt begins along the Trail Kiosk by the restrooms, take a moment to review the map. Head down toward the main Preddy Creek Loop and make an immediate left, staying to the left past the first trail intersection. We will ride the main loop in a clockwise direction, just follow the Preddy Creek Loop Trail markers.

0.3 Continue to the left past these two intersections. The first will be Sue's Trail and the second Reuben's Trail. We will ride both of these trails after we complete the main loop.

0.5 Continue straight along the Preddy Creek Loop Trail. The trail to the right is Mundy Place Trail. We will climb Mundy a little later.

0.6 Continue to the left following the Preddy Creek Loop Trail. The trail to the right is a connector trail to Otty's Trail.

0.7 Continue straight on the Preddy Creek Loop Trail. The trail to the right is Cuddin's Trail.

1.0 Turn left into the designated Advanced Mountain Bike Loop. Don't be intimidated by the sign. The trails are narrower and a little harder, definitely fun. They offer a little more severe elevation changes and occasional obstacles. When in doubt, dismount.

1.24 The first of the trails obstacles is a small "gap jump." Just ride the short bridge to the right.

2.0 This section of the trail offers several branches where most of the more advanced options in the loop are. All branches will basically connect a little further along the trail. We will stick along the main trail to the right.

2.1 The "branches" mentioned in 2.0 merge back into the main trails.

2.2 You are back on the main loop. Turn left to continue following the Preddy Creek Loop Trail in a clockwise direction. We'll take a little detour to ride the portion of the main loop we skipped when entering the Advanced Mountain Bike Trail.

2.3 Turn right onto the connector. This will be a short trail that will take us up to Cuddin's. Turn right immediately when you reach the next intersection.

2.4 Continue straight past Otty's Trail and then turn right to hop back on the Preddy Creek Loop trail.

2.6 You're back at the entrance of the Advanced Mountain Bike Loop. Continue straight along the Preddy Creek Loop Trail. The next section of trail is super fun.

3.1 Continue on the Preddy Creek Loop Trail past the exit to the Advanced Mountain Bike Loop; or, give it a shot in the opposite direction.

3.2 Continue left on the Preddy Creek Loop Trail past the connector trail we rode on a little while ago.

3.8 Continue on the Preddy Creek Loop Trail past the next three intersections. The first intersection to the right is Cuddin's Run Trail, the next one to the left is the Creekside Trail (hiking only), finally, the third intersection, to the right, is Mundy Place. We'll revisit this section in a few minutes.

3.9 Continue straight along the Preddy Creek Loop Trail past Otty's Trail to the right.

4.3 Turn right onto Sue's Trail. Now we'll hit most of the internal trails before finishing up the loop. If you want to be done, continue straight along the Preddy Creek Loop Trail until you reach the starting point of the ride.

4.6 Continue along Sue's Trail past Mullaney Crossing to the left.

4.7 You reach the Preddy Creek Loop trail, turn right and immediately right again to hop on Reuben's Trail. The next downhill section is sketchy. Be careful!

4.9 Continue straight (slight left/slight right) to merge onto Otty's Trail; a nice covered bench will be to your right. A sharp right turn will take you down to the Preddy Creek Loop Trail and intersection 3.9.

5.1 Back in familiar territory. Turn right onto Cuddin's Run Trail. We rode up this short section of trail earlier. Follow Cuddin's all the way down to the bottom to the Preddy Creek Loop Trail.

5.2 The trail to the left is the connector trail we rode on at 2.3–2.4. Stay on Cuddin's Run.

5.6 Turn right on the Preddy Creek Loop Trail and then immediately right again to climb along Mundy Place all the way back to the top side of the Preddy Creek Loop Trail.

5.8 Continue straight through this intersection, Otty's Trail. The covered bench will be to your right.

5.9 Turn left on the Preddy Creek Loop Trail to get a taste of the main loop in the counterclockwise direction.

6.1 Go past Reuben's Trail and turn left onto Sue's Trail. We'll head all the way back to the bottom of Sue's and the Preddy Creek Loop Trail.

6.2 Continue straight along Sue's Trail past Mullaney Crossing. If you want to finish the ride, turn right on Mullaney Crossing.

6.5 Back on the Preddy Creek Loop Trail, turn right to finish out the loop.

6.7 Continue following the main loop across the gravel road. The spur to the left will lead you up toward the Meadow Loops.

7.1 You're pretty much back at the starting point. You can turn left to finish the ride or make a right to follow Mullaney Crossing. We'll do that—let's ride as much as we can!

7.2 You reach Sue's Trail. Turn left to climb back up to the Preddy Creek Loop Trail.

7.3 Back on the Preddy Creek Loop Trail, turn left to complete the ride.

7.6 Turn right to head back up to the trail kiosk, the loop is complete.

Ride Information

Bike Shops

Blue Ridge Cyclery: blueridgecyclery.com
Bike Factory: bikefactory.com
Blue Wheel: www.bluewheel.com

Local Events and Attractions

Visit Charlottesville has a comprehensive list of events and attraction in downtown Charlottesville and Albemarle County: www.visitcharlottesville.org
Charlottesville is home to the University of Virginia (UVA), check out UVA's calendar for a myriad of events from arts to athletics: calendar.virginia.edu
Thomas Jefferson's Monticello: www.monticello.org
Walnut Creek has a 23-acre lake with a beach; if hit the trails during a hot and muggy Virginia Summer, a dip in the lake is a welcome end to any ride.

Restaurants

Beer Run: beerrun.com
Sticks Kebob Shop: www.stickskebobshop.com
Jack Brown's Beer & Burger Joint: www.jackbrownsjoint.com
Three Notch'd Brewing Company: threenotchdbrewing.com (bring your own food)

Honorable Mentions

Compiled here is an index of great rides in Virginia's Piedmont region that didn't make the A list this time around but deserve recognition. Check them out and let us know what you think. You may decide that one or more of these rides deserves higher status in future editions, or perhaps you may have a ride of your own that merits some attention. Some of these rides are documented on our website, www.mtbdc.com

O. Rivanna River Trail (RTF)—Observatory (O) Hill: At 23 miles, the RTF is a challenging outing for any mountain biker looking for a good ride. The trail circumnavigates the city of Charlottesville, and is generally flat as it follows the path of various drainages. Along the western border of the RTF, you'll find the Observatory (O Hill) trail network, a dense maze of unmarked trails over a small ridge adjacent to the University of VA. The "urban" nature of the RTF allows you to access it from several locations throughout the city, enabling you to ride only certain portions, incorporating restaurants and local watering holes in the city along the way. If you do choose to ride the entire trail, follow the white "RTF" blazes that mark its path. For more detailed information about the RTF, including maps and access points, visit www.rivannatrails.org/

P. Powhite Park: Powhite Park, located just off the Chippenham Parkway and across from the Chippenham Medical Center is an optional riding destination in Richmond's urban landscape. The development and revitalization of the trails along the James River and Pocahontas State Park diverted some attention from this Richmond destination, but they remain a local favorite. Located within the confines of a 100-acre park are nearly 8 miles of tight, twisty, and technical trails guaranteed to keep you busy for a couple of hours. Expect punchy, steep climbs, and descents. As a warning, it's best to try and avoid Powhite after substantial rainfall, since the lower portions of the system are located within a swampy area that does not drain very well.

GPS coordinates: 37.518187, −77.527819

Southern Virginia

Virginia's "Southside" is part of the Virginia Piedmont, but it certainly deserves recognition for some of its own unique characteristics. Framed by the Blue Ridge Mountains to the west, the James River to the north, and the fall line to the east, Southern Virginia is a region full of character and natural resources to be explored.

Early settlers to this region came for the richness of the soil. Virginia's south, along with much of the settled lands in southern bordering states, were well known for their tobacco crops. As you ride the trails within IC Dehart, near the Woolwine community, you'll understand why; your tires will roll over some of the "reddest" Virginia dirt in the state. The nutrient rich "dirt" provides the perfect conditions for growing tobacco and other hardy plants, including cotton and soybeans.

In the early 1940s, communities in Southern Virginia began manufacturing textiles. Cotton fiber from nearby plantations was converted into fabric at newly constructed mills, most notably along the Dan River in the city of Danville. Low labor and low operating costs, along with the region's proximity to regional trading centers such as Richmond helped the textile industry in the Southside of the state flourish.

Unfortunately, globalization began to take a toll in not only Virginia's textile industry, but also on its once thriving tobacco industry. Many of the mills closed and work was outsourced to other countries, including China, India, and Mexico. Demand for tobacco also waned, as cigarette manufacturers imported more of their product from cheaper markets, including South America, Africa, and China.

With the decline in these industries, southside Virginia has begun to redefine itself. Communities such as Danville are reshaping their downtown districts, and have begun to take advantage of the rich mix of rural and cosmopolitan life present in their communities. New crops are taking hold, and smaller cities are luring other industries with tax incentives and the promise of low operating costs and high quality of living.

Despite the changes, however, Southern Virginia's proud heritage continues to be present. The communities that were shaped by the once bustling tobacco and textile markets are finding ways to continue to thrive, albeit differently. Once such community, along the plains of the Blue Ridge Mountains, is the town of Floyd. Floyd, approximately 1 hour from Martinsville (Mountain Laurel Trails, Ride 18) and only 20 minutes from IC DeHart (Ride 17) offers visitors a bustling main street with shops and restaurants that highlight the region's artisans and take advantage of the surrounding scenery. Trust me, it's worth visiting.

16 Angler's Ridge

Old School—The Anglers Ridge mountain bike paradise has a little bit of an old school feel to it. With over 30 miles of trails, there are tons of options to choose from, and regardless of your ability, you're bound to be satisfied with what this Southern Virginia destination has to offer. The system is pretty much divided into three sections: In Anglers Ridge, the relatively flat and easy Riverside Drive Trail splits the system in two halves, with Little Pisgah and Crooked Stick to the east and Camelback, Hot Tamale, and Witchback to the west. On the opposite side of Rte. 58 is the Hidden Hollow Trail in Dan Daniel Memorial Park. No matter what option you choose, be ready to get a good workout. The Riverside Trail is appropriate for beginners since it offers little elevation change and only a few TTFs. It does, however, include several bridge crossings with no railings, which may "intimidate" younger or beginner riders.

Start: Start from the first trailhead to the left as you drive into the main parking area for Anglers Park.
Length: 5.7–30 miles of trails
Ride time: 45 minutes–1 hour
Difficulty: Novice to expert.
Trail surface: Rolling hard packed and rooty singletrack trails several TTFs.
Lay of the land: Rolling twisty singletrack trails through dense forestland along the Dan River watershed.

Land status: Public
Nearest town: Danville
Other trail users: Hikers, trail runners
Trail contacts: Virginia Mountain Bike Association, www.svmba.org
Schedule: Dawn to dusk
Fees: Free to public

Getting there: From 29/58 South, take the Ricer Park Drive Exit toward Dan Daniel Memorial Park and turn left. Follow River Park Drive for approximately 1/10 mile and turn right on Stinson Drive and then left on Northside Drive. Follow Northside toward the water treatment facility and turn left into the park. Continue straight into the main Anglers Park parking area, the trailhead will be to your left as you enter the parking area. **GPS coordinates:** 36.55904, -79.35643.

The Ride

The trails at Anglers Park and Dan Daniel Park are the result of a collaborative effort between volunteers from the Southern Virginia Mountain Bike Association (SVMBA), and the city of Danville. In late 2002, the city of Danville and SVMBA signed an MOU that allowed SVMBA to extend the trails at Anglers Park. Today, thanks to that effort, there are over 30 miles of trails to enjoy at this Southern Virginia destination.

All the trails in Anglers Park and Dan Daniel Park are easily accessible from the Riverwalk Trail, a paved path that parallels the Dan River. The path highlights the city of Danville's natural resources and has contributed to the reshaping of the area's future. Known as the "Last Capital of the Confederacy," Danville was once a major

SVMBA has done a fine job of marking the trails at Anglers Park. A detailed map is available near the trailhead and bike wash area.

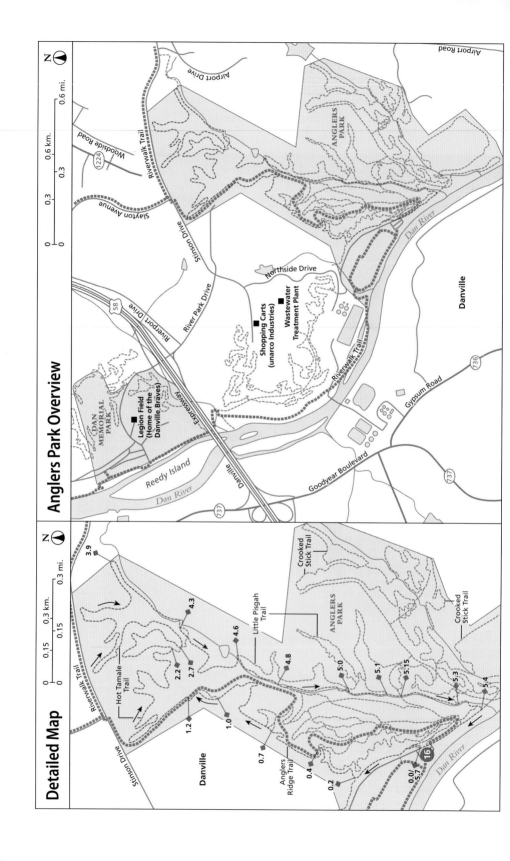

Detailed Map

N

0   0.15   0.3 km.

0   0.15   0.3 mi.

Riverwalk Trail

Stinson Drive

3.9

Hot Tamale Trail

4.3

4.6

2.2

2.7

Little Pisgah Trail

4.8

Danville

1.2

1.0

0.7

5.0

5.1

5.15

5.3

Crooked Stick Trail

ANGLERS PARK

Crooked Stick Trail

5.4

Anglers Ridge Trail

0.4

0.2

0.0/ 5.7

16

Dan River

Anglers Park Overview

N

0   0.3   0.6 km.

0   0.3   0.6 mi.

Airport Drive

Riverwalk Trail

Woodside Road
1224

Slayton Avenue

Stinson Drive

River Park Drive

Riverport Drive

58

Expressway

Danville

737

Reedy Island

Dan River

DAN MEMORIAL PARK

Legion Field
(Home of the Danville Braves)

Northside Drive

Shopping Carts
(unarco Industries)

Wastewater
Treatment Plant

Riverwalk Trail

Dan River

Gypsum Road

Goodyear Boulevard

737

736

ANGLERS PARK

Danville

Airport Road

tobacco-trading hub. The arrival of the railroad in the mid-1850s made it strategically much more important. During the Civil War, the city played a critical role for the South, as its rail link to Richmond, the Southern Capital, made it a major resupply depot.

In early April of 1865, shortly after the fall of Petersburg, Southern leadership, including Confederate President Jefferson Davis, fled Richmond to Danville to establish a new Capital for the Confederacy. But upon learning of Lee's surrender at Appomattox, the City was abandoned as the seat of Southern Government. After the War, tobacco markets continued to flourish, and in addition, a new textile industry was born along the banks of the Dan. Danville's cotton mills thrived for years, but competition from overseas finally forced the closing of the mills in 2006. Since then, the city has begun a transformation to redefine itself to attract new businesses and industries.

The trails at Anglers Park are clearly marked. You can choose from one of five marked loops (Green: 2 miles; Blue: 5 miles, Purple: 7 miles; Orange: 6.2 miles, and Red: 12 miles), all begin and end at the trailhead where my "sample" ride begins. All of the loops can be ridden in both directions and combined to create a myriad of routes to suite your taste.

The ride I document here will give you a good taste of what Anglers has to offer. I highly recommend you explore this great destination at your own pace to craft a loop that suits you. If you are looking for a mellow/kid-friendly ride, I recommend you ride the Riverside Trail out and back. The Riverside Trail is nice and flat and offers you the opportunity to access several of the park's other more challenging trails, including Camelback, Hot Tamale, Little Pisgah, and Crooked Stick (my personal favorite).

Miles and Directions

0.0 As you enter the parking area, look for the small trailhead sign along the wood line. There are two trailheads, one closer to the parking lot entrance (the one we want) and one closer to the restrooms and vending machines. Enter this trailhead and head to the left, as if leaving the park. Immediately upon entering, you'll reach an intersection, stay left. The trail to the right will take you toward the second trailhead.

0.2 Stay to the right at this intersection, the trail to the left is the Witchback Trail. Witchback is blazed with Orange markings, we will follow the Green and Red arrows to remain on the Anglers Ridge Trail.

0.4 You reach the intersection of Anglers Ridge, Camelback, and Broken Arrow. Turn left to hop onto Camelback.

0.7 Continue following Camelback straight ahead. You are now following the Red Loop, the green loop will go to the right.

1.0 Continue to the left, the trail to the right is a short connector to the Riverwalk Trail (paved).

1.2 You reach the end of Camelback. Cross over the Riverwalk Trail (paved) and enter Hot Tamale.

2.2 Continue to the left to stay on Hot Tamale, the branch to the right is Flying Squirrel, a shortcut to the next section of Hot Tamale and the Riverside Drive trail.

2.7 You reach the intersection of Hot Tamale and Flying Squirrel. Flying Squirrel is a short connector to the Riverside Drive Trail, we'll reach that intersection a little later on. Continue to the left to remain on Hot Tamale and continue to follow the Red Loop.

3.9 You reach the end of Hot Tamale at the Riverside Trail; turn right. The left fork will take you toward a dead end and Stinson Drive. We will now remain on the Riverside Trail for the remainder of the ride. You'll parallel the creek and cross it several times.

4.3 You reach the intersection with Flying Squirrel. A right turn will take you back up toward Hot Tamale (mile marker 2.7). Continue straight on Riverside Trail. Continue following the red markers.

4.6 Go over the short bridge and continue following Riverside Drive to the right. The left fork will take you up along Little Pisgah. Little Pisgah is a longer alternative to the same destination we are heading to. It offers a little more elevation and technical features. You are now following the blue loop.

4.8 After crossing the creek, continue following the trail to the left toward the Copperhead Twist, a small TTF. Immediately after the TTF, the trail will split; the right fork on the near side of the creek is Eagle Scout Trail. Follow the left fork to the left across the creek to remain on Riverside Drive.

5.0 After a couple of bridge crossings, you'll reach a connector trail to Little Pisgah, continue straight along Riverside Drive.

5.1 Continue straight along Riverside Drive, the trail to the left is another connector to Little Pisgah.

5.15 Cross Gravity Hill to remain on Riverside Drive.

5.3 You reach a fork in the trail; either branch will take you to the same spot. The left branch contains a short deck that marks the "entrance" to Little Pisgah. Continue following the Riverside Drive Trail.

5.4 After a long bridge crossing, the trail will veer to the left and split again along two parallel routes. The right fork is an easy track while the left fork offers you the opportunity to ride a series of rock features. The trail will merge within 50 yards and you'll hit the intersection of Eagle Scout to the right. Continue straight on Riverside Drive to the doubletrack and turn right on the gravel road. Follow the gravel road back toward the parking area and bike wash.

5.5 Continue straight along the gravel road, the trail to the right is an entrance point to Eagle Scout. Shortly after the intersection, the gravel will turn to pavement.

5.7 You reach the starting point. The loop is complete.

Ride Information

Local Information

Danville, VA—www.danville-va.gov/
Danville Parks and Recreation—www.playdanvilleva.com/264/Riverwalk-Trail

Bike Shop

Bicycle Medic, 2024 Riverside, Dr. Danville, VA, 24540-4305, (434) 799-3133

Local Events and Attractions

Riverwalk Trail—playdanvilleva.com/264/Riverwalk-Trail
Visit Danville, Virginia—www.danville-va.gov
Legion Field—visible from the Hidden Hollow Trail; If you're into baseball, it's the home of Minor League Baseball's Danville Braves—www.dbraves.com
Virginia International Raceway—virnow.com

Restaurants

Me's Burgers and Brews: www.mesburgers.com (closed Sunday and Monday)
2 Witches Winery & Brewery: www.2witcheswinebre.com (bring your own food)

Restrooms

Available next to the Bike Wash.

17 IC DeHart

The best trails you've never heard of. Sitting at the base of the Blue Ridge Mountains, this varying terrain singletrack trail has a little bit of everything a true mountain biker could ask for. Incredible rock gardens, fast-flowing sections, scorching fast downhills, beautiful singletrack climbs, and an all-around top-notch mountain bike course. There are numerous advanced options throughout this hidden gem in the shadow of the Blue Ridge Mountains.

Start: From the parking area adjacent to the IC DeHart pavilion, ride down the paved path to the trail kiosk. All loops begin there.
Length: Up to 12 miles
Ride time: 1.5–3 hours
Difficulty: Novice to expert
Trail surface: Rolling singletrack with advanced features, including rock gardens, TTFs, and natural obstacles.

Lay of the land: Rolling lower Blue Ridge Mountains singletrack. Trails built specifically for cross-country riding.
Land status: Public
Nearest town: Woolwine
Other trail users: Hikers, trail runners
Trail contacts: IC DeHart Memorial Park, Woolwine, VA 24185, (276) 930-2127
Schedule: Dawn to dusk
Fees: Free to public

Getting there: From I 81, take the exit 144, VA-8 toward Christiansburg/Floyd and continue S/W toward Floyd. Continue on VA-8 for approximately 32 miles. Turn left on VA-40 E and continue for 2.5 miles. IC DeHart Memorial Park will be on your left. **GPS coordinates:** 36.8148, –80.25589.

The Ride

Over the past several years that I have been traveling to document rides for my cycling guides, I've had the opportunity to ride a considerable number of great trails in the DC, MD, and Virginia Regions. But on very few occasions, have I been surprised by a particular trail system like the way I was by the ribbons that have been cut at IC DeHart Memorial Park near Woolwine.

IC DeHart Memorial Park, named after local resident Isaac "Ike" DeHart, includes quite possibly the best trails you've never heard off, until now. Before there were trails, the land where the current park sits belonged to grist mill and legal distiller Isaac "Ike" DeHart. Over the course of his life, Isaac and his brother Joseph built a thriving business that took advantage of Virginia's rich soil and ran a farm, raised cattle, operated a roller and grist mill, and ran a legal distillery that shipped Corn and Rye Whiskey to markets throughout the state and beyond.

Like all good things, their distilleries came to a close in the early part of the twentieth century when prohibition took over the state. The alcohol business gave way to other endeavors, and ultimately, Ike DeHart's heirs donated the land that is now the park, to Patrick County.

The land stood idle for some time until 2009 when local resident Eric O'Connell approached Patrick County officials with a proposal to build a mountain bike trail within the confines of the park. The County gave him the green light, and in 2009, Eric—along with his wife—headed into the woods to begin building the trails.

At first, work went slowly, and Eric began to get discouraged, but then something clicked in his mind. Eric approached the local Sheriff and pitched him an idea to use some of the current incarcerated prisoners in the County to help build the trails. He figured some of those guys, who were in for small crimes, would love to be outside. In the process, they could help build a trail system that would eventually benefit their community.

The Sheriff agreed to the proposal and Eric selected a couple of guys, Bobby and Jason, who gladly volunteered to help. Together, they set out to build an 8-mile loop in the fall of 2010. By spring of the following year, they had completed it. The guys worked rain or shine, cold or heat, and despite the back braking labor, they loved the opportunity Eric and the County Sheriff provided them with. With the trails completed, Eric organized the first Shiner's Revenge Mountain bike race at IC DeHart, a regional favorite event.

In September 2015, a devastating flood hit Patrick County. In addition to destroying a local historical landmark, the Bob White Covered Bridge, the rains also had a devastating effect on the trails. Faced with rebuilding them, Eric set out to flag a new route, and once again utilized the same resources and program he used for the initial trail system. This time around, however, the new trails were rebuilt using sustainable methods, and instead of a two-man crew, Eric had solicited the help of five guys.

Eric is incredibly proud of the trail system, but more of the program he helped develop. "Some of the guys that helped cut the trail had no quality of life," he told me. "When riders told them how much they enjoyed the fruits of their labor, they felt a sense of purpose; that they had given something back to their community. Seeing their reactions was priceless; it meant something to them."

Eric has also helped organize a few regular races at IC DeHart, including the Shiner's Revenge, a mountain bike race that pays homage to the area's distillery history. All of the proceeds from the event go back to the community that made the trails happen, including the establishment of a scholarship fund for students interested in law enforcement.

When I arrived to IC DeHart, I came with little expectations of finding a great trail system; and I walked away wanting to come back for more. And, once I found out how they were built, and what they have meant for this community, I was even more impressed. Do yourself a favor; make the trip to Woolwine to sample some of the best trails Southern Virginia has to offer. You will not be disappointed.

The rock armoring at IC DeHart is extraordinary.

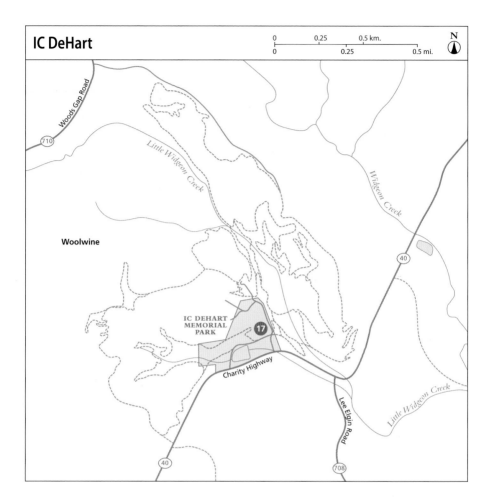

IC DeHart

0 0.25 0.5 km.
0 0.25 0.5 mi.

N

710

Woods Gap Road

Little Widgeon Creek

Widgeon Creek

Woolwine

40

IC DEHART
MEMORIAL
PARK

17

Charity Highway

Lee Elgin Road

Little Widgeon Creek

40

708

Miles and Directions

The Terrain at IC DeHart is Rolling; there will be climbing, but the trail builders have ensured that none of that climbing is "steep." For the most part the trails are all fast rolling, hard packed red Virginia dirt. A few TTFs and several rock features have been added to the trail. All, with the exception of the easy to roll rock armoring, have ride arounds. All the trails are clearly marked with colored diamond-shaped blazes.

There are five pre-marked loops that are easy to follow. When you arrive at the park, park in front of the Pavilion and make your way down the paved path away from the park entrance toward the Woodline. The entrance to all trails is clearly marked with a map and kiosk. Depending on your ability, select from one of the following pre-marked courses:

All white—10 miles

White to yellow to white—9.5 miles

White to blue to white—5 miles

White to red to white—3.5 miles

Ride Information

Local Information

Patrick County, VA—www.visitpatrickcounty.org/

Bike Shop

Chain of Fools: www.chainoffoolsbicycles.com

Blue Ridge Bike Shop: www.facebook.com/blueridgebikeshop/

Local Events and Attractions

Shiner's Revenge: www.shinersrevenge.com

The Town of Floyd: visitfloydva.com

The Blue Ridge Parkway: www.nps.gov/blri

Restaurants

El Charro Mexican Grill: 302 Locust St, Floyd, VA 24091 (540) 745-5303

Restrooms

Available in the park.

18 Mountain Laurel Trails

The Mountain Laurel Trails, built by Bob Norris, on his property are a testament to a rider/builder who has embraced the sport of mountain biking full heartedly. The trails offer novice and expert cyclists alike a challenging and fun network that have been packed into a relatively small parcel of land.

Start: As you enter the main property, follow the signs for "trail parking." The trailhead is clearly marked with a kiosk with trail conditions information and a map of the trail system.
Length: Up to 9 miles (and growing)
Ride time: 1-2 hours
Difficulty: Novice to expert
Trail surface: Hard-packed singletrack

Lay of the land: Rolling bi-directional singletrack in a forest setting. Creek side trails with few TTFs
Land status: Private property
Nearest town: Martinsville
Other trail users: Trail runners, hikers
Trail contacts: Bob Norris, www.mountainlaureltrails.com
Schedule: Open year-round, dawn to dusk.
Fees: Free for public

Getting there: From US Hwy. 58 West to the Horsepasture Price Road. 1 and ½ miles out on the right is Mountain Laurel Trail. Travel approximately ½ miles to the day-use trailhead on the right after the fork in the road. There is plenty of parking onsite. **GPS coordinates:** 36.60639, -79.95703.

The Ride

Every trail has a story, and Mountain Laurel's is as interesting as they come. In 2013, Bob Norris visited his physician and was diagnosed with type 2 diabetes. His doctor recommended a change in diet and that he start exercising to lose some weight and get on track to a healthier lifestyle. Not knowing what to do, Bob asked for advice, and his doctor told him to "mountain bike."

Bob had very little idea of where to begin, but there was a fire road and a couple of trails within his 110-acre property line in Martinsville, so he bought a bike and set out to ride them. At first, he couldn't get very far, but gradually he began to get better, and enjoy his daily outings. With very little singletrack nearby, Bob decided he would put his former construction background into use, and began building his own trails. Armed with research, IMBA's trail building guide, and a newly purchased Ditch Witch, Bob set out to build the Mountain Laurel Trails in 2014. The rest, as they say, is history.

But what fun is riding and building trails alone? Knowing that he could not do it all by himself, Bob set up a website (mountainlaureltrails.com) and invited the local community to come and see what he was doing. His progress energized riders in the region, and many showed up to help him with his project, making the trail on his property a community endeavor. Within 2 years, he, along with an army of volunteers, had cut nearly 8 miles of trails. And, they are not finished. When I showed up to ride Mountain Laurel, Bob told me that he was planning on adding at least 4–5 additional miles and will continue to work so that riders in the area have a quality place to ride.

In addition to building the trails, Bob has built a kiosk at the trailhead that provides incoming riders with on-trail status updates. There is a map of the property that gives users a pretty good idea of what they are heading into, and he has clearly marked all trails so that you can easily follow a selected loop. Plans are in the work for a small building to provide additional amenities, including take away maps, drinks, tools, and shelter to just hang out after a ride in the woods.

The thing that Bob is most excited about is the fact that so many riders are enjoying the fruits of his labor. Bob estimates that around fifty riders hit the trail each week. Some he knows, and others have just heard of the trails through word of mouth. Bob actively advertises scheduled rides on Facebook and through his website, including a series of beginner rides to get people out on the trails. "These trails changed my life," he told me. "I lost a considerable amount of weight, I'm healthier, and love being in this stress-free zone; I want other riders, beginner and advanced, to benefit from the trails and enjoy them as well."

The trails are a joy to ride. Because Bob and his team used sound sustainable building techniques, the trails drain well and roll beautifully over the terrain. The trails can be strenuous though, and experienced riders will love them because they can provide a great workout, one in which they can build on their "speed" skills. Beginner and intermediate riders will also enjoy them because they offer a stress-free place where they can improve their bike handling skills.

Bob is also building a healthy community competition. A Strava club has been set up so that riders can compete on the Yellow Loop Challenge or other rotating competitions, regardless of ability. These challenges provide an incentive for riders to get out on the trails and enjoy them on a regular basis. Winners of the challenges are often recognized at the trailhead for their efforts.

Ride Information

Local Information

Martinsville, Henry County—www.visitmartinsville.com/
Bike Shop: Chain of Fools—www.chainoffoolsbicycles.com

Local Events and Attractions

Martinsville Speedway—www.martinsvillespeedway.com/

Bob Norris (right), Mountain Laurel's builder and proprietor, has started a friendly competition with local riders.

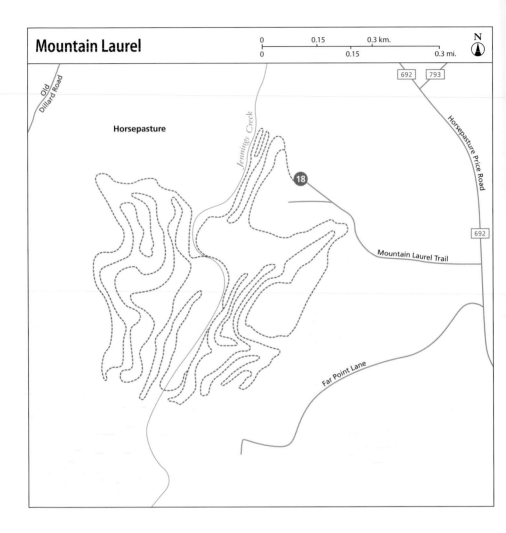

Restaurants

Mtn' Jax Restaurant & Pub

43 E Chruch St, Martinsville, VA 24112 (276) 403-4529 www.facebook.com/
MtnJaxRestaurantAndPub/

Hugo's 10 East Church St. (lower level) Martinsville, VA 24112 (276) 632-3663
www.martinsvillehugos.com

Restrooms

Not available at the trail.

Honorable Mention

Compiled here is an index of additional rides in Southern Virginia that didn't make the A list this time around but deserve recognition. Check them out and let me know what you think. You may decide that one or more of these rides deserves higher status in future editions, or perhaps you may have a ride of your own that merits some attention. Some of these rides are documented on our website, www.mtbdc.com

Q. Mount Rogers Recreation Area—Iron Mountain Trail: There's a reason why Damascus is known as Trail Town USA. This small community in Southwestern Virginia sits at the crossroads of several noteworthy trails, including the Appalachian Trail, The Virginian Creeper Trail, the Transamerica Bike Route, and the Iron Mountain Trail. Of special interest to us, is the Iron Mountain Trail (IMT), a 20-mile ribbon of challenging singletrack along the mountain that bears its name. Despite being home to one of the region's most popular endurance races, the Iron Mountain 100, the IMT continues to be one of those "best kept secret" trails that only the locals seem flock to. The trails are reminiscent of those old school West Virginia singletrack epics we used to (still do) venture to in the early and mid-1990s; they are rugged and full of character; they're mature. If you like long fire road climbs with equally technical, sketchy, as well as rock and root infested descents, then this is the place for you. Sounds ominous, right? It is. But, once you get a taste for this challenging type of riding, you'll know why you got into the sport in the first place. The IMT can be accessed from several places within the Mount Rogers Recreation Area. The most popular access points are from the Virginia Creeper Trail along Beach Grove, or right from downtown Damascus, along Rebel Circle on the eastern side of town.

GPS coordinates: 36.63488, −81.77943

Virginia Mountains and the Shenandoah Valley

Two of Virginia's most distinct features, and perhaps its most celebrated, are its mountains and the fertile valley between them. The Blue Ridge Mountains, part of the greater Appalachian Range, and the Shenandoah Valley, part of the Great Appalachian Valley, mark the western borders of the Old Dominion. Considered Virginia's frontier by early settlers, the Blue Ridge and Shenandoah Valley became the home for generations of families because of the ample resources they provided. Today, the region is home to not only one of our nation's most visited National Parks, the Shenandoah Valley National Park, but also two National Forests, The George Washington National Forest (GWNF) and Jefferson National Forest (JNF).

Occupying over 1.6 million acres in Virginia alone, the forests are one of the largest preserved natural areas in the eastern United States. An additional 125,000 acres in West Virginia and 961 in Kentucky account for the balance. It is within the confines of Virginia's 1.6 million acres that the rides I've selected for this section of this guide will take place.

Most people don't equate remote backcountry with Virginia, but that is precisely what you'll find within Virginia's Blue Ridge Mountains and the Shenandoah Valley, as well as in the vast expanses of the George Washington and Jefferson National Forests. Hundreds of miles of backcountry trails traverse the Blue Ridge Mountains and span the long linear ridges that make up the Blue Ridge. Built by Roosevelt's Army of the unemployed (the Civilian Conservation Corps—CCC) in the 1930s, the backcountry trails would eventually ignite an interest in backcountry travel and cycling.

In 1933, approximately 100—300 out-of-work young men based out of Camp Edith (now camp Roosevelt, see Kennedy Peak ride) set out to implement Roosevelt's New Deal. Roosevelt's plan, enacted into law as the Emergency Work Act, provided eligible out-of-work young men between the ages of 17 and 25 a steady monthly paycheck in an otherwise dismal economy for "building infrastructure" in inaccessible lands. Managed by the multiple Federal Agencies, The Emergency Work Act proved to be a success that garnered strong public support. By 1942, when the program ended, nearly 3 million men in more than 2,600 camps modeled after Camp Edith would find employment and build not only trails but also be responsible for reforestation efforts, building wildlife shelters, restoring historic battlefields, and clearing campgrounds for the nation's enjoyment. In the Corp's near decade of existence, its workers built nearly 1,000 parks and planted billions of trees, in the process, fulfilling Roosevelt's vision of a "tree army" that promoted conservation and universal youth service.

Documenting everything that's available for mountain biking in this region would require the writing of its own book. The rides selected here will give you a sampling of what is available and hopefully inspire you to craft some loops of your own. I've divided the region into four "ride centers": Front Royal/Strasburg, Harrisonburg, Clifton Forge/Lexington, and Roanoke.

The epicenter for riding in the region is Stokesville, home of the Stokesville Lodge and Chris Scott's Shenandoah Mountain Touring company, one of the driving forces behind the development of the Virginia Mountain Bike Trail, a 480-mile ribbon of [mostly] singletrack that connects the public lands from the northern to southern borders of Virginia.

None of Scott's effort would be possible without the "other" force in the region, the Shenandoah Valley Bicycle Coalition (SVBC). The SVBC is an advocate organization that promotes all things cycling and works, at a grass roots level, with city and county governments and the national forest to ensure the preservation of natural spaces. The SVBC has secured hundreds of thousands of dollars for trail development and conservation efforts that have propelled the region to the forefront of mountain biking and have helped make the Blue Ridge Mountains and the Shenandoah Valley not only a regional, but national destination for mountain biking.

No visit to Harrisonburg, home of the SVBC, would be complete without also paying a visit to the Shenandoah Bicycle Company. Located only a few blocks away from the city's center, and a quick ride from Harrisonburg's Rocktown trails at Hillandale Park, the Shenandoah Bicycle Company is a hub of activity for the region's advocacy scene. Thomas Jenkins, the shop's owner, is very much active with the SVBC, and is one of the many volunteers responsible for navigating the necessary requirements to secure $600,000 of Federal RTP Grants that the SVBC obtained to finance much of the trail revitalization going on in the valley.

As you ride through the selected routes, including the trails along Lookout Mountain, the new downhill portions of Festival, and the highly enjoyable Tillman downhill, you'll appreciate how much that effort has paid off. The astonishing thing about these trails is that despite being in a backcountry setting, they are so easily accessible. This accessibility allows regional and visiting riders to sample what else they may encounter in the more "secluded" trails that abound in the region. Ride any of the aforementioned trails, and you'll have a pretty good idea of what you may encounter elsewhere within the forest's more than 1.5 million acres. That way, when you are ready to commit to a more extensive ride like Reddish Knob, Dowell's, or the Epic Southern Traverse you'll know what lays ahead.

That said, many of the trails within the confines of the GWNF and the TJNF are indeed backcountry trails and you must be prepared. Bring plenty of water and fuel. Let someone know where you are headed and when you'll be back; study the route before heading out and be familiar with it. Carry a map and know your alternatives. Cell coverage is spotty at best and a minor mechanical can turn into a day-long (even overnight) ordeal.

My recommendation is that when you do venture out into the vast expanses of the Blue Ridge and Shenandoah, that you do so in a group. The stories you'll tell afterwards will be with you for the rest of your life.

Front Royal/Strasburg Ride Center

Front Royal and Strasburg have been a long time favorite destination for mountain bikers in the Washington, D.C., Northern Virginia, and Shenandoah Valley regions. Countless gravel roads, and rocky technical singletrack—like the trails at Elizabeth Furnace (Ride 20)—have been a rite of passage for cyclists in the area for years. During the early 1990s, many cyclists in Northern Virginia and Maryland made the trek to ride the trails around Front Royal simply because they were some of the few that were open to bikes at the time. Today the mountain biking landscape has changed considerably, but the riding in the George Washington National Forest around these two small Virginia towns remains some of the best in the region.

Virginia's mountains are a mountain bike destination for riders from all over the eastern United States.

19 Mill Mountain: Little Stoney to Big Schloss

Not for the timid. If there is a ride in this book that will test your determination, it's this one. It's hard up and down, and the brief moments of rest you encounter along the way are to simply deliver you to the next technically demanding section of trail. Mill Mountain is where you get to test all the technical riding skills you've developed as you've explored the other rides in this book; it is your final exam.

Start: Little Stoney Trailhead along FR 92.
Length: 9.3 miles
Ride time: 2–4 hours
Difficulty: Intermediate to expert. Difficult. Technically challenging climb and descent. This ride is NOT for beginners.
Trail surface: Mountainous rocky/technical singletrack.

Lay of the land: Rocky and technical singletrack. Little Stoney is a "creek" trail, very wet when it rains.
Land status: Public
Nearest town: Woodstock
Other trail users: Hikers
Trail contacts: George Washington National Forest (GWNF), www.fs.usda.gov/gwj
Schedule: Open year-round
Fees: Free to public

Getting there: From Northern VA. Take I-66 W to I-81 South toward Roanoke. Take exit 283 for VA-42 toward Woodstock. Stay on 42 for approximately 5.2 miles and make a right on VA 768. VA 768 is a short access point to Rte. 623 and 675. Merge onto 623 and then make a right onto Rte. 675. Continue on 675 for half a mile and turn right on State Rte. 608/Johnstown Road. Continue on 608 for 2.5 miles, shortly after the road turns to gravel, turn left onto FR 92. FR 92 is not marked, however, it is the first gravel road to the left. Continue on FR 92 for 3.3 miles. The parking area will be to your left and the trailhead to your right.
GPS coordinates: 38.93795, –78.6463.

The Ride

At 9.3 miles, the Mill Mountain Big Scholls Ride seems relatively short, but what this ride lacks in distance is made up for in the demanding nature of trails you'll be riding. Don't let it dissuade you though, this is a rite of passage every mountain biker in Virginia has gone through, and one every rider should experience.

The ride starts with a gradual climb along the aptly named Little Stoney Creek Trail before turning into a steep technical singletrack climb. Once you reach the high point of the ride, you'll experience some of the most technically rewarding ridge trails in the area. Despite its difficulty, the trail is a blast to ride. And, even though you'll be heading downhill for virtually 5 miles, the descent will prove just as difficult as the ascent.

As you reach the final 2 miles of the trail, you'll be treated to a phenomenal white-knuckle descent to the starting point of the ride. At this final cutoff, if you still

The overlook views of West Virginia from the Mill Mountain Trail are worth the climb.

have the legs for it, you can detour toward the Big Schloss Overlook to view the large rock outcropping for which the area is known.

German settlers once populated this region of the Shenandoah Valley, and they named the large visible rock outcropping along on this 2,964 ft. peak "Big Schloss" because of its resemblance to a castle.

Nearby Woodstock, established in 1761, has served as the County's seat since 1772; and its historic courthouse, designed by Thomas Jefferson and built in 1795, is the oldest working courthouse west of the Blue Ridge Mountains.

Woodstock is also known for Lutheran pastor and Revolutionary war officer John Peter Gabriel Muhlenberg. It is said that Muhlenberg delivered his famous speech from his church on main street calling for area volunteers to join the County Militia and the Continental Army. During the sermon, Muhlenberg removed his Lutheran clerical robes at a key moment to reveal his Colonel's Uniform. The speech, in which he eloquently declared, "this is the time of war," convinced 162 men to enlist on the spot. And, within a day's time, Muhlenberg led 300 men to form what would become Virginia's 8th Regiment.

Miles and Directions

0.0 From the trailhead, head into the woods along the Little Stoney Creek Trail, blazed with yellow markings. The trail will parallel the Little Stoney Creek for nearly its entire length it gradually (1.2 miles), then drastically ascends toward the Sugar Knob Cabin. For this reason, it is advisable you don't ride this trail shortly after heavy rainfall. The trail will become an extension of the creek during heavy rain.

3.2 You reach the Sugar Knob Cabin. Continue past the cabin, the trail will widen.

3.3 Turn left onto the blue blazed Tuscarora Three Ponds Trail. Will climb for only a little bit longer.

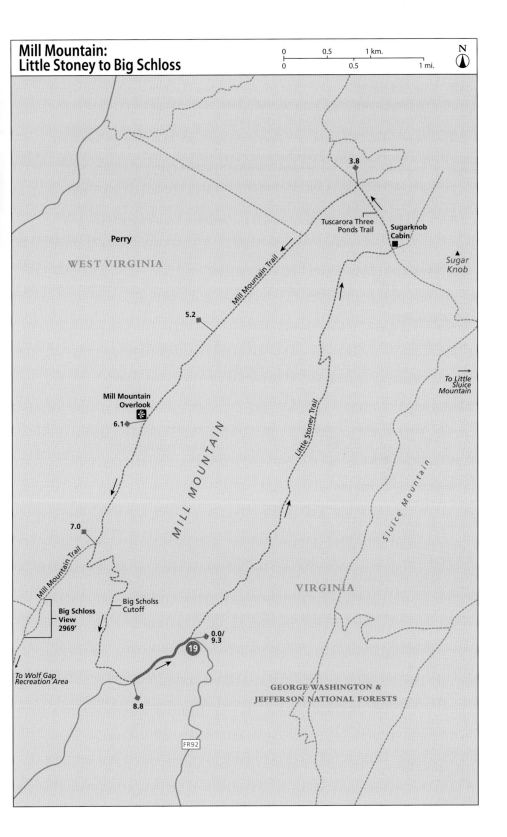

Mill Mountain:
Little Stoney to Big Schloss

0   0.5   1 km.

0   0.5   1 mi.

N

3.8

Tuscarora Three
Ponds Trail

Sugarknob
Cabin

Perry

WEST VIRGINIA

Sugar
Knob

Mill Mountain Trail

5.2

Little Stoney Trail

To Little
Sluice
Mountain

Mill Mountain
Overlook

6.1

M I L L   M O U N T A I N

Sluice Mountain

7.0

Mill Mountain Trail

VIRGINIA

Big Scholss
Cutoff

Big Schloss
View
2969'

**0.0/
9.3**

19

To Wolf Gap
Recreation Area

8.8

GEORGE WASHINGTON &
JEFFERSON NATIONAL FORESTS

FR92

3.8 Turn left onto the Mill Mountain Trail, blazed with orange markings. You're almost done with the climbing.

4.3 You're done with the climbing, it's all downhill from here. That, actually may not be a good thing. Stay alert and sharp, some downhill portions of this trail are just as difficult as their uphill counterparts and come up at you quickly.

5.2 Cross Deep Gutter Run along Sandstone Spring. You'll know you are here because of the rather long and intense rock garden.

6.1 You reach the Overlook. This is a nice spot to take a break and have a good look at West Virginia form the Overlook. The Mill Mountain Trail actually crosses in and out of West Virginia along its run.

7.0 You reach the intersection with the Big Schloss Cutoff trail. Turn left and get ready for a super fun descent.

8.8 You reach FR 92. Turn left and roll back to the starting point.

9.3 You're back at the starting point, the ride is complete.

Ride Information

Local Information

Front Royal, VA—www.discoverfrontroyal.com
Strasburg—www.strasburgva.com

Bike Shops

Element Sports, Winchester, VA, (540) 662-5744, www.elementsport.com
Hawksbill Bicycles, Luray, VA, (540) 743-1037, www.hawksbillbicycles.com
Bicycle Outfitters, Winchester, VA, (540) 431-5525, www.bikeoutfitters.com

Local Events and Attractions

Front Royal, VA: www.discoverfrontroyal.com
Strasburg: www.strasburgva.com

Where to Eat

Jalisco Mexican Restaurant
Front Royal, VA
(540) 635-7348

Cristina's Café
Strasburg, VA
(540) 465-2311
www.cristinascafe.net

Backroom Brewery
Middletown, VA
(540) 869-8482

www.backroombreweryva.com
PaveMint Taphouse & Grill
Front Royal, VA
(540) 252-4707
www.paveminttaphouse.com

Woodstock Brewhouse
Woodstock, VA
540-459-BREW (2739)
www.woodstockbrewhouse.com

20 Elizabeth's Furnace

This is by far one of the most difficult rides in the book, but one of the most rewarding. I won't sugarcoat it—this ride is demanding, technical, steep, fast, and dangerous. If the ride itself doesn't do you in, a bear might. When you finish, you'll ask yourself "Why?" And then, out of nowhere, you'll start planning your return, or researching other rides in the forest—there are plenty, more than 400 miles of singletrack, to choose from. This demanding and technical ride has become a rite of passage for mountain bikers in the Washington, D.C., region and serves as the perfect introduction to type of trail you'll find elsewhere in the George Washington National Forest and the Catoctin Mountains to the north.

Start: Massanutten Mountain/Signal Knob parking area
Length: 11.7 miles
Ride time: 2–3 hours
Difficulty: Difficult
Trail surface: Mostly singletrack; one section of gravel road

Lay of the land: Rugged trails of the Appalachian Mountains
Land status: State forest
Nearest town: Front Royal
Other trail users: Hikers
Trail contacts: GWNF Supervisor's Office, (540) 265-1000 (information only)
Schedule: Open year-round

Getting there: From Washington take 66 West toward Front Royal. Take exit 6 for US 340/ US 522 South toward Front Royal. Turn right on US 55W, Strasburg Road, and then left onto Fort Valley Road. The parking area will be to your right and clearly marked as you enter the George Washington National Forest. **GPS coordinates:** 38.924428, –78.332176.

The Ride

I remember the first time I ventured out into the George Washington National Forest (GWNF). I thought it would be the last. I headed out west of Washington on Rte. 66 to Front Royal with a group of friends from MORE to ride Elizabeth Furnace for the first time. I had already been riding my mountain bike in the region for several months and had ridden Wakefield, Patapsco, and Loch Raven Reservoir to the north in Baltimore, and all the other usual spots. But none of those rides would prepare me for what I was about to experience in the foothills of the GWNF and the Appalachian Mountains.

The first part of our ride will follow a gravel road that was once used to transport the pig iron created in the furnace below to the other side of Massanutten Mountain. Iron ore was mined in the area and then brought to the Elizabeth Furnace, where it was purified. Unfortunately, not much is left of the furnace that produced nearly three tons of pig iron daily until the Federals burned it during the Civil War.

The furnace was rebuilt shortly after the war, but it only stayed in operation for a short time and then never operated again. Today some of the structure remains, but it is in disrepair and often covered by overgrown vegetation during the spring and summer months.

Once past the dirt road, which really is a pleasant climb, we will enter the canopy and begin a journey toward the Strasburg Reservoir and Signal Knob. The singletrack trails continue in an upward direction and offer a series of highly enjoyable technical sections with several creek crossings. They are technical enough to keep you focused on the ride and what lies ahead. The beauty of this ride is that at its midpoint you can veer right and visit Strasburg Reservoir, and during a hot summer day, take a dip in its cool waters before confronting the hike-a-bike to Signal Knob, the high point of the ride.

To get to Signal Knob, however, you must endure one of the toughest 0.5-mile sections of trail in the region. Once up high, you'll be treated to fantastic panoramic views of the valley below. It's no surprise that Confederate soldiers climbed the very

The trails at Elizabeth Furnace are very challenging.

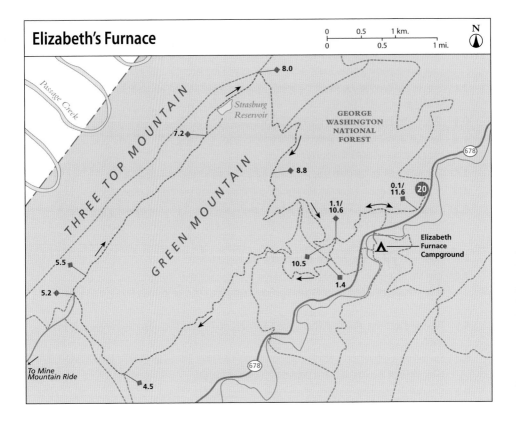

Elizabeth's Furnace

0   0.5   1 km.
0   0.5   1 mi.

N

Passage Creek

THREE TOP MOUNTAIN

8.0

Strasburg Reservoir

7.2

GEORGE WASHINGTON NATIONAL FOREST

678

GREEN MOUNTAIN

8.8

0.1/ 11.6   20

1.1/ 10.6

Elizabeth Furnace Campground

5.5

10.5

5.2

1.4

To Mine Mountain Ride

678

4.5

same trail you will use to observe Union troop movements and relay signals from its peak to their counterparts. After enjoying the view and recovering your strength, you'll descend on what is perhaps one of the best downhill runs in the region. Boulder gardens that will tame the most seasoned mountain biker will open up and treat you to one of the most technical

▶ **The Appalachian Mountains are more than 450 million years old and were once as tall as the Alps and the Rocky Mountains.**

and rewarding downhills you'll ever experience, and before you know, it deliver you to the starting point of the ride. You'll likely spend a quarter of the time in this last section, and although exhausted, you will undoubtedly be asking for more.

If more is what you want, don't fret. There are literally hundreds of miles of trails in the forest and lots of them have been documented in another guide: *Mountain Biking Virginia*, by my good friend Scott Adams, with whom I coauthored *Mountain Biking the Washington, D.C./Baltimore Area.*

Miles and Directions

0.0 Start from the Massanutten Trail, Signal Knob parking area. The trailhead is on the west side of the parking area. Enter the trail and stay to the left.

0.1 Stay to the right as you reach the group camping sign. The trail will be blazed with orange markings.

0.4 Stay to the right and follow the blue blazes.

1.1 Turn left at this trail intersection. Massanutten Mountain West is on the right fork; this is the direction we will be returning in.

1.4 Turn right on the fire road and get ready for a nice grinder up the mountain.

4.5 The fire road ends. Enter the singletrack and then stay to the right at the trail fork.

5.2 Cross Mudhole gap and then turn right on the gravel road. Continue following the orange blazes. (**Option**: A left turn will take you toward the Mine Mountain Ride, described elsewhere in this book.)

5.5 Continue straight through the gate on the gravel road.

7.2 Turn left and follow the signs for Signal Knob. (If you continue straight, less than 0.25 mile ahead is the Strasburg Reservoir. On a blistering hot day, you can take a dip in the reservoir.)

8.0 Turn right into the Blue Trail. This is the beginning of the last, and most brutal, climb of the ride.

8.8 You've reached the top. I highly suggest you take a break and prep yourself for the downhill ride. The trail is to the left and blazed with blue markings.

10.5 Stay left at this intersection and continue on the Blue Trail.

10.6 Stay to the left at this intersection. (You can turn right and do the entire loop again if you want.) At this point, we'll be backtracking on the trail we initially started on.

11.6 Stay to the left.

11.7 Turn right to return to the parking area and close out the loop.

Ride Information

Local Information

Front Royal, VA—www.discoverfrontroyal.com
Strasburg—www.strasburgva.com

Bike Shops

Element Sports, Winchester, VA, (540) 662-5744, www.elementsport.com
Hawksbill Bicycles, Luray, VA, (540) 743-1037, www.hawksbillbicycles.com
Bicycle Outfitters, Winchester, VA, (540) 431-5525, www.bikeoutfitters.com

Local Events and Attractions

Front Royal, VA: www.discoverfrontroyal.com
Strasburg: www.strasburgva.com

Where to Eat

Jalisco Mexican Restaurant
Front Royal, VA
(540) 635-7348

Cristina's Café
Strasburg, VA
(540) 465-2311
www.cristinascafe.net

Backroom Brewery
Middletown, VA
(540) 869-8482

www.backroombreweryva.com
PaveMint Taphouse & Grill
Front Royal, VA
(540) 252-4707
www.paveminttaphouse.com

Woodstock Brewhouse
Woodstock, VA
540-459-BREW (2739)
www.woodstockbrewhouse.com

21 Mine Mountain

This ride combines several of the elements for which the GWNF is widely known: its long fire road climb, its technical ridge, and its screaming singletrack descent. The section of the Massanutten Trail we will be riding is rocky and technical, but extremely rideable. Along the way toward Mudhole gap, you'll experience beautiful views of the North Fork of the Shenandoah River and the valley below.

Start: Start from the small parking area along FR 66 adjacent to the Mine Gap Trailhead. This ride can be easily combined with the Elizabeth Furnace Loop.
Length: 9.9 miles
Ride time: 1.5–3 hours
Difficulty: Intermediate to expert. Difficult due to the long road climb and technical trails along the ridge. This ride is NOT for beginners.
Trail surface: Mountainous, rocky singletrack, and gravel forest roads.

Lay of the land: Rocky and technical singletrack along the George Washington National Forest.
Land status: Public
Nearest town: Front Royal
Other trail users: Hikers
Trail contacts: GWNF, www.fs.usda.gov/gwj/
Schedule: Open year-round
Fees: Free to public

Getting there: From Northern VA. Take I-66 W to exit 6 for US-340/US-522 toward Front Royal/Winchester. Turn left onto US-340 S/Winchester Road. Continue for a little over a mile and turn right onto VA-55 W/W Strasburg Road. After approximately 5 miles, turn left onto Fort Valley Road (Rte. 678). Continue to follow Fort Valley Road for 8.6 miles and turn right onto Boyer Road. After 1 mile, bear right at the Y intersection to continue on the gravel road toward Mine Mountain. FR 66 will be on your right approximately 0.5 miles ahead (it is not marked). Turn right and continue for 0.1 miles to the small parking area on the right. There are additional parking areas (remote campgrounds) along FR 66 should this parking area be full. **GPS coordinates:** 38.898437, -78.404444.

The Ride

Much of what I wrote about Elizabeth Furnace and Mill Mountain could very well fit in this chapter of the book, but the Mine Mountain ride detailed here offers enough variety within its 9.9 miles that it deserves its own chapter. The riding you'll experience at this location is very similar to the two previously mentioned rides, but it includes at least three distinct features that sets it apart from the others: its nearly 3-mile gravel road climb, its outstanding views of the North Fork of the Shenandoah River and the Valley below, and its fast and furious singletrack descent back to FR 66.

Our ride will take you gradually up Mine Mountain until you reach the Woodstock Tower trailhead, before hitting the orange blazed Massanutten Trail to Mudhole Gap.

The ridge trail is challenging and highly rewarding.

Mine Mountain Loop

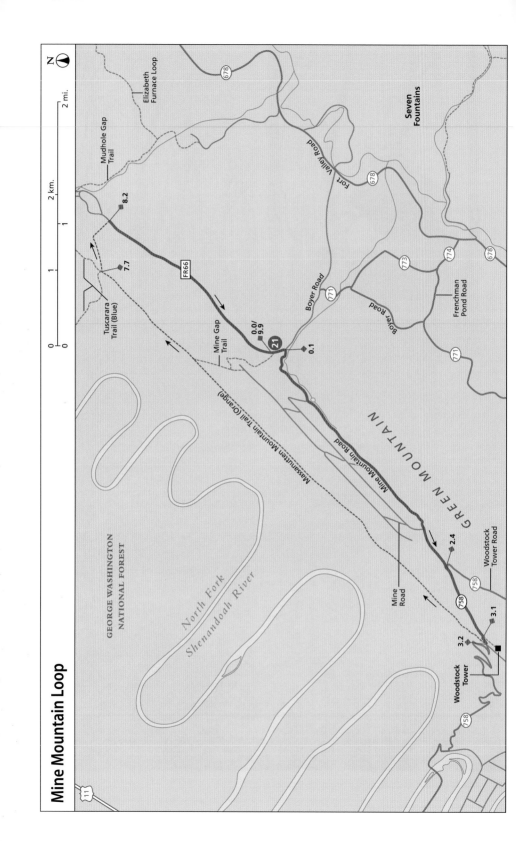

The climb is a little monotonous, but it's very well worth the effort, and once you hit the Massanutten Trail, you'll be glad you stuck with it. As you venture into other Valley rides in the book, especially those in the "Burg" (Harrisonburg Area), you'll understand why this fire road climb is a "recurring" feature of the George Washington National Forest.

Unlike several of the other trails in the George Washington National Forest, which were built by the Civilian Conservation Corps, the Massanutten Trail had its origins in the Revolutionary War. Originally known as Morgan Road, a portion of the Massanutten Trail was built as a contingency in case the Continental Army was defeated at Yorktown, the Revolutionary War's last major land battle. George Washington himself ordered the construction of the road near Veach Gap (just to the south of our ride) to serve as an avenue of retreat. Thankfully, the contingency was not needed, and today, the Massanutten Trail, including portions of Morgan Road has become part of the trail's 71-mile circuit.

Portions of the ridge trail we will be riding will likely have been used by Union and Confederate troops alike on their way to Signal Knob, the northern peak of Massanutten Mountain. Although we won't make it up to the Signal Knob on this ride, you will still get a chance to soak in some of the panoramic views the peak offers. When you do, it will be clear why the Signal Corps fought for its control. Our turn off point, before the trail continues toward Signal Knob, will offer you with an exhilarating descent, another one of the forest's distinct features. After several miles of technical ridge riding, you'll welcome this gravity-assisted portion of the ride. Despite not having to pedal, you'll still have to work considerably before reaching the bottom of the descent and the final portion of the ride.

Miles and Directions

0.0 From the Parking area, head back along FR 66 to Mine Mountain Road.

0.1 Turn right on Mine Mountain Road and get ready for a 3-mile grinder to the trailhead.

2.4 Continue following the road to the right, you'll now be on Woodstock Tower Road.

3.1 You reach the summit, the entrance to the trail that leads to the Woodstock Tower will be to your left. Continue on the road as it begins to descend. Pay close attention to the right side for the Massanutten Trail trailhead. It is not far, if you descend for more than 0.10of a mile, you'll have passed it.

3.2 Turn right onto the Massanutten Mountain trail, blazed with orange markings. We'll now ride the ridge for a little over 4 miles. Get ready for some classic George Washington National Forest ridge riding!

6.6 You reach the intersection of the Mine Gap Trail, blazed with purple markings. Had enough? Turn right and follow the trail straight down to the parking area.

7.7 You reach the intersection of the Tuscarora Dolly Ridge trail. Continue straight for approximately 30 yards. The trail will be blazed with both orange and blue markings. Tuscarora Ridge will continue up to the left (blue) and the orange Massanutten Trail will continue down to the right. Follow the trail to the right toward Mohole Gap. Get ready for a fast and technical descent.

8.2 You reach FR 66. Turn right to complete the loop. A left turn will take you toward the Mudhole Gap trail. You can combine this ride with the Elizabeth Furnace loop to increase your mileage.

9.9 You're back at the starting point, the loop is complete.

Ride Information

Local Information

Front Royal, VA—www.discoverfrontroyal.com
Strasburg—www.strasburgva.com

Bike Shops

Element Sports, Winchester, VA, (540) 662-5744, www.elementsport.com
Hawksbill Bicycles, Luray, VA, (540) 743-1037, www.hawksbillbicycles.com
Bicycle Outfitters, Winchester, VA, (540) 431-5525, www.bikeoutfitters.com

Local Events and Attractions

Front Royal, VA: www.discoverfrontroyal.com
Strasburg: www.strasburgva.com

Where to Eat

Jalisco Mexican Restaurant
Front Royal, VA
(540) 635-7348

Cristina's Café
Strasburg, VA
(540) 465-2311
www.cristinascafe.net

Backroom Brewery
Middletown, VA
(540) 869-8482

www.backroombreweryva.com
PaveMint Taphouse & Grill
Front Royal, VA
(540) 252-4707
www.paveminttaphouse.com

Woodstock Brewhouse
Woodstock, VA
540-459-BREW (2739)
www.woodstockbrewhouse.com

22 Shenandoah River State Park

The trails at Shenandoah River Raymond R. "Andy" Guest Jr. State Park (yes, it's a mouthful—Guest State Park for short) have been recently rerouted and rebuilt with the help from IMBA's Doug Vinson and MORE's regional trail liaisons. The paths offer a combination of flowy doubletrack and singletrack trails that are bound to satisfy the most demanding mountain bikers. The trails are fast and rolling, and the elevation changes are "just right." The trails along the river are perfect for beginners, while the trails along the hillsides are perfect for intermediate and expert riders.

Loop #1 starts at the intersections of the Hemlock Hollow and bluebell trails in the farthest lot to the left as you drive into the park from Daughters of Stars Drive. The trails are clearly marked and labeled.

Loop #2 starts at the trailhead adjacent to the Virginia Canopy Building.

Length: Loop #1: Up to 14 miles; Loop #2: 5.7 miles

Ride time: Loop #1: 2-3 hours; Loop #2: 1-2 hours

Difficulty: Novice to expert. The easier trails tend to be along the river; other trails include steep climbs and fast descents.

Trail surface: Single and doubletrack trails. Flowy and minimally technical trails.

Lay of the land: Single and doubletrack trails along the Shenandoah River and adjacent hillsides.

Land status: Public

Nearest town: Front Royal

Other trail users: Hikers, trail runners, equestrians

Rail contacts: Shenandoah River State Park: www.dcr.virginia .gov/state-parks/shenandoah-river

Schedule: 8 a.m. and dusk

Fees: VA State Park fees apply (depending on season and State license plates)

Restrooms: Available in the park visitor center.

Getting there: From Washington, D.C. Take I-66 W to exit 6 for US-340 toward Front Royal/ Winchester. Turn left onto Rte. 340 and continue straight for 2 miles. Turn left W 14th St. 14th St. will curve right onto North Royal Avenue. Continue on North Royal (340) for almost 9 miles and turn right onto Daughter of Stars Drive, the entrance to Shenandoah River State Park. Continue following Daughters of Stars toward the river and turn left for loop #1 or right for loop #2 at the T intersection. **GPS coordinates:** 38.863350, -78.310385.

The Ride

Shenandoah River State Park is a relatively new property in Virginia's repertoire of State Parks. The Park, which opened its doors in 1999, inherited a system of unsustainable trails that had very little appeal to many of the park's early users. Within the park's first decade of existence, however, that would change.

In early 2007, the park began a transformation that would eventually see those legacy trails disappear. The park's revitalization called for a new visitor center along with other amenities, including parking, RV, and camping facilities. Much of the work to be done, however, required heavy equipment that would have an impact on the existing trails.

Park management relied on the advice of then Ranger Doug Vinson for his recommendations on what to do. Doug, who had been tasked with maintaining the existing trail infrastructure, knew he had little to work with, so he recommended that the park solicit the advice of trail building expert Rich Edwards of IMBA.

Rich visited the park several times and recommended an overhaul of the trail system. And, together with Doug, set out to flag nearly 20 miles of trails that would fit within the parks new infrastructure. While the planning took place, the park also worked on securing Recreational Trail Program (RTP) funds to pay for the project, and worked internally to get the necessary approvals to build the proposed system.

With the necessary RTP funds and internal approvals on hand, and with a crash course in trail building from IMBA, Doug and his team set out to build the trails documented on this ride. Along the way, Doug worked with the local community, including the SVBC and MORE, to organize several trail workdays. In addition to the internal building efforts from the park, local riders also came by to help throughout the process.

Doug would eventually leave the park in 2009 and only saw the completion of the trails along the first loop documented here. The process, however, had a profound impact on him. He went on to work for the BLM where he eventually led the build effort at the Meadowood Recreation Area (Ride 11). Eventually, the experience he gained at Shenandoah River State Park and with the BLM at Meadowood helped him land a position with IMBA. Today, he is building trails across the Mid-Atlantic for all of us to enjoy.

The trails at Shenandoah River State Park are a textbook example of multiuse trails. Early park users who had experienced the previous legacy trails welcomed the change wholeheartedly. Those who loved it most were the park's many equestrian users. The width of the trail is perfect for them, but also perfect for intermediate and advanced riders looking for a challenging ride. Although the initial 20 miles of flagged trail were not entirely built, the park offers hikers, cyclists, and horse enthusiasts over 15 miles of sustainable trails to enjoy.

Take a moment to visit Cullers Overlook for a fantastic view of one of the Shenandoah River's famous bends.

Shenandoah River State Park

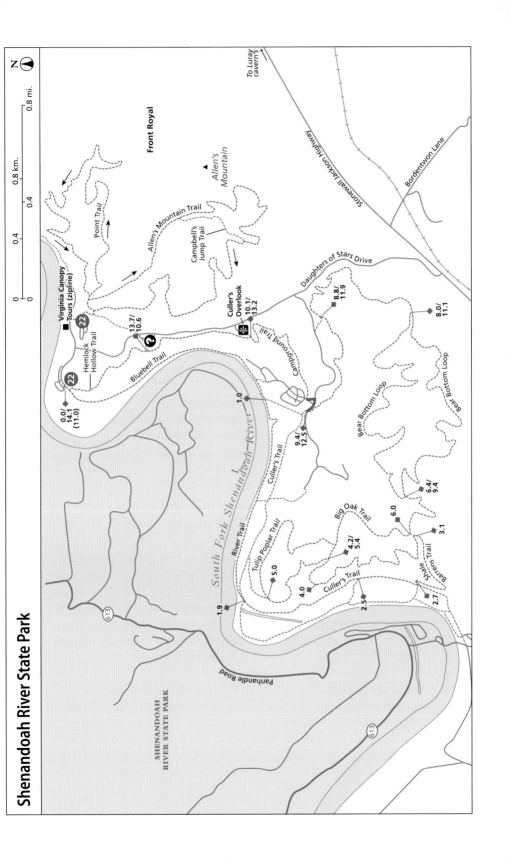

Young and beginner riders will appreciate the level paths along the river's frontage while intermediate to advanced riders will enjoy the undulating trails along the park's hillsides. The trails are really a joy to ride; they offer a less strenuous alternative to the rugged trails of neighboring George Washington National Forest. Since their completion in early 2011, they have become a regional favorite with the rider communities of Northern Virginia and the Shenandoah Valley.

Miles and Directions

Loop 1 starts at the intersections of the Hemlock Hollow and bluebell trails in the farthest lot to the left as you drive into the park from Daughters of Stars Drive. The trails are clearly marked.

0.0 Start from the trail sign at the far end of the lot and follow the blue blazes along the bluebell trail. Immediately after entering the trail, stay to the right to stay on the bluebell trail. We will finish out the ride along the trail to the left, Hemlock Hollow. The first portion of our ride will take us along a flat and easy to ride riverside trail. This portion of the ride is perfect for young kids.

0.9 Continue following the trail to the right. The left spur takes you to the RV campground.

1.0 You've reached the River Trail. Continue to the right along the crushed fine gravel. Still flat. The river trail is blazed with green markings.

1.9 Hop on the doubletrack to enter the orange blazed Culler's Trail. The right fork is the continuation of the River Trail; either fork will eventually lead you to the same spot, but for the sake of this ride, follow the Culler's Trail toward the Shale Barren's Trail.

Note: If you are riding with young children, I suggest you continue to the right along the River Trail and then make your way back along Culler's Trail and back to bluebell. There is very little elevation change and you'll ride a little over 4 miles.

2.5 Continue straight, the fork to the right will take you toward the River Trail.

2.7 Make a sharp left onto the Shale Barren's Trail and get ready to climb. You'll encounter a tight and steep switchback to the right, get ready!

3.1 Turn left to hop on the Redtail Ridge Trail (blazed with red markings) and get ready for some super fun-rolling trail. During winter, early spring, and late fall, you can see the river through the trees.

4.0 The spur to the left takes you to a scenic overlook, continue following the Redtail Ridge Trail to the right. The overlook is only a tenth of a mile to the left.

4.2 Continue to the right along the Big Oak Trail (blazed with white markings) and make the second left to hop on the pink blazed Tulip Poplar Trail. We will doubletrack along this portion of the Big Oak Trail on our way back.

5.0 Continue following the trail to the left to hop back on the Big Oak Trail, it will now be blazed with white markings. The fork to the right will take you down along the Big Oak Trail toward Culler's Trail, a bail out point.

5.4 Turn left to continue on the Big Oak Trail. If you turn right, you'll go back on the Redtail Ridge Trail. We're now doubletracking along the Big Oak Trail. Turn right at the next intersection and continue to follow the white blazes. A left will put you back on the pink blazed Tulip Poplar Trail (intersection 4.2).

6.0 Continue to the left following the white blazes along the Big Oak Trail. The spur to the right will take you back to the Shale Barren's Trail and the point where we turned left to hop on the Redtail Ridge Trail (intersection 3.1). This is another alternate bail out point.

6.3 You reach the Bear Bottom Loop trail. We'll follow the trail to the left and "possibly" come back to this intersection once again. If so, you'll ride this portion of trail once again.

8.0 Decision point. If you continue straight/slight left, you will finish out the ride and bypass one of the best sections of trail in the park. I urge you to make a sharp right and head back toward the intersection at 6.3. You'll add a little over 3 miles to your ride; you can thank me later.

9.4 If you chose to follow my advice you're back at the intersection we detailed a short while ago (6.3). Make a sharp right and doubletrack back along the Teal Blazed Trail you rode a few minutes ago.

11.1 You're back at the "Decision Point." This time, continue to the left to finish out the ride.

11.9 (8.8) Continue following the trail to the left. The spur to the right will take you to the Horsebarn Area.

12.5 12.6 (9.4–9.5) Turn right on the road and then immediately left onto the Campers Loop. The Campground Trail will be immediately to your right as you enter Campers Loop. Turn right to hop on the Campground trail, blazed with purple markings.

13.2 (10.1) The spur to the right will take you up to Culler's overlook, worth a visit. Continue to the left toward the Hemlock Hollow Trail and the end of the ride.

13.7 (10.6) Continue following the trail to the left. The spur to the right will take you up to the visitor center. You can also access Allen's Mountain and the Point Trail from here (via the Turkey Roost Trail across Daughters of Stars Drive) and add a few more miles to the ride. See Loop#2 for more details.)

14.1 (11.) You've reached the bluebell trail. Turn right to finish out the ride. The loop is complete.

Loop 2, Allen's Mountain and Point Trail Loops

This is an alternate, albeit shorter loop, that will give you a taste of what the Shenandoah River State Park Trails have to offer. You can ride either or both the Allen's Mountain or Point trails to sample the terrain in the park. The best access point for both loops is the parking area alongside the Virginia Canopy Tours building. If you want to add a little variety to your day, I suggest doing a zip line tour and then hitting the trails.

0.0 Start at the trailhead from the Virginia Canopy Building. The trail will shoot straight down and cross a small creek. Follow the trail as it curves to the left and follow the signs for the Allen's Mountain Trail. You'll also notice the exit point of the Allen's Mountain Trail above to the right; we will be coming back that way. It's worth noting that you can follow the Allen's Mountain Trail in either direction and you will end up roughly in the same spot. For the sake of this ride, we will follow the Allen's Mountain Trail in a clockwise direction (my preference). Both directions will require you to climb toward the summit of Allen's Mountain before shooting back down to the starting point of the loop.

0.1 Veer right from the Cotton Wood Trail onto the white blazed Allen's Mountain Trail and begin your climb (either direction will begin with a climb, and end with a descent).

0.6 You reach the intersection of Campbell's Jump Trail. Continue straight on Allen's Mountain. (**Option:** Campbell's Jump can shorten Allen's Mountain Trail. If you've had enough of the climbing, this is a good point to turn right. If you really want to ride Campbell's, I suggest hitting it from the other direction.)

1.3 Now we begin descending!

1.6 You reach the opposite end of the Campbell's Jump Trail. (***Option:*** If you want to ride it, I suggest you turn right here since it will be mostly down toward mile marker 0.6.) We'll bypass it now and continue straight on Allen's Mountain.

3.0 You're back on the Cotton Wood Trail; turn right and doubletrack over the short section of trail we rode at the beginning.

3.1 Go past the entrance to the Allen's Mountain Trail and continue straight to access the Point Trail. The Point Trail will be blazed with gold markings.

5.2 The Point Trail ends at a boardwalk; this is the Cotton Wood Trail. Turn left and follow the Cotton Wood Trail back to the creek and up to the Virginia Canopy Tours Building.

5.6 Follow the trail to the right across the creek and up to the parking area. The Turkey Roost Trail will be to your left immediately after crossing the creek.

5.7 You're back at the trailhead, the loop is complete.

Ride Information

Local Information
Front Royal, VA—www.discoverfrontroyal.com
Strasburg—www.strasburgva.com

Bike Shops
Element Sports, Winchester, VA, (540) 662-5744, www.elementsport.com
Hawksbill Bicycles, Luray, VA, (540) 743-1037, www.hawksbillbicycles.com
Bicycle Outfitters, Winchester, VA, (540) 431-5525, www.bikeoutfitters.com

Local Events and Attractions
Front Royal, VA: www.discoverfrontroyal.com
Strasburg: www.strasburgva.com

Where to Eat
Jalisco Mexican Restaurant
Front Royal, VA
(540) 635-7348

Cristina's Café
Strasburg, VA
(540) 465-2311
www.cristinascafe.net

Backroom Brewery
Middletown, VA
(540) 869-8482

www.backroombreweryva.com
PaveMint Taphouse & Grill
Front Royal, VA
(540) 252-4707
www.paveminttaphouse.com

Woodstock Brewhouse
Woodstock, VA
540-459-BREW (2739)
www.woodstockbrewhouse.com

23 Kennedy Peak

This ride will lead you over a steep and rocky climb to a gentle rolling doubletrack trail and then back up and over a brutally technical ascent to Kennedy Peak, where you can enjoy the panoramic views of the Shenandoah Valley. The return leg will be a rewarding piece of trail that is technically challenging and grin inducing. You'll thank yourself for putting the effort to get to over 2,500 feet once your wheels start rolling downhill.

Start: Start from the Camp Roosevelt Trail Parking area. You can take the singletrack up to the Kennedy Peak trailhead or follow the "easier" road climb to the top.
Length: 8.9 miles
Ride time: 1.5–3 hours
Difficulty: Difficult due to technical rocky trails. This is NOT a ride for beginners.
Trail surface: Mountainous, rocky singletrack and doubletrack trails.

Lay of the land: Rocky and technical singletrack with steep climbs and descents.
Land status: Public
Nearest town: Front Royal
Other trail users: Hikers
Trail contacts: George Washington National Forest, www.fs.usda.gov/gwj/
Schedule: Open year-round
Fees: Free to public

Getting there: Head west on I-66 and take exit 6 for US-340 toward Front Royal/Winchester. Turn left onto Rte. 340 and then right onto Rte. 55/W Strasburg R. Stay on Rte. 55 for approximately 5 miles and then turn left onto Fort Valley Road. Follow Fort Valley for approximately 20 miles to Camp Roosevelt Road. Turn left onto Camp Roosevelt Road and continue for 3.7 miles. The Camp Roosevelt and Stephen's Trail Parking area will be to your left. **GPS coordinates:** 38.728045, –78.515210.

The Ride

The Kennedy Peak ride and trails documented herein hold great significance in our Nation's history. In 1933, when President Franklin Delano Roosevelt took office, the country was in dire straits, both financially and spiritually. In late 1929, an economic crisis within the stock market in the United States triggered a global financial collapse that had devastating consequences for both rich and poor nations around the world.

In the United States, a great number of people lost everything they had. Along the central portion of the country, a severe drought exasperated conditions; severe dust storms greatly damaged America's crops and forced thousands of families to abandon their homes in search of new financial opportunities. Elsewhere in the country, manufacturing and construction came to a halt. Unemployment reached extraordinary levels, and foreign trade virtually stopped. Attempts to revitalize the nation's economy fell short, and there seemed to be no end in sight to the hopeless situation that so many of our nation's citizens fell upon.

In an effort to help those most in need, President Roosevelt introduced a bill to congress early during his presidency to try to alleviate the situation. His efforts resulted in the Emergency Work Act of 1933 and set the stage for the creation of the CCC in March of the same year. The plan was simple, put young, unmarried, unemployed, and out-of-school men between the ages of 17 and 25 to work toward environmental conservation in camps around the country. The men received shelter, clothing, food, and medical treatment and were paid $30 a month, $25 of which was sent to their families. Those who did not have families had their money held in an account until they were released from the CCC. A typical enlistment lasted up to two years.

The CCC was administered by several agencies, with the Army and Navy providing supervision of camp construction, and the National Park Service and Forest Service providing much of the leadership, training, and projects to be worked on. Camp Roosevelt (aka National Forest Camp 1—NF-1), near the beginning of our

The relatively smooth doubletrack of the Kennedy Peak trail is the proverbial "calm before the storm" that waits ahead. Enjoy the relative ease of this section of trail before the more technical portions to come.

Kennedy Peak

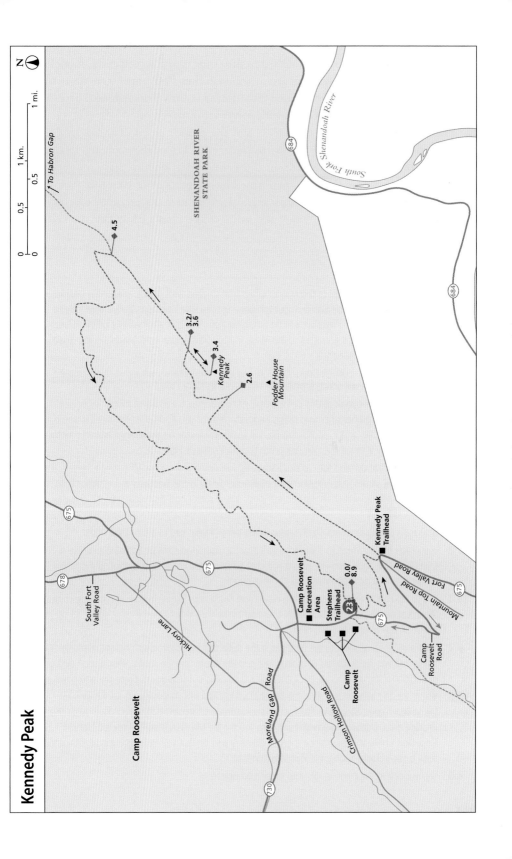

ride, was the first CCC camp established in the country and served as the model for others to follow. By the time the program would end in 1942, there were more than 2,500 similar camps around the country, with over 60 in Virginia alone. The camps housed several 48-men crews tasked with conservation work.

The CCC was an immediate success, and the money sent to families by CCC recruits proved to be one of the most vital triggers that helped the economy rebound. The program's legacy, however, lays in the lasting contributions and conservation efforts that resulted from the work performed by the millions of men that took part in the program. Even now, more than eight decades after the program was implemented, we are continuing to enjoy the fruits of the crew's labor that worked to preserve our national forests.

Miles and Directions

0.0 We'll start measuring where the Massanutten Trail (blazed with orange markings) begins from the entrance to the Camp Roosevelt parking area. The Stephens Trail, at the far end of the parking area is where we will be returning from. You can alternatively ride up Camp Roosevelt Road to the entrance of the Massanutten Trail across from Mountain Top Road. We'll stick to the singletrack.

0.8 You reach Camp Roosevelt Road. Turn left and then immediately left again to continue on the orange blazed Massanutten Trail, this is the Kennedy Peak trailhead entrance. There is a nice overlook at this point where you can enjoy the views of the valley below; they'll be much better once you reach Kennedy peak. If you had taken the road, it would have been a little longer, approximately 1.4 miles. We'll stay on the orange blazed trail for approximately 2 miles until we reach the spur to Kennedy Peak.

2.6 The trail will narrow and turn to singletrack as you reach a sharp switchback to the left. It's a tough one; hopping to position your bike accordingly is the best way to negotiate this obstacle. The trail will shoot upwards a long, a very rocky, and technical trail. It's rideable, but very difficult.

3.1 Stay right at this intersection, the spur to the left will take you to a small overlook.

3.2 You reach the entrance to Kennedy Peak. You can continue straight and skip the hike a bike up to the peak, but why would you—the technical downhill from the top is incredibly rewarding. Turn right and head up to the overlook.

3.4 You've reached the top. Soak in the views and catch your breath before you ride down the technical descent back to the main trail and make your way to the starting point; it's pretty much all downhill from now; really...

3.7 Continue heading down to the right along the main trail, still blazed with orange markings. We are on our way back toward Stephens Trail and the return leg of our ride. After a short section of additional technical singletrack, the trail will smooth out (relatively). Enjoy the ride down.

4.5 You reach the intersection with the Stephens Trail. Turn left. At this point, we will stay on the yellow blazed Stephens Trail for the approximately the next 5 miles until we reach the parking area. Continuing straight will take you on the Massanutten Trail toward Habron Gap. Don't miss this turn since there is no easy way back if you keep going straight—other than back-tracking along the Massanutten trail.

8.9 You're back at the parking lot; your loop is complete.

Ride Information

Local Information

Front Royal, VA—www.discoverfrontroyal.com
Strasburg—www.strasburgva.com

Bike Shops

Element Sports, Winchester, VA, (540) 662-5744, www.elementsport.com
Hawksbill Bicycles, Luray, VA, (540) 743-1037, www.hawksbillbicycles.com
Bicycle Outfitters, Winchester, VA, (540) 431-5525, www.bikeoutfitters.com

Local Events and Attractions

Front Royal, VA: www.discoverfrontroyal.com
Strasburg: www.strasburgva.com

Where to Eat

Jalisco Mexican Restaurant
Front Royal, VA
(540) 635-7348

Cristina's Café
Strasburg, VA
(540) 465-2311
www.cristinascafe.net

Backroom Brewery
Middletown, VA
(540) 869-8482

www.backroombreweryva.com
PaveMint Taphouse & Grill
Front Royal, VA
(540) 252-4707
www.paveminttaphouse.com

Woodstock Brewhouse
Woodstock, VA
540-459-BREW (2739)
www.woodstockbrewhouse.com

Harrisonburg

Harrisonburg, originally known as Rocktown, was renamed for one of its earliest residents, Thomas Harrison. Harrison, the son of English settlers, brought his family to the Shenandoah Valley in 1737 and quickly laid claim to over 12,000 acres of land. His home, built in 1750, still stands within the city limits. In 1779, one year after the Commonwealth of Virginia officially recognized Rockingham County, Harrison donated 2.5 acres of his land for the construction of a courthouse to serve as the seat for the new County. Within a year, he added 50 acres to what would become Harrisonburg's Historic Downtown District.

The city continued to grow over the years and welcomed new residents into its borders, including two universities. In 1908, the Virginia General Assembly established the State Normal and Industries School for Women, known today as James Madison University (JMU). In 1917, only one year after Harrisonburg was incorporated as an independent city, Eastern Mennonite University (EMU) was also founded. Today, over 20,000 students call Harrisonburg home, and form a large portion of the city's population. The Universities have also played an important role in the city's development, fueling a vibrant arts community, as well as a Virginia culinary destination.

Like many small cities throughout the Old Dominion, Harrisonburg began to see a period of revitalization in the early part of the twenty-first century. The city started several rejuvenation projects that have culminated with Harrisonburg being named to the national register of Historic Places and being designated a Virginia Main Street Community.

The designations, however, did not stop the city's revitalization efforts. Continuing through 2008, the city worked on several "streetscaping" projects to improve infrastructure, develop new signage to highlight historical landmarks, and improved sidewalks, lighting, and landscaping. It was during that year that the SVBC was formed by merging two long-standing bicycle groups, the Shenandoah Bicycle Club and the Shenandoah Mountain Bike Club. The formation of the SVBC and its organization fueled another form of growth for the city; making Harrisonburg a national cycling destination. The SVBC has ensured that cyclists of all disciplines have an active voice in the development of their community.

Since its inception, SVBC's leadership has worked extremely hard to develop positive and constructive relationships with the city and the National Forest Service that have resulted in Harrisonburg being named a Bicycle Friendly Community by the League of American Cyclists, and a Bronze Level IMBA Ride Center. The accolades have not slowed down the SVBC—the group has continued to work to improve the already vast number of available cycling opportunities for local residents and regional visitors.

Part of the SVBC's efforts on the off-road cycling front have been to ensure there is connectivity across the vast number of trails in the city's vicinity and the National Forests, that are within a short driving distance of Harrisonburg. One of the Coalition's biggest advocates for this connectivity is Chris Scott, owner and operator of Shenandoah Mountain Touring and the man behind the now famous Shenandoah 100 endurance bicycle race. Chris' dedication to the sport is second to none, and his vision to connect nearly 500 miles of backcountry trails in the George Washington and Jefferson National Forests spanning the length of Virginia's Allegheny and Blue Ridge Mountains is well on its way to becoming a permanent reality.

In 2011, after years of scouting and riding, Chris and a group of other adventurers completed the first step of this vision by riding a 480-mile route of mostly single-track trails over the course of 12 days along Virginia's public lands, from Strasburg to Damascus. Ultimately, Chris told me, the goal is to have a hut-to-hut system that other singletrack lovers can take advantage of. In order to fulfill that vision, however, there has to be a lot of volunteer involvement to make it happen, and the SVBC has been busy laying the foundation for the future. In 2016, the Coalition obtained over $500,000 in RTP funds to perform improvements on key sections of the route. Today, thanks to that effort, Shenandoah Mountain Touring leads groups of riders along portions of the route from its base of operations in Stokesville, to other regional cycling hotspots like Douthat State Park (Ride 30).

The SVBC has also forged a partnership with private landowners, including the Massanutten Resort (www.MassResort.com). Locally known as "The Nut," the resort has miles of trails expertly built by SVBC volunteers. Visit svbcoalition.org/our-riding/mountain-biking/massanutten/ for additional info and to learn how you can obtain a daily, weekly, or annual trail pass to these excellent trails.

As you ride the trails at Hillandale Park, Lookout Mountain, Narrowback Mountain, or the buttery smooth ribbons of Dowell's Draft, you'll understand why this VA destination gets all the praise it does. Riders from around the region, and from around the country keep coming back, simply because the riding and local hospitality is second to none. The vision and dedication of volunteers from the SVBC has really made Harrisonburg the unofficial Virginia Bike Capital, and has helped the city of Harrisonburg usher in a new chapter in its history.

24 Lookout Mountain

The Lookout Mountain loop has a little bit of everything you'll find when riding the trails around the Stokesville and Harrisonburg (Burg) areas; long gravel/road climbs, and challenging technical ridge trails with equally demanding descents. Like many of the trails around the Burg, the Lookout Mountain Trail has benefited from an influx of redevelopment as a result of the Shenandoah Valley Bicycle Coalition's efforts. As you descend toward the North River, you'll experience some of the region's most unique and challenging stonework.

Start: Start from the Wild Oak trailhead parking area that is immediately to your right as you enter FR 95.

Length: 13.1 miles

Ride time: 2–4 hours

Difficulty: Difficult due to technical rocky trails and a long climb to start things out. This is NOT a ride for beginners.

Trail surface: Mountainous rocky singletrack with a long paved/unpaved ascent.

Lay of the land: Long forest road climb to technical and rocky singletrack ridge trails. Fast and technical singletrack descent.

Land status: Public

Nearest town: Stokesville/Harrisonburg

Other trail users: Hikers

Trail contacts: GWNF, www.fs.usda.gov/gwj/; Shenandoah Valley Bicycle Coalition, www.svbcoalition.org

Schedule: Open year-round

Fees: Free to public

Getting there: From Harrisonburg: Head south on VA-42 S/S High St. for 19 miles and turn right on Rte. 747, Mossy Creek Road. At the T intersection, turn left onto Rte. 613. Rte. 613 will curve right in approximately 2.5 miles; stay straight to continue onto Rte. 747, Mossy Creek Road. In approximately 1 mile, turn right onto Rte. 731, Natural Chimney Road and continue for 1 mile to Rte. 730, North River Road. Turn left on Rte. 30 and continue to the T intersection. Turn right onto Stokesville Road and continue for an additional mile to FR 95. Turn left onto FR 95; the Wild Oak Trailhead will be 0.1 miles to your right. **GPS coordinates:** 38.367043, –79.164506.

Miles and Directions

0.0 We'll start from the Wild Oak parking area that is immediately to your right as you enter FR 95 from Stokesville road. From the parking area, turn right onto FR 95 and get ready for a gradual and steady long climb with a couple of breaks.

2.4 The Wild Oak Trail (#716) is to your right. Wild Oak leads back down to the parking area.

2.8 The Trimble Mountain Trail (#375) is to your left directly across from the gravel road that leads, continue climbing on FR 95.

3.0 Continue following the road to the left. Your climb will get a little harder now, but you'll be rewarded with a fast descent to a T intersection. The right fork leads to Todd Lake.

4.4 You reach the T intersection. Turn left to hop on the gravel road that parallels Broad Run.

Lookout Mountain

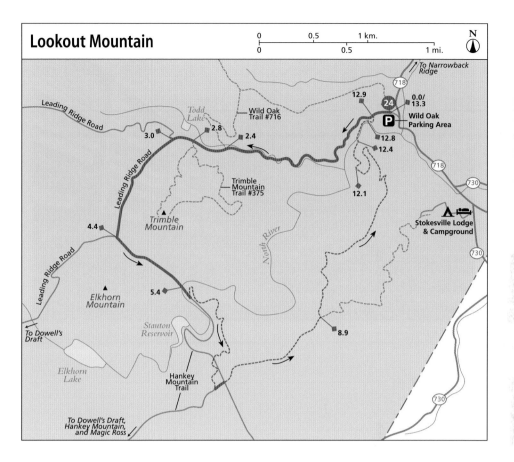

5.4 Enter the North River area and go over two small bridges. Immediately after the second bridge, make a sharp left to begin the climb up the gravel road for an additional 2 miles. There is a signpost labeled "Hankey Mountain, 425."

7.4 You reach the intersection of the Wild Oak Trail (#716) also known as Lookout. Turn left and continue to climb; almost done!

7.6 Turn left and continue to follow the Wild Oak Trail, singletrack heaven is looming.

8.9 Continue following 716 to the left. Trail 513, Shaffer Hollow is to the right. You can take Shaffer Hollow down to the fire road and then left to the Stokesville Lodge, the next.

12.1 Reach the Overlook Trail; continue following the trail to the right. The next section of trail will get pretty technical.

12.4 Smiling yet? You reach the North River Trail. Make a right and then make an immediate left to go over the bridge. Immediately after the bridge turns left, head up the switchbacks. For good measure, we'll finish the ride with a short climb.

12.8 Turn left and follow the whit blazes.

12.9 Turn right and FR 95 and coast down to the starting point.

13.3 Your loop is complete.

The Bridge over the North River signals the end of the phenomenal Lookout Mountain descent. A perfect chance to rest your arms and soak in the views of the river.

Ride Information

Local Information
www.visitharrisonburgva.com

Bike Shops
Shenandoah Bicycle Company: www.shenandoahbicycle.com
Rocktown Bicycles: www.rocktownbicycles.com/

Local Events and Attractions
Shenandoah 100: www.mtntouring.com
Stokesville Lodge: www.stokesvillelodge.com
Massanutten Resort: www.massresort.com

Where to Eat
Harrisonburg is quite possibly one of the best dining destinations in the Old Dominion. There are a ton of restaurants, breweries, and other places to enjoy great food and drink. Here's a couple of my favorite places:
Cuban Burger: www.cubanburger.com
Jack Brown's Beer and Burger Joint: www.jackbrownsjoint.com
Bella Luna Wood Fired Pizza: bellalunawoodfired.com
Brothers Craft Brewing: brotherscraftbrewing.com/
Three Notch'd Brewing Company: threenotchdbrewing.co

25 Dowells Draft/Magic Moss

If you must pick one ride in this book, do this one. This is a bold statement, considering the other gems documented throughout these pages, but this ride manages to sample two of the best Burg area trails in one loop. Both Dowells Draft and the Magic Moss trails have benefited from significant work thanks to the Shenandoah Valley Bicycle Coalition securing nearly $600,000 in grant money for trail development. Every foot you climb throughout the ride's length will be worth the effort, and once you're done you'll want to come back for more. If you really want to make it even more of an epic ride, you can easily combine this ride with either (or both) the Lookout Mountain ride or the Narrowback ride.

This ride can be easily modified and shortened. I'll present alternatives along the way so that you can customize your own adventure.

Start: Start from the parking area in the Braley Pond recreation area. Alternate (limited) parking is available along Braley Pond Road at the entrance of the Dowells Draft trailhead
Length: 22.2 miles
Ride time: 3–4 hours
Difficulty: Intermediate to advanced riders. Difficult due to length, elevation, and TTFs.
Trail surface: Rocky mountainous singletrack and gravel roads.

Lay of the land: Rocky and technical singletrack along the GWNF
Land status: Public
Nearest town: Stokesville/Harrisonburg
Other trail users: Hikers
Trail contacts: GWNF, www.fs.usda.gov/gwj/; SVBC, svbcoalition.org/
Schedule: Open year-round
Fees: Free to public

Getting there: From Harrisonburg take VA 42 south for approximately 20 miles to VA 736. Turn right on 736 (Jennings Cap Road) and continue for 3.5 miles to US-250 West, Hanky Mountain Highway. Continue for 6.4 miles and take a right onto Braley Pond Road. Immediately turn left into the Braley Pond Recreation area and park in the main lot by the pond. Alternatively, you can continue on Braley Pond Road for approximately 0.5 miles and park at the Dowells trailhead—there is limited parking at the trailhead. **GPS coordinates:** 38.280533, -79.293643.

Miles and Directions

0.0 Start from the Braley Pond Picnic Parking area. The parking area is approximately 0.6 mile from the main road (Braley Pond Road). We'll begin measuring from the intersection of the entrance of the parking area and the main Braley Pond access road. Head back toward the Braley Pond Road.

0.6 Turn left onto Braley Pond Road.

0.8 Turn right into the access area to Dowells Dr. 449. There is enough parking here for a couple of cars. This is an alternate starting point. Go through the gate and begin the initial climb on the doubletrack.

1.2 Turn left onto the clearly marked singletrack. Now we climb. Pay attention to the trail as you head up, we'll come down this on the way out.

3.9 You reach the intersection with trail 651, locally known as Magic Moss. This is your first decision point. You can turn around and head back for a quick out-and-back and enjoy nearly 3 miles of absolutely glorious singletrack downhill (what you just climbed). You can also continue straight and continue to climb for 2 more miles and turn around and backtrack and descend for a little over 5 miles of absolutely glorious singletrack. An alternate option includes continuing straight and connecting with Lookout Mountain ride; study both route maps closely to see how you can easily combine the two rides. We will turn left and ride Magic Moss. Do get ready; the next 3 miles are going to make you smile.

4.5 Continue following the trail to the left. The trail to the right (716) will take you back up toward Dowells Draft. Trail 716 is part of the main Wild Oak Trail loop.

6.4 You reach Braley Pond Road (FR 96). This is your second decision point. You can turn left and follow the road for a little over 3.5 miles back to the entrance of the Braley Pond Picnic Area. Alternatively, you can turn around, climb back up Magic Moss, and descend Dowells Draft. We'll turn right and continue on. There is also an alternate parking area directly across the trail exit point.

8.4 Turn right onto FR 95 toward Todd Lake and Elkhorn Lake.

9.0 Pass the entrance to Elkhorn Lake and the entrance to trail 505, Flat Run, to the left. Continue straight; you are now on FR 533.

10.47 Continue straight through this intersection toward the North River Area. A left turn will take you toward the starting points of the Lookout ride and the Narrowback Tillman ride. We are actually now riding a portion of the Lookout loop.

11.6 Turn left and begin hating the author. You'll climb for nearly 5 miles before closing out the ride.

13.4 You reach the entrance to the Lookout Mountain Trail to the left. We'll continue straight.

15.6 You reach the gate and entrance to the singletrack, we're almost done climbing.

16.2 You've reached the top! Now it's time to begin loving the author. We'll descend and then hit short "speed scrubber" before plummeting down to the start of the ride.

17.7 Continue following the trail to the left. The right branch will take you toward Magic Moss and mile marker 4.5.

18.1 You reach the intersection worth trail 651. Looks familiar? We were here at 3.9. Brace yourself for a phenomenal downhill.

20.8 You reach Dowells Drive. Turn right and back track to the starting point.

21.0 Look closely to the left. The trailhead to the left is an extension of Dowells Draft to Rte. 250; we will continue back tracking to Braley Pond Road and the Braley Pond Picnic Area.

21.2 Go through the gate and turn left on Braley Pond Road.

21.4 Turn right to enter the Braley Pond Picnic area.

22.0 You reach the entrance to the Braley Pond Picnic area parking area. The loop is complete.

Dowells Draft and Magic Moss

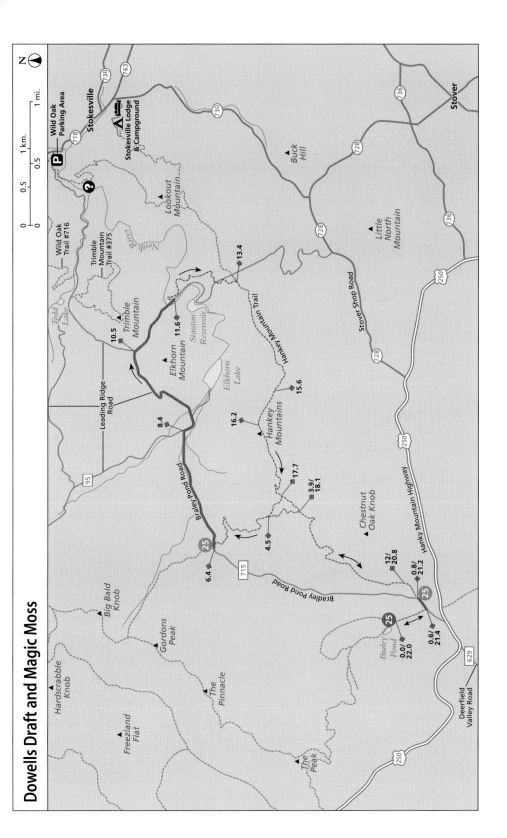

Short rocky sections are scattered throughout the Dowells Draft descent.

Ride Information

Local Information
www.visitharrisonburgva.com

Bike Shops
Shenandoah Bicycle Company: www.shenandoahbicycle.com
Rocktown Bicycles: www.rocktownbicycles.com/

Local Events and Attractions
Shenandoah 100: www.mtntouring.com
Stokesville Lodge: www.stokesvillelodge.com
Massanutten Resort: www.massresort.com

Where to Eat
Harrisonburg is quite possibly one of the best dining destinations in the Old Dominion. There are a ton of restaurants, breweries, and other places to enjoy great food and drink. Here's a couple of my favorite places:
Cuban Burger: www.cubanburger.com
Jack Brown's Beer and Burger Joint: www.jackbrownsjoint.com
Bella Luna Wood Fired Pizza: bellalunawoodfired.com
Brothers Craft Brewing: brotherscraftbrewing.com/
Three Notch'd Brewing Company: threenotchdbrewing.co

You May Run Into: Harlan Price

I think it's fitting to include Harlan Price in this "You May Run Into" sidebar, considering that as I ventured into Harrisonburg and the Stokesville area to document the rides for this guide, I literally ran into him on practically every ride I set out to do.

During my first outing, I stayed at the Stokesville Lodge with a group of friends, and as I headed out to document Lookout Mountain, I met Harlan and his dog, Gertie, for the first time. Weeks later, I returned to document Reddish Knob, and once again, I ran into him. Finally, on the day I set out to document the Dowells/Magic Moss ride, I bumped into him not once, but twice, as he led a group of riders on one of his riding clinics.

Harlan permanently moved to the valley in 2015 after years of visiting on a regular basis. In the short time, since he's called Harrisonburg home he's managed to make a name for himself. He owns and operates Take Aim Cycling (takeaimcycling .com), a mountain bike skills and instruction company that helps riders improve their abilities. "I raced bikes professionally for 8 years, and the Valley offered a great place to train," he told me. "In the time I kept coming back I noticed that although racing was important, the locals put a great emphasis on just having fun. If you focus too much on racing, you ended up missing some great trails. After years of training hard, I decided I would follow their lead and shifted my focus to share what I had learned in my racing career with other riders. Moving to Harrisonburg to do that was the next logical step."

"The biking culture in Harrisonburg is great," he told me. "People really love the sport and are making this region the place to be if you are a mountain biker. The hospitality and camaraderie that exists with riders in this area is great, and the effort that the volunteers from the SVBC are putting into the regional trails is phenomenal. Harrisonburg is a great town. There's good food, great trails and the people are incredibly welcoming. That's why I decided to make it my home."

Harrisonburg has quickly become a regional Mountain bike "go to" destination with riders from Washington, D. C., Maryland, Northern Virginia, Richmond, and Roanoke flocking to ride some of the best trails in Virginia. So, it's understandable that Harlan chose it as his base of operations. In addition to his years of professional racing experience, Harlan has received certifications from IMBA, and completed a Professional Mountain Bike Instructor (PMBI) Certification Program. His enthusiasm for the sport, along with his desire to help others achieve their best when riding their bikes, is what has fueled his efforts with Take Aim Cycling.

"My primary goal is to offer high quality MTB Skills Camps and instruction for groups or individuals," he said. "Cycling instruction has been focused on the fitness side of things and skills instruction has been missing. The trails in Harrisonburg and elsewhere in Virginia are technical, and having the right skills are critical. My goal is to help people learn or improve those skills so that they can have more fun when they are out there."

Judging by the grins on the group of people Harlan was leading the last time, I ran into him, I'd say he's doing a good job. If you want to take your riding to the next level, I highly recommend you give Harlan a call. Better yet, just head out on a ride in the Burg, chances are you'll run into him leading another group of riders in one of his clinics or just having a good time in his new home.

26 Narrowback

The classic Burg ride. Narrowback Mountain is a longtime favorite with regional cyclists, because it is the one of the most accessible rides in the Stokesville/Harrisonburg areas. The Narrowback ride allows cyclists to ride a relatively "quick" loop in an area dotted with lots of backcountry trails. The loop documented here can be ridden as a figure 8, or broken down into a quick loop ride that includes some of the best flow trails in the area.

Start: Start from the Tillman trailhead along Tillman Road.
Length: 12.6 miles
Ride time: 1.5-3 hours
Difficulty: Difficult due to technical rocky trails. The loop can be cut in half, making it suitable for intermediate to beginner riders to experience what backcountry Burg riding is like.
Trail surface: Mountainous rocky singletrack with a section of forest road and doubletrack.

The ride ends along one of the best flow trails in the region.
Lay of the land: Rocky and technical singletrack with a glorious descent along Tillman trail.
Land status: Public
Nearest town: Stokesville/Harrisonburg
Other trail users: Hikers
Trail contacts: GWNF, www.fs.usda.gov/gwj/; SVBC, svbcoalition.org/
Schedule: Open year-round
Fees: Free to public

Getting there: From Harrisonburg: Head south on VA-42 S/S High Street for 19 miles and turn right on Rte. 747, Mossy Creek Road. At the T intersection, turn left onto Rte. 613. Rte. 613 will curve right in approximately 2.5 miles; stay straight to continue onto Rte. 747, Mossy Creek Road. In approximately 1 mile, turn right onto Rte. 731, Natural Chimney Road and continue for 1 mile to Rte. 730, North River Road. Turn left on Rte. 30 and continue to the T intersection. Turn right onto Stokesville Road and continue onto Tillman Road—the road will turn to gravel. Remain on Tillman road for approximately 3 miles (from the spot where it turned to gravel) to a small parking area to the right. You'll see the Tillman trailhead along the tree line. **GPS coordinates:** 38.396758, -79.155588.

Miles and Directions

0.0 From the parking area, head north on Tillman Road for a little over a mile. The first portion of our ride will be a gradual climb along this road.

1.1 Turn right away from Tillman Road; there is a gate and several grave markers. This is a pet cemetery. Continue up on the doubletrack.

1.3 Go through the logging plot and go through the gate into the singletrack.

2.4 Turn right onto the trail as it shoots up and to the right.

The Narrowback builders have taken full advantage of the natural features along the trail. This section is much easier than the photo suggests.

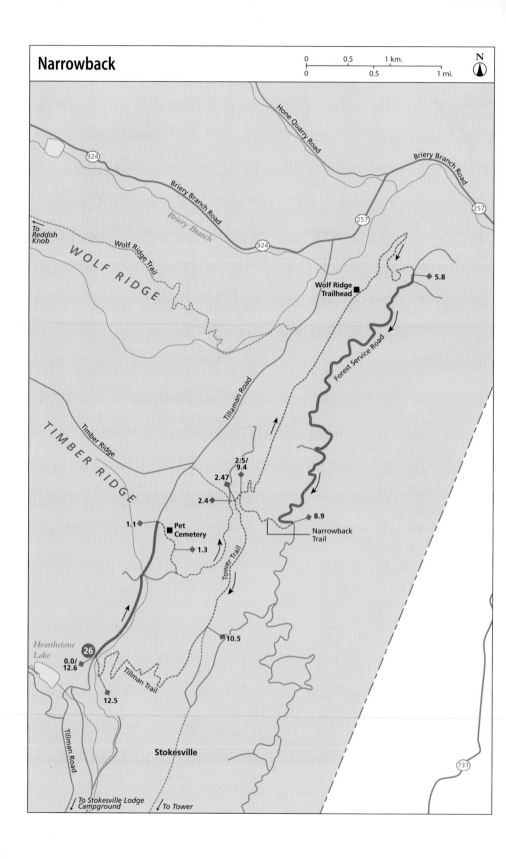

Narrowback

0   0.5   1 km.
0   0.5   1 mi.

N

Hone Quarry Road

924

Briery Branch Road

Briery Branch Road

257

257

Briery Branch

924

To Reddish Knob

Wolf Ridge Trail

W O L F   R I D G E

Wolf Ridge Trailhead

5.8

Forest Service Road

Tillaman Road

T I M B E R   R I D G E

Timber Ridge

2.5/ 9.4

2.47

2.4

1.1

Pet Cemetery

1.3

8.9

Narrowback Trail

Tower Trail

10.5

Hearthstone Lake

26

0.0/ 12.6

Tillman Trail

12.5

Tillman Road

Stokesville

731

To Stokesville Lodge Campground

To Tower

2.47 You reach a T intersection. Continue to the left on Festival. If you are limited on time, turning right will make the ride a little shorter. You'll still hit some of the best flow trail in the region either way. We'll close out the "long" loop along the right path on the way back.

2.5 Continue following the yellow blazes straight. We will return from the trail to the right (Narrowback Trail).

5.8 You exit Festival; turn right on the doubletrack to head back toward Narrowback Trail.

8.9 Turn right onto trail #432, Narrowback Trail. Get ready to climb!

9.4 You reach the intersection of Festival, turn left and continue straight past the next intersection to hop onto Tower Trail. You'll climb steadily for the next mile.

10.5 You reach Tillman Trail, turn right and get ready for a glorious descent back to the starting point.

12.5 You reach the exit to Tillman; turn right on the doubletrack and head back toward the starting point.

12.6 Cross the creek and come out onto Tillman Road, the loop is complete.

Ride Information

Local Information
www.visitharrisonburgva.com

Bike Shops
Shenandoah Bicycle Company: www.shenandoahbicycle.com
Rocktown Bicycles: www.rocktownbicycles.com/

Local Events and Attractions
Shenandoah 100: www.mtntouring.com
Stokesville Lodge: www.stokesvillelodge.com
Massanutten Resort: www.massresort.com

Where to Eat
Harrisonburg is quite possibly one of the best dining destinations in the Old Dominion. There are a ton of restaurants, breweries, and other places to enjoy great food and drink. Here's a couple of my favorite places:
Cuban Burger: www.cubanburger.com
Jack Brown's Beer and Burger Joint: www.jackbrownsjoint.com
Bella Luna Wood Fired Pizza: bellalunawoodfired.com
Brothers Craft Brewing: brotherscraftbrewing.com/
Three Notch'd Brewing Company: threenotchdbrewing.co

27 Reddish Knob

This is one of those truly epic rides that every local in the Burg raves about. Most locals will recommend you do it as a shuttle, but that has never discouraged adventurous cyclists from climbing the 4,400-foot Reddish Knob, the second highest peak in Augusta County. If you choose to ride to the top, make sure you are well fueled and both physically and mentally ready, because the unforgiving climb to the Knob will test all of your determination and commitment. I personally prefer to shuttle this ride, and that is how I am presenting it here. Shuttling will allow you to conserve your energy. Despite it being a "downhill," this ride will require all of your skill and strength.

The first portion of the ride along Timber Ridge is highly technical. Within the first 0.5 mile, you will encounter a difficult rock garden that is bound to demoralize even the most technically able riders. This first rock garden is the most difficult, and what lies beyond is some of the most exhilarating trail in the region. As you descend onto Wolf Ridge, you'll enjoy some of the most fun-rolling trail in the area. As with several of the other trails documented here, the SVBC has devoted a considerable amount of effort and dollars to making it highly enjoyable. The descent will end with a great section of flow trail that will make you want to shuttle right back up to do it all over again. Combine this ride with the Narrowback loop for a fantastic day of riding.

Start: If shuttling: Park one vehicle at the Wolf Ridge Trailhead (38.431646, -79.127808) along Tillman Road and drive up Briery Branch Road to FR 85 to the Reddish Knob staging area (dead end). From there, select either one of the two trailheads, the first one, up top, offers a technical entrance into the trail with a set of large steps. The second one, less than 0.25 mile down the knob is a little easier to drop into. If riding as a loop, park at the Wolf Ridge Trailhead parking area (N38 27.740' / W79 14.502') and ride up Briery Branch Road to Reddish Knob. We'll be "shuttling" this ride.
Length: 8.4 miles
Ride time: 1–2 hours
Difficulty: Intermediate to expert. This "downhill" has nearly 800 feet of climbing and lots of technical rock gardens. While novice riders can do it, it will be physically demanding and technically challenging. An alternative is to bike/hike up Lynn Trail to Wolf Ridge. Riders will still experience an exhilarating downhill but avoid the more technically and demanding upper section of the ride.
Trail surface: Mountainous rocky singletrack.
Lay of the land: Rocky and technical singletrack trails several technical rock gardens and fast and steep descents.
Land status: Public
Nearest town: Stokesville/Harrisonburg
Other trail users: Hikers
Trail contacts: GWNF, www.fs.usda.gov/gwj; SVBC, svbcoalition.org/
Schedule: Open year-round
Fees: Free to public

Getting there: If shuttling: From Harrisonburg: Head south on VA-42 S/S High Street for 19 miles and turn right on Rte. 747, Mossy Creek Road. At the T intersection, turn left onto Rte. 613. Rte. 613 will curve right approximately 2.5 miles, stay straight to continue onto Rte. 747, Mossy Creek Road. In approximately 1 mile, turn right onto Rte. 731, Natural Chimney Road and continue for 1 mile to Rte. 730, North River Road. Turn left on Rte. 30 and continue to the T intersection. Turn right onto Stokesville Road and continue onto Tillman Road—the road will turn to gravel. Remain on Tillman Road for approximately 5 miles (from the spot where it turned to gravel) to the Wolf Ridge Trailhead parking area to the left. Leave one vehicle there and continue straight along Tillman Road to Briery Branch Road. Turn left on Briery Branch and continue up to FR 85, turn left and then slightly left again at the Reddish Knob Spur. The trailheads are slightly before reaching the Reddish Knob staging area and on the actual staging area; Graffiti marks the entrance point. **GPS coordinates:** 38.46234, -79.2417.

Nothing but smiles on the way down from Reddish Knob.

Reddish Knob

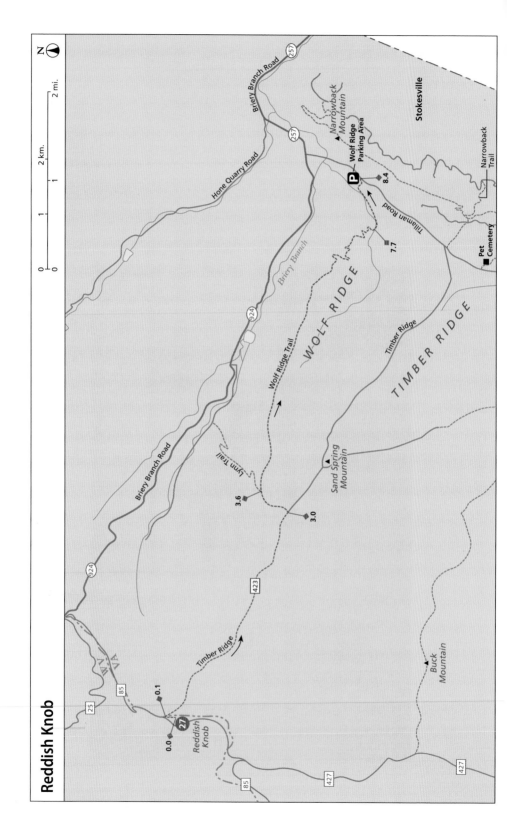

Miles and Directions

0.0 Drop down the technical steps from Reddish Knob and follow the trail as it curves to the left and then to the right.

0.1 Cross FSR 85 and continue following the trail on the opposite site. This is the second trailhead; first if you bypassed the technical entry point. Brace yourself, the descent begins in earnest and will deliver you into a very technical rock garden. Over your head? Don't worry, this first rock garden is the hardest, the rest are much easier.

3.0 Turn left at this intersection; the trail is clearly marked and easy to follow. Follow it toward the Wolf Ridge Trail. The right (straight) fork will take you toward Sand Spring Mountain and ultimately down to Tillman Road.

3.6 Continue straight on Wolf Ridge Trail (378). Lynn Trail (436) is to the left. Lynn will take you toward Briery Branch Road, an alternate/bail-out descent point. Get ready for some amazing trail.

7.7 Cross the small creek and continue on Wolf Ridge Trail toward Tillman Road.

8.4 Reach the Wolf Ridge parking area, the ride is complete. You can easily combine this ride with the Narrowback Loop for a little extra distance.

Ride Information

Local Information

www.visitharrisonburgva.com

Bike Shops

Shenandoah Bicycle Company: www.shenandoahbicycle.com
Rocktown Bicycles: www.rocktownbicycles.com/

Local Events and Attractions

Shenandoah 100: www.mtntouring.com
Stokesville Lodge: www.stokesvillelodge.com
Massanutten Resort: www.massresort.com

Where to Eat

Harrisonburg is quite possibly one of the best dining destinations in the Old Dominion. There are a ton of restaurants, breweries, and other places to enjoy great food and drink. Here's a couple of my favorite places:
Cuban Burger: www.cubanburger.com
Jack Brown's Beer and Burger Joint: www.jackbrownsjoint.com
Bella Luna Wood Fired Pizza: bellalunawoodfired.com
Brothers Craft Brewing: brotherscraftbrewing.com/
Three Notch'd Brewing Company: threenotchdbrewing.co

28 Rocktown Trails at Hillandale Park

The Rocktown Trails at Hillandale Park have something for every level of mountain biker. Planned, built, and maintained by the SVBC, the Rocktown Trails have a mix of easy, intermediate, and advanced trails in a relatively small (74 acres) park within the limits of the City of Harrisonburg.

SVBC began work on the trails in 2007 and officially opened it to the public in 2009. Since then, the trails have evolved and have been expanded. Today, there are approximately 6 miles of singletrack along with a pump track within this urban destination. The trails are immensely popular not only with cyclists, but with walkers and runners because of their proximity to the center of Harrisonburg. The trails are easily accessible from at least three locations, including two pedestrian/cyclist trailheads at South Avenue and Circle Drive and one vehicular entrance within the park across from shelter #11 along Hillandale Avenue.

The stacked loops have become a focal point and popular recreational resource for the City of Harrisonburg. Volunteers from the SVBC have amassed over 4,000 hours of work to build and maintain the trails. Built with the help and guidance of expert trail builders from the International Mountain Biking Association (IMBA), the trails follow IMBA's guidelines for sustainable shared-use.

Start: Start from the trailhead adjacent to the last parking area on the right as you head into Hillandale Park on Hillandale Avenue.

Length: 5+ miles

Ride time: Dependent on route

Difficulty: Novice to expert. Hillandale Park has several trails for all rider abilities.

Trail surface: Smooth and rocky twisty singletrack.

Lay of the land: Small neighborhood park. Hillandale includes a small pump track and one section of flow trail along the power line.

Land status: Public

Nearest town: Harrisonburg

Other trail users: Hikers, trail runners

Trail contacts: City of Harrisonburg, www.harrisonburgva.gov; SVBC, www.svbcoalition.org

Schedule: Open year-round

Fees: Free to public

Getting there: Head southwest on S High Street (Rte. 42) toward W Bruce Street and turn right onto Hillandale Avenue. Continue to the far end of the park and access the trailhead from the parking area to the right just before the traffic circle. You can also park in downtown Charlottesville and ride your bike to Hillandale. Pedestrian access is available along Circle Drive (near the intersection with Oak Drive) and along South Avenue where South Avenue intersects with South Dogwood Drive. The access point along South Avenue will put you right on the powerline flow trails.

GPS coordinates: 38.443916, −78.897236.

Rocktown Trails at Hillandale Park

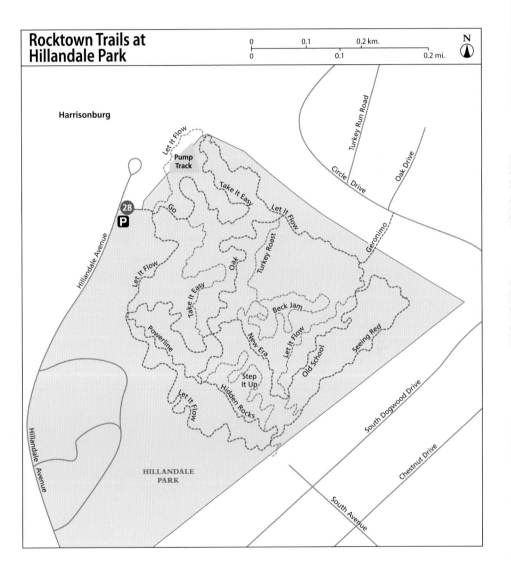

Harrisonburg

Turkey Run Road

Circle Drive

Oak Drive

Let It Flow

Pump Track

Take It Easy

Let It Flow

Go

Geronimo

Hillandale Avenue

28
P

Let It Flow

Oak

Turkey Roast

Take It Easy

Beck Jam

Powerline

New Era

Let It Flow

Old School

Seeing Red

Step It Up

Hidden Rocks

Let It Flow

South Dogwood Drive

Chestnut Drive

Hillandale Avenue

HILLANDALE PARK

South Avenue

The Ride

The trails at Hillandale Park are well blazed and marked with clear and easy to read difficulty ratings. You really will not have too much trouble finding out where you are and will find that it's difficult to get lost within the confines of this 74-acre city park. For a great starter loop, begin at the trailhead across from shelter #11 adjacent to the furthest parking area in the park and follow the green "Let it Flow" trail in a counter clockwise direction until you reach the starting point. This will give you a taste of the "easy" trails within the park. Following Let it Flow all the way around is a suitable loop for beginner and young mountain bikers (aka groms). All of the other trails can be easily accessed from this loop, and with the exception of Seeing Red and Old School, are within the inside perimeter of the green Let it Flow loop. Half-way through the outer loop, you'll reach the top of the power lines (South Avenue trailhead), where you'll get a chance to descend and ride a super fun flow/jump trail. Locals will often session this section of trail, descending down the Powerline Trail and climbing back up along Let it Flow.

I highly recommend you park in one of the public lots in downtown Harrisonburg and then ride your bike from town to Hillandale Park. Harrisonburg is a very friendly cycling community and getting around town on two wheels is super easy. A visit to Harrisonburg is also not complete until you've spent some time at the Shenandoah Bicycle Company (SBC). SBC is a local shop that has become a staple in the Mountain Biking Community of the region. If you've never visited the region, the staff at SBC will gladly point you in the right direction and recommend rides beyond those documented in this guide. The SBC often leads rides straight from their shop and often has demo days, where you can sample some of the best bikes on the market on the trails at Hillandale Park.

Clifton Forge/Lexington

lthough Clifton Forge and Lexington's neighbors to the north and south, Harrisonburg and Roanoke, have been recently stealing the mountain bike spotlight, this small nook in Virginia's Alleghany Highlands along the southern tip of the Shenandoah Valley still remains one of the top mountain bike destinations in the state. The reason is the miles of trails at Douthat State Park and along the ridges of the Blue Ridge Parkway, including the Sherando Lake Recreational Area.

29 Torry Ridge/Big Levels–Sherando Lake

This particular loop is a bit different than what most people will ride when they tackle the trails near and around Sherando Lake. The "classic" loop is a bit longer and starts along Coal Road to the Mills Creek trail, then onto the switchbacks before descending to Torry Ridge and the White Rock Gap Trail. Instead, our ride will take us up along the White Rock Gap Trail and over the majority of the Torry Ridge trail, a technically demanding ribbon with glorious views of Sherando Lake and Waynesboro, before we descend rapidly to the Torry Furnace.

This is not a beginner's ride. The start along the White Rock Gap Trail can be deceiving. The gently rolling trail will turn right and drastically ascend before joining the Torry Ridge Trail. Advancing beginner riders, or those looking for a "quick out an back," can ride the White Rock Gap Trail from its genesis along the Upper Sherando Lake to the Blue Ridge Parkway before turning back for an exhilarating downhill to the starting point.

Start: Start from the small parking area along the entrance to the Sherando Lake recreation area.
Length: 14.4 miles
Ride time: 2–4 hours
Difficulty: Difficult due to long climbs and rocky ridge trails. This is NOT a ride for beginners
Trail surface: Mountainous, rocky singletrack and some paved roads.
Lay of the land: Rocky and technical singletrack with one long steep climb. Ride includes two sections of paved road at the beginning of the ride, and at the end along Mt. Torrey Road.

Land status: Public
Nearest town: Waynesboro
Other trail users: Hikers
Trail contacts: GWNF, www.fs.usda.gov/gwj; Sherando Lake Recreation Area, www.fs.usda.gov/recarea/gwj/recarea/?recid=73959
Schedule: Open year-round
Fees: Between Apr 1 and Oct 31, there is a nominal fee to use the area. Cyclists, if riding in, pay only a nominal fee to enter the area. If you opt to drive in, it will cost you a little more.

Getting there: From Charlottesville: Take I-64 W to exit 96, State Rte. 624 toward Waynesboro/Lyndhurst; turn left onto 624 and continue for 9.1 miles to the entrance of the Sherando Lake Recreation Area. Turn right and park immediately to the left after crossing the bridge over the Back Creek. You will ride into the recreation area. **GPS coordinates:** 37.930003, -78.979514.

The Ride

In all my years, riding around the DC Region and neighboring MD and Virginia, the trails around Sherando Lake and Big Levels often eluded me. Most of my "serious" riding friends often exalted about the merits of the rides around this popular recreational area in the Blue Ridge Mountains. They mentioned rocky and technical ridges with phenomenal views of the lake, thigh busting climbs to the ominous sounding peaks of Torry Ridge and Devil's Knob, and long white-knuckle descents to the peaceful lakes in the Sherando Recreation Area. My friends often boasted about these epic outings, so it left me wanting to partake in a similar adventure.

Finally, when the time came to document the trails for this guide, I naturally had to head out to Sherando to see for myself why the lakes and surrounding trails are often referred to as the Jewel of the Blue Ridge Mountains. After doing lots of research on the available loops in the area, I turned to my good friend Mark Humbertson, one of those "serious" riders, for advice. Mark jumped at the opportunity to show me around one of his favorite riding destinations.

The Sherando Lake recreation area and complex is one of the many CCC projects that dot the Virginia mountain landscape (see Kennedy Peak ride). The lower lake and supporting facilities were one of the first projects tackled by the CCC in the early 1930s. Built first, the lower lake, serves both as a recreational destination and as a flood control device. The second and smaller upper lake was built later, in the 1960s,

The views of Sherando Lake from Torry Ridge are spectacular.

Torry Ridge

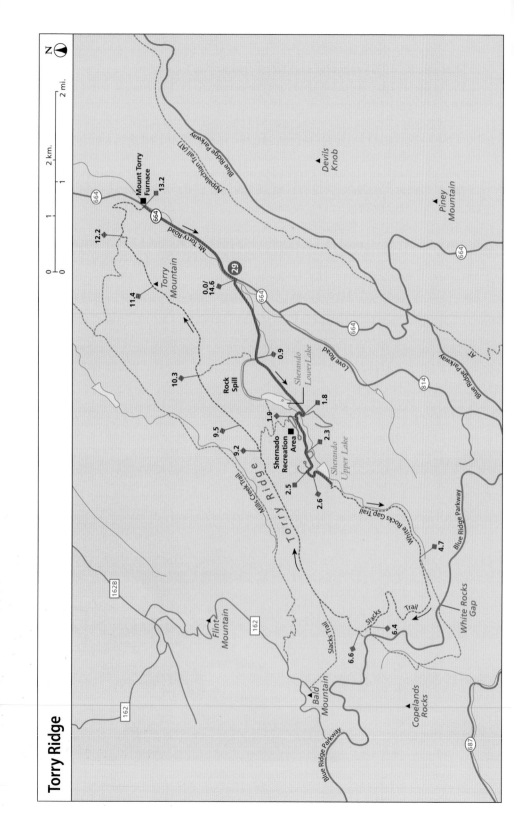

to provide additional flood protection. Today, the lower lake is popular for swimming and boating while the upper lake is known for its great fishing.

In addition to the lake, the CCC worked extensively in the area around the lake building trails, planting trees, and helping with major construction efforts on areas of the Blue Ridge Parkway. Until the early 1940s, CCC recruits lived in nearby Camp Lyndhurst, an isolated complex that served as their base of operations. With the looming prospect of America's involvement in WWII, the camp was closed in 1941, albeit for a short period of time, and then reopened in 1944 to house a different kind of "recruit," German POWs.

These POWs continued to work on the surrounding area. With the majority of the young American male population participating in the war effort, the POWs filled a labor void left in the home front, and even provided local Shenandoah Valley farmers with much needed labor. Ultimately, at the end of the war, the POWs were sent back to their homelands.

Miles and Directions

0.0 We'll start the ride from the small parking lot that's immediately to the left as you enter the Sherando Lake Area. This lot is way before the entrance gate to the park. You will continue on the road all the way past the lower lake and up to the upper lake, approximately 3 miles.

0.9 Continue on the main road once you go over the small bridge. The road to the right will take you to the north side of the lake.

1.8 The road will descend and make a sharp "U" turn to the right and then sweep left.

1.9 Turn left to continue following the main loop toward the main camping areas, including the White Oak Loop and the Amphitheater.

2.3 The RV parking area will be to your left.

2.5 The road will curve to the right. Continue past the Work Center and Volunteer Village to your right and make an immediate left along the gravel road and past the gate. There is a small "trail" sign adjacent to the gate and arrow pointing to the "Upper Lake." This is pretty much the last "civilized" point of our ride until we descend to the Torry Furnace 13 miles from now...

2.6 The gravel road will end and curve left into doubletrack, the entrance to the White Rock Gap Trail will be visible ahead to the right.

2.7 Enter the White Rock Gap Trail (blazed with orange markings) and begin the climb to the Torry Ridge Trail. The upper lake will be immediately to your left for a short while. The first couple of miles will ascend gradually. Enjoy the singletrack, it's great!

4.7 Turn right to follow the Slacks Trail toward the Slacks Overlook, the trail will turn considerably steeper now. If you want to make this a short ride, continue for an extra half mile to the left to the Blue Ridge Parkway and return along the same route. You'll enjoy a great downhill along Rock White Rock Gap trail.

6.4 Continue straight along the Slacks Trail. The fork to the left will take you to the Slacks Overlook. One more mile until you reach the Torry Ridge Trail. Some riders will park here and shuttle to the starting point of our ride, or use the overlook as a starting point for this loop. The Overlook label for the area above is a little deceiving since there is not much of a view from the parking area above. Perhaps when the parkway was first built in the 1930s, the view was not obstructed by today's vegetation.

6.6 The trail to the left is an alternate access point to the Slacks Overlook.

7.2 You reach the Torry Ridge Trail, turn right. The left fork will take you up toward the Blue Ridge Parkway and Bald Mountain. The "classic" loop generally comes down from the left; riders who take the mills trail to Bald Mountain will descend along the trail to the left and bomb down to the White Rock Gap Trail along the climb we just endured. The next section of trail is absolutely phenomenal, get ready to enjoy Torry Ridge and GWNF riding at its finest.

9.2 Continue following the Torry Ridge Trail to the left. The trail to the right is the Blue Loop Trail and descends straight down to Lake Sherando. There is an overlook approximately 0.2 miles down the Blue Trail; I recommend against going to the overlook, the hike down is steep and hard. If you choose to bail out at this point, be prepared to walk, the trail is steep and technical.

9.5 After a short technical descent, you'll reach the rock spill. Approximately 50 yards down the rock spill is a large rock that offers phenomenal views of the lake below. If you choose to make the site trip, walk carefully! The rock slide is a little treacherous, especially in cycling shoes!

10.3 You reach the Blue Loop Trail. Continue straight along the Torry Ridge trail. The portion of the Blue Loop Trail to the right will take you straight down, much like the previous one to Sherando Lake. This one, however, will deliver you to the access road we passed along mile marker 0.9.

11.4 You've reached the top of Torry Mountain, 2,781 feet, congratulations! Now we go down—check your brakes and get ready for a fast, sometimes technical descent to Torry Furnace.

12.2 The trail to the left is Mills Creek Trail. We'll head right along the Torry Ridge Trail. If you were to turn left and head up along the Mills Creek Trail, you could access the beginning of the classic loop; this is one way to extend your ride.

13.2 You reach the Mount Torry Furnace. Turn right on Mount Torry Road and head back along the black top to the starting point of the ride. The old iron furnace was built in 1804 and destroyed six decades later during the Civil War. It was rebuilt and operated for an additional 20 years processing iron ore from the nearby mountains until it finally closed in 1884.

14.6 Turn right into the Sherando Lake Area and the parking area to the left. Your ride is complete.

Ride Information

Local Information

Visit Waynesboro—www.visitwaynesboro.net/

Bike Shop

Rockfish Outfitters—www.rockfishgapoutfitters.com/

Local Events and Attractions

Waynesboro—www.visitwaynesboro.net/

Restaurants

Jakes Bar and Grill—jakesbarandgrill.net/
Blackjack & Company—www.facebook.com/greatfood4U
Seven Arrows Brewing Company—www.sevenarrowsbrewing.com

Restrooms

Available in the Sherando Lake Recreation Area.

30 Douthat State Park

Douthat State Park is a hidden gem just north of historic Clifton Forge with a myriad of riding opportunities. Honestly, the most difficult thing about the trails at Douthat is selecting which to ride. With over 20 trails, totaling over 40 miles of rideable terrain, it's no wonder that Douthat has been dubbed "Mountain Bike Disneyland." The trails, along with all the park's other facilities and amenities, will keep you coming back season after season.

Start: Both rides start from the Stoney Creek trailhead, located on the left side of Douthat State Park Road shortly before you reach the Contact Station. Do visit the Park Rangers at the visitor center to pay the appropriate park fees.
Length: 9.3/18.3 miles
Ride time: 1.5-2 hours/3-4 hours
Difficulty: Intermediate to expert trails with lots of elevation change.
Trail surface: Smooth and technical single-track in a mountainous landscape.

Lay of the land: Smooth and technical singletrack in a mountainous landscape with sweeping Panoramic views along several of the park's trails. The park has several trails with long climbs with equally long descents.
Land status: Public
Nearest town: Clifton Forge
Other trail users: Hikers, trail runners, and equestrians
Trail contacts: Douthat State Park, www .dcr.virginia.gov/state-parks/douthat
Schedule: 6 a.m.–10 p.m.
Fees: VA State Park fees apply.

Getting there: From I-64, take exit 27 near Clifton Forge. Turn north onto State Rte. 629 and continue 5 miles to the trailhead on the left. The Park's visitor center is approximately 0.5 miles beyond the Stoney Run parking area. **GPS coordinates:** 37.887668, -79.803466.

The Ride

Douthat State Park is a hidden gem just north of historic Clifton Forge. The location is packed with a myriad of riding opportunities. The most difficult thing about the trails at Douthat is choosing which to ride and how much time to spend on these rich trails. The trails at Douthat are phenomenal. You will find yourself wanting to visit every season.

Listed in the National Register of Historic Places, Douthat State Park (pronounced "dowthat") is a jewel in Virginia's State Park and mountain bike inventory. The park was one of the first built by the CCC (see the Narrowback ride for more info) and continues to be a model for other parks around the country. Recruits from the CCC dammed the waters of Wilson Creek to form the 50-acre Douthat Lake and built virtually all the amenities visitors continue to enjoy today, including the log cabins, the guest lodge, a gift shop and camp store, and a full-service restaurant with great views of the lake.

Douthat is best enjoyed over the course of a few days since it gives you the chance to roll out from one of the many available campsites along the lake, or from one of the many cabins or lodges available for rent in the park. The starting point for any ride at Douthat, if you chose to stay the night, will undoubtedly be your front door, or front flap. For the sake of giving you a set of predetermined loops, I've chosen the Stoney Run parking area, one of the more popular starting points, to begin the two loops documented here.

▶ Between the first Saturday in April to June 15 and from September 16 to October 31, Douthat Lake is stocked twice a week with trout. During these times, if you are planning on fishing, you are required to have a Virginia freshwater fishing license and a daily fishing permit, both sold right in the park.

The two loops I've written up will give you a pretty good feel for what is available within the park. The first loop is a relatively short ride along the east and west sides of Douthat Park Road (Rte. 629) that can be easily broken down

Trails like this one are why people keep coming back to ride Douthat over and over again.

Douthat State Park

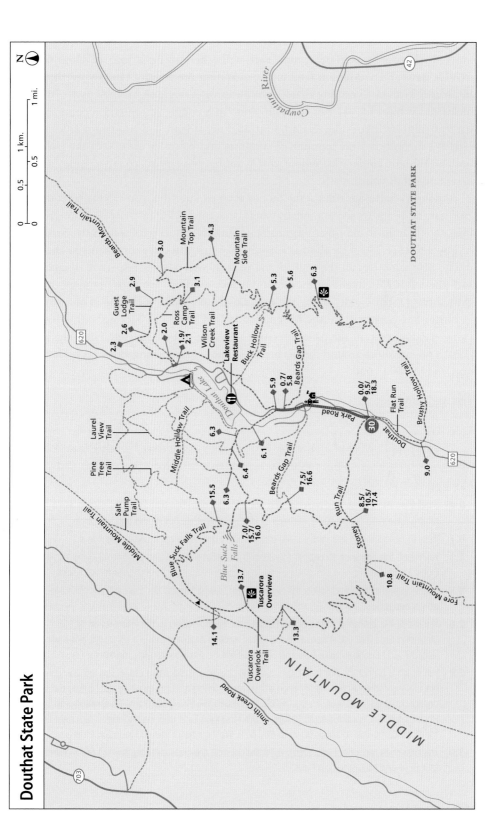

into two shorter loops. The second ride will take you on a tour of Douthat's premier trails and prominent landmarks, including the Brushy Hollow overlook, the Brushy Hollow Swinging Bridge, the Tuscarora Overlook, and the park's Blue Suck Falls. While ride #1 can be easily done in a couple of hours, I recommend that you allocate a considerable amount of time, at least 4–5 hours, for ride #2. Ride #2 includes a large amount of climbing and passes by several of the park's most prominent landmarks, where you'll definitely want to pause to enjoy the views and catch your breath.

Although I start both rides at the Stoney Run parking area, you can easily modify your starting point to accommodate where you are staying in the park. The great thing about Douthat and other Virginia State Parks is that all trails are clearly marked for easy reference. The park also has a handy map that you can grab when you check in. The map annotates all the trails in the park, as well as their respective distances. Both the loops I highlight here can also be accessed from the park's campgrounds by modifying them slightly. Study the map closely to modify your loop as necessary.

Note: The park map has the Mountainside Trail labeled as "Hiking" only. This is a long-standing typo in the park's literature that's yet to be corrected. The only "off limits" trails are those around the perimeter of the lake, including Buck Lick, Heron Run, and the YCC trail.

Miles and Directions

Ride #1

This ride will give you a taste for what it's like to climb at Douthat State Park. We'll chew off a small chunk so that you get a sense for what may come should you decide to do ride #2.

0.0 Start from the Stoney Run parking area and turn left onto Douthat State Park Road. We'll hit the pavement for a couple of miles to warm up the legs before the first big climb.

0.7 Pass the entrance of the Park's main office. This is the connection point with ride #1.

1.9 You reach the entrance to cabins 12–31 and 33–35, turn right and begin your climb to Guest Lodge Trail.

2.3 Go through the gate and follow the signs toward "Guest Lodge," the road will get considerably steeper now.

2.6 You reach the entrance of the Guest Lodge Trail. We're headed to the intersection of the Mountain Side Trail 0.6 miles ahead. The first section of this climb is a bit tough, but it will level out and become more bearable. The trail will be blazed with blue markings.

2.9 You reach a branch on the trail. Either side will take you to the same place. The left branch will gradually climb while the right branch will descend before sharply climbing up. I prefer the left branch. In about 400 feet, IF YOU CHOSE THE RIGHT BRANCH, reach the intersection with the Ross Camp Trail, continue straight toward the Mountain Side trail. Had enough? Turn right on the Ross Camp Trail to shoot down to Rte. 629. We'll continue toward Mountain Side.

3.0 The branches reconnect at a sharp right switchback, continue climbing toward the Mountain Side and Mountain Top Trails.

3.1 Turn right onto the clearly marked Mountain Side Trail. Want to keep climbing? Head up to mountain top to the left, eventually you'll end up at the next marker point, albeit a little further.

4.3 Turn right onto mountain top and continue following the yellow blazes. Pay attention here! This also marks the intersection of the Buck Hollow Trail. A sharp right will put you on the Buck Hollow Trail (blazed with blue markings), stay on the Mountain Side Trail.

4.6 You reach the intersection with the Beard's Gap Trail; a shelter and park trail post marks it. This also marks the end of the Mountain Top Trail and the beginning of the Brushy Hollow Trail (see ride #3). Turn right onto Beard's Gap and get ready for a screaming descent.

5.8 You reach the main park office. Continue through the office driveway and turn right onto the Rte. 629, Douthat State Park Road. Had enough? Turn left and head back to the Stoney Run Parking area.

5.9 Turn left onto the gravel road toward the Camp Carson Picnic Area and the Discovery Center.

6.1 Go over Wilson Creek and bear right through the parking area to the trail marker ahead. At the trail marker, turn right and follow the doubletrack toward the Blue Suck Falls trail.

6.3 Bear left onto the clearly marked Blue Suck Falls trail. The trail to the right (Heron Run) will go over a short bridge and follow the perimeter of the lake. Heron Run is hiking only. We're making our way to the Locust Gap Trail.

6.4 Continue following the Blue Suck Falls Trail past the next two intersections. To the left is the Tobacco House Ridge trail, and to the right, shortly after crossing the creek, is Huff's Trail.

6.6 You reach the intersection with the Laurel View trail. Unlike other intersections in the park, this one is a little confusing. Fortunately, there is a shelter that makes it a little obvious. Turn left and continue following the Blue Suck Trail.

7.0 You reach the Locust Gap Trail. Turn left. This is my favorite trail on the park.

7.5 Continue following the Locust Gap Trail to the right. The Beard's Gap Trail is to the left.

8.3 You reach Stoney Run. Turn left and head down to the starting point of the ride. Over the course of the next mile, you will cross the creek several times. If it's a hot summer day, you'll appreciate the cool refreshing water. It is possible, however, to gingerly cross the creek without getting wet.

9.3 You're back at the Stoney Run Parking area; the loop is complete.

Ride #2

Ride #2 is a little more challenging than ride #1. We'll hit a few more trails and more than double the climbing distance we saw in ride #1. The pay-off? We'll descend nearly twice as much!

0.0 Start from the Stoney Run Parking Area and turn left on Douthat Park Road.

0.8 Turn right into Creasy Lodge and follow the gravel driveway to the entrance of the clearly marked Wilson Creek Trail. The Wilson Creek Trail parallels the road for a short distance. **Note:** You can continue along Douthat Park Road and follow the same directions for ride #1 until you reach the entrance of the Guest Lodge Trail. Distances will vary slightly. We'll stick to the trails for this loop.

1.3 Continue through this intersection, Buck Lick Trail. A left turn will take you to the Lakeside Restaurant and camp store in less than a tenth of a mile. The trail will descend quickly, go over a small bridge and reach a T intersection, continue to the left following the Wilson Creek Trail white blazes.

2.0 You reach the Ross Camp Trail. A right turn will take you up toward the Mountain Top Trail. We'll turn left instead and then climb up to the Guest Lodge Trail along the road.

2.1 You reach the road, turn right and then immediately right again to begin the climb to the Guest Lodge Trail. The entrance is marked: "Cabins 12-31 and 33-35."

2.5 Go through the gate and follow the signs toward "Guest Lodge," the road will get considerably steeper now.

2.6 You reach the entrance of the Guest Lodge Trail. We're headed to the intersection of the Mountain Side Trail 0.6 miles ahead. The first section of this climb is a bit tough, but it will level out and become more bearable. The trail will be blazed with blue markings.

2.9 You reach a branch on the trail. Either side will take you to the same place. The left branch will gradually climb while the right branch will descend before sharply climbing up. I prefer the left branch. In about 400 feet, IF YOU CHOSE THE RIGHT BRANCH, reach the intersection with the Ross Camp Trail, continue straight toward the Mountain Side Trail. Had enough? Turn right on the Ross Camp Trail to shoot down to Rte. 629. We'll continue toward Mountain Side.

3.0 The branches reconnect at a sharp right switchback, continue climbing toward the Mountain Side and Mountain Top Trails.

3.1 You reach the intersection of the Mountain Side and Mountain Top Trails. Stay left and continue to climb. You'll hit at least half a dozen switchbacks. If you've never ridden switchbacks, this is the perfect place to learn.

4.3 You're at the top! Continue following the yellow blazes. The trail to the left is an access point to the George Washington National Forest.

5.3 You reach the intersection of the Mountain Top, Mountain Side, and Buck Hollow trails. You will continue straight and remain on the Mountain Top Trail until you merge with the Brushy Hollow Trail. Had enough? A right turn will take you down toward the lake along the Buck Hollow Trail. A sharp right (almost U-turn) will take you down toward the Guest Lodge Trail along Mountain Side.

5.6 You reach the Beard's Gap Trail. We will continue straight onto the orange blazed Brushy Hollow Trail. This is your last opportunity to bail for the next 3.4 miles. We'll begin a steady climb for the next mile before descending to the park road for nearly 2.5 miles. Brushy Hollow has some phenomenal views and one of the best descents in the park. Enjoy!

6.3 You reach the Brushy Hollow Overlook. Take a minute to soak in the view before the final short push of our climb.

9.0 You reach the bottom of the Brushy Hollow Descent. Cross over the hanging bridge and turn right on Flat Run Trail. Enjoy the next flat mile, a BIG climb awaits!

9.5 Turn left, cross the road and enter the Stony Run Parking area and the Stony Run Trail.

10.5 Continue straight past the Locust Gap Trail. We will return from the right and descend the short portion of the Stoney Run Trail we just climbed. Follow the signs to the Tuscarora Overlook.

10.8 Continue straight through this intersection; the trail is marked with a no horses sign. We are still on the Stoney Run Trail.

11.1 Follow the trail to the right as it crosses the creek and continues to climb. This is another nice spot for a break. The branch to the left proceeds through a dense Rhododendron tunnel to a scenic waterfall.

13.3 You reach the entrance to the Tuscarora Overlook Trail. Turn right. A left turn will take you up higher toward the Middle Mountain Trail. We want to enjoy the views from the overlook, a well-earned reward for the 3 miles we just climbed.

13.7 You reach the entrance to the overlook, continue climbing to the left. Before you continue, take a short detour to the overlook, soak in the views, you won't be disappointed. Plus, you need a break from all that climbing. After you've enjoyed the view and taken a short break, continue the ride.

14.1 Continue following the trail to the right; you're pretty much done with the climbing for today. The trail to the left is a connector to the Middle Mountain Trail. If you want to extend your ride even further, turn left and then right on Middle Mountain and follow Middle Mountain to the Pine Tree Trail and then Blue Suck Falls. We will descend along the Blue Suck Falls Trail.

15.5 You reach the intersection with the Pine Tree Trail. If you chose to extend the ride as described above, this is where you'd end up. Continue to the right along the Blue Suck Falls Trail.

15.7 You reach the Blue Suck Falls, time for another break to soak in the park's scenery. The trail beyond will get considerably more technical as it descends along the creek on the way to the Locust Gap Trail.

16.0 Turn right onto the Locust Gap Trail and away from the creek. Locust Gap will be blazed with yellow markings. You'll shortly reach another intersection; continue straight on the Locust Gap Trail. The next section couple of miles will be pure joy. We'll finish out the ride in style.

16.6 Continue following Locust Gap to the right. Beard's Gap Trail will be to your left.

17.4 You're back at Stoney Run. This time, we'll ride it downhill to the starting point, turn left. Over the course of the next mile, you will cross the creek several times. If it's a hot summer day, you'll appreciate the cool refreshing water. It is possible, however, to gingerly cross the creek without getting wet, but you'll be going so fast that you'll hardly notice the splashes on the way down.

18.3 You're back at the Stoney Run Parking area. Your ride is complete.

Ride Information

Local Information, Events, and Attractions

Clifton Forge—www.cliftonforgeva.gov/visit/
Clifton Forge Main Street—cliftonforgemainstreet.org/
Lexington—lexingtonvirginia.com/
Alleghany Highlands—www.visitalleghanyhighlands.com/main/index.php

Bike Shop

Lexington Bicycle Shop: (540) 463-7969

Restaurants

Douthat Lakeview Restaurant—www.dcr.virginia.gov/state-parks/douthat
Jack Mason's Tavern—jackmasonstavern.com (Clifton Forge)
Brew Ridge Taps—www.brewridgetaps.com (Lexington)
Blue Lab Brewing Company—www.bluelabbrewing.com (Lexington)
Devil's Backbone Brewing Company, Outpost Brewery—dbbrewingcompany.com (Lexington)

Restrooms

Available in the park.

Roanoke Ride Center

Early explorers came to the area that is now known as Roanoke as early as the seventeenth century, however, most of the of the land they found in the flat and fertile region between the mountains along the upper Roanoke River remained largely undisturbed. It wasn't until the late 1700s, when the lands to the east of the mountains began to get developed. It's in that region that small communities along the southern edge of the Shenandoah Valley began to appear. It took another 100 years for these communities to grow into towns— one of the most notable is Big Lick.

Chartered in 1874, it only took Big Lick—known as such for the salty marshes that attracted deer, elk, and buffalo—eight years to become a city. By 1882, after the arrival of two railroads, the Shenandoah and the Norfolk & Western, Big Lick grew ten-fold from 500 to 5,000 residents and the community transformed into an industrial crossroads. By 1884, it was renamed "Roanoke" after the river that flows through it.

The city that once thrived on coal, timber, and limestone from the nearby mountains benefited from the advent of the railroads, and shifted its industry to manufacturing railroad cars, textiles, and other enduring and profitable businesses. The once humble town of Big Lick soon annexed several neighboring communities to accommodate its growth. The expansion, however, would be limited to the valley and ridge region that lies between the Blue Ridge and Alleghany Mountains, leaving its neighboring slopes untouched.

The geographical location of Roanoke makes it one of the most unique cities in the Old Dominion. The self-proclaimed capital of the Blue Ridge offers its residents the conveniences of both an urban and rural lifestyle. Roanokans from the city's center can find themselves riding the urban trails of Mill Mountain, hiking into one of the Appalachian Trail trailheads, or riding one of the trails at Carvins Cove, the nation's second largest municipal park, within just minutes of a short drive.

The proximity to so many natural resources has prompted local cyclists to get involved and get organized. In 2012, the Roanoke mountain bike community came together to become a chapter of the International Mountain Biking Association.

Since then, Roanoke IMBA has been working hard to build positive relationships with land managers and city officials to ensure mountain bikers continue to enjoy access to the hundreds of miles of trails available just outside their doorstep.

Roanoke is already a League of American Bicyclists "Bicycle Friendly Community," and now Roanoke IMBA is following the lead of its neighboring communities, such as Harrisonburg and Richmond, with an effort to become an IMBA Ride Center. Roanoke IMBA leadership has a standing ten-year trail plan at Carvins Cove that will result in the development of nearly 40 miles of rideable singletrack. Plans are also in the works for expanding and improving the trails at Explore Park (HM-V), including the addition of a pump track and skills area. Efforts are also ongoing to maintain other area trails, including those within the city's limits. The overall goal is to create riding facilities for mountain bikers of all skill levels.

Roanoke IMBA is well on the way to make its vision a reality. As you ride the Cove, or the backcountry trails along North Mountain, or even the descents along Spec Mines and Dody Ridge, you'll understand why this Southwestern Virginia destination is definitively a regional favorite.

31 Carvins Cove

Carvins Cove is a huge mountain biking playground with over 30 miles of singletrack trails that are bound to satisfy the most demanding off-road cyclists. The trails at the Cove can be, and are generally very demanding, but there is a little for everyone. Along with the loop I detail here, I also offer you a 1-mile quick loop that is perfect for kids—although it has a little elevation (no matter which way you ride it), it offers young cyclists an opportunity to experience "real" mountain biking. More advanced riders can choose from a myriad of challenging options.

The longer loop I detail here will introduce you to real Roanoke riding—strenuous climbs followed by phenomenal descents. I urge you to study the map and craft your own loop. Remember, however, that paper is flat and what may look easy can end up being a rather brutal challenge.

Start: Start from the Bennett Springs Parking Area along Carvins Cove Road.
Length: 9.1 (up to 40) miles
Ride time: 1–3 hours
Difficulty: Novice to expert
Trail surface: Smooth and technical single-track. Contains trails for all ability levels.
Lay of the land: Watershed recreation area, second largest municipal park in the nation
Land status: Public
Nearest town: Roanoke

Other trail users: Hikers, equestrians, and trail runners
Trail contacts: Roanoke Parks and Recreation, www.playroanoke.com; Roanoke IMBA, www.roanokeimba.org
Schedule: Open year-round
Fees: Daily fees apply. Trail access passes can be purchased at the Bennett Springs and Timberview parking lots. Annual passes can be purchased at a discount from the boat dock.

Getting there: From Roanoke: Take 581 North to 81 South and then take exit 141 for VA-419 toward VA-311. Turn right onto Rte. 311, Catawba Valley Drive. Continue on Catawba Valley Drive for approximately 2 miles and turn right onto Carvins Cove Road. The Bennett Springs parking area will be approximately 3.5 miles on the right and is located on the opposite side of the street from the parking area. As you drive in and turn right into the parking area, look to the left to see the trailhead. Our first loop begins there. **GPS coordinates:** 37.384708, –80.005784.

The Ride

There's a good reason why this municipal park, the second largest in the nation, just 8 miles north of Roanoke, is known as the jewel of the southeast when it comes to mountain biking. With nearly 60 miles of trails, you can easily spend multiple days at the Cove and not ride the same sections twice. Within its nearly 13,000 acres, the park has trails to satisfy virtually all levels of mountain bikers. Whether you want to roll out on a flat rolling ride, crank out a lung-busting climb, or fly down a purpose-built downhill trail, there is something for you at this regional destination.

The Cove holds the major water source for the city of Roanoke, and contains recreational opportunities that include not only mountain biking, but also hiking, horseback riding, fishing, and boating within the 600-acre lake, provided their engines not exceed 10 hp. Because of the myriad of recreational opportunities, the Cove has become one of the most visited destinations in the east.

In addition, the Cove is an important cog in the area's natural infrastructure. Carvins is connected to both national and state trail systems, including 4 miles of the Appalachian Trail (AT). If you have time, I highly encourage a hiking side trip to the AT. The section of the AT that traverses the Carvins watershed area includes the most photographed point from the AT, McAfee Knob. Chances are you've seen images from this glorious spot in literature describing the AT or in any serious hiker's photo album. Roanoke.com calls the spot "the AT's postcard image." The Knob's risky overhang offers adventurous hikers a nearly 270-degree panoramic view that includes Catawba Valley and Dragons Back / North Mountain ride to the west, Tinker Cliffs to the north, and the Roanoke Valley to the east. Being photographed or taking a photograph from the knob is an AT tradition. In addition to McAfee Knob, thru- and day hikers can enjoy great views of the area from other points, including Tinker Mountain, Hay Rock, and Angel's Gap.

Carvins Cove is a mountain biker's dream. There are over 30 miles of challenging singletrack trails to choose from.

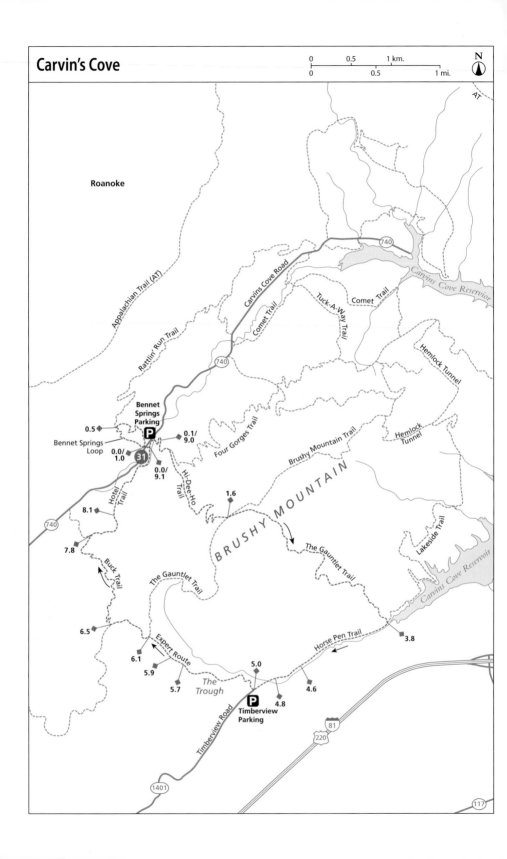

Carvin's Cove

| 0 | 0.5 | 1 km. |
| 0 | 0.5 | 1 mi. |

N

Roanoke

740

Carvins Cove Reservoir

Appalachian Trail (AT)

AT

Carvins Cove Road

Comet Trail

Tuck-A-Way Trail

Comet Trail

Rattlin' Run Trail

740

Hemlock Tunnel

Bennet Springs Parking

0.5

0.1/9.0

Bennet Springs Loop

0.0/1.0

P

31

0.0/9.1

Four Gorges Trail

Brushy Mountain Trail

Hemlock Tunnel

Hi-Dee-Ho Trail

1.6

B R U S H Y   M O U N T A I N

The Gauntlet Trail

Lakeside Trail

Hotel Trail

8.1

740

7.8

Buck Trail

The Gauntlet Trail

Carvins Cove Reservoir

6.5

Expert Route

6.1

Horse Pen Trail

3.8

5.9

5.0

5.7

The Trough

P

4.6

4.8

Timberview Parking

81

Timberview Road

220

1401

117

There are several points from which to access the trails at Carvins Cove, but the most popular is the Bennett Springs parking area. From this spot, riders have access to nearly 60 miles of trails. The trails at the Cove are managed by the Roanoke's Department of Parks and Recreation with the help of several volunteer groups, including IMBA's regional chapter, Roanoke IMBA. In 2002, the Roanoke Parks and Recreation Department met with several user groups to finalize an overall system map and trail naming convention. Today's trail markings and signage are a result of that initial endeavor. Since then, the Parks and Recreation Department has continued to work constructively with several user groups to ensure all their needs are met within the park's vast trail network while minimizing user conflict. To fulfill that vision, the Parks and Recreation Department drafted and approved a trail management plan in mid-July 2010 with input from all stakeholders. The plan, currently in effect, is used to ensure existing trails and any new ones added within the park's 12,000 acres are sustainable and appropriate for all users.

▶ **It's worth noting that Carvins Cove is a very popular destination for mountain bikers, hikers, trail runners, and horseback riders. Stay alert and be prepared, chances are you will run into other trail users during your ride. Always be polite and courteous and yield to other users.**

The department continues its efforts to include and solicit input from all users of the Cove, which has resulted in a trail system that has become not only a valuable local resource, but also a regional Virginia destination. A day spend at Carvins will not disappoint you; it will entice you to come back for more.

Miles and Directions

Both of the rides I detail here and the recommended easier loop start from the Bennett Springs parking area along Carvins Cove Road.

Bennett Springs Loop—short 1-mile loop suitable for kids

0.0 Immediately after entering the trailhead, you'll reach a "T" intersection. You can go in either direction; we'll head right to follow the loop in a counterclockwise direction. Either way you go, you'll climb, gradually, for the first 0.5 mile.

0.5 You reach the intersection with Rattling Run, a black diamond trail. Continue straight and begin your descent back to the starting point.

1.0 Arrive back at the starting point. The loop is complete.

Classic Loop

This is one of the "classic" Carvins Cove loops and it will give you a pretty good taste of what climbing and descending is like in the Roanoke region. I suggest you ride the Bennett Springs loop first to warm up your legs a little before heading into this ride. This loop starts at the main kiosk at the far end of the parking area. Our ride will take us up along Hi-Dee-Ho, down The Gauntlet to Horsepen and then back up the Trough before descending back to the lot via Buck Trail and Hotel.

The majority of intersections are clearly marked. Other than one intersection along Hi-Dee-Ho (0.3), every other turn has a sign along it.

0.0 Drop into the trail and follow it to the right as it curves over a short bridge.

0.1 Turn left at this intersection and follow the signs to Hi-Dee-Ho. The trail to the right is Hotel, we will return along Hotel.

0.2 Continue following Hi-Dee-Ho to the right. The trail to the left will take you back toward Carvins Cove Road. The climbing begins, gradually at first.

0.3 Continue following the trail to the right past the next two intersections. Both left forks lead you toward the Four Gorge Trail. Climbing will get considerably more difficult now.

1.6 You reach the top of Hi-Dee-Ho. Take a minute to catch your breath. Turn left onto Brushy Mountain Fire Road and then immediately right onto The Gauntlet. You're about to lose all the elevation you just climbed. Use caution over the next 2.2 miles. The descent is fast and technical in places.

3.8 You reach the intersection of the Lakeside Trail and Horsepen. Turn right to continue on Horsepen; the creek will be to your left.

4.1 Go over a small bridge and continue following Horsepen to the right. You'll now begin your gradual climb back up to Brushy Mountain Fire road.

4.6 You reach the first entrance to First Deck. If you want to add a little mileage to your ride, you can hop in on First Deck and hook back with Horsepen a little further down. First Deck also allows you to access Royalty, and alternate climb back up to Brushy Mountain Fire road. I highly recommend you climb via the trough though.

4.8 You reach the second intersection with First Deck, continue straight.

5.0 Turn right and begin the climb back up to Brushy Mountain Fire Road along the trough. The climb will be gradual at first and then get steeper toward the end. It will not be as difficult as the ascent we encountered earlier along Hi-Dee-Ho though.

5.7 The trail will split; follow the "mortals" option to the left. The "Expert" fork to the right is meant more for "downhill" riders and is a considerably more difficult climb.

5.9 The expert and mortals options rejoin. Continue climbing. You can make a right and do a quick loop to experience the expert route in a downhill direction.

6.1 You're back at Brushy Mountain Fire Road. The bulk of your climbing has now been completed. Other than a couple of speed scrubbers along the last leg of the route, it's all downhill from here.

6.5 Turn right on Buck to begin the final descent back toward Hotel and the Bennett Springs parking area.

7.8 You reach Hotel. Turn right to continue on Hotel. A left turn will take you along Buck back toward Carvins Cove Road; this is an alternate ending point.

8.1 Continue following the trail to the left, the right fork is an old trail; hopefully, by the time you read this, it will have been closed permanently.

9.0 You reach the first intersection we encountered during our ride. Turn left and head back up toward the parking area.

9.1 You're back at the trail kiosk; the loop is complete.

If you want to experience a "less extreme" loop at Carvins, I recommend you follow the following trails.

From the Bennett Springs parking area:

Ride north along Carvins Cove Road for approximately 1.1 miles and turn right on Comet. Continue on Comet and turn left on Tuckaway. At the road, turn right and then right again onto Enchanted Forest. At the road, cross onto Little Bell then once again onto Schoolhouse; Schoolhouse will end on Happy Valley Fire Road, turn left and follow the Fire Road all the way back to Carvins Cove Road. Turn right onto Carvins Cove Road and then right onto Songbird. Songbird will eventually end on Carvins Cove Road at which point you can turn right to finish the ride. This loop is relatively flat and about 10 miles long.

Ride Information

Local Information, Events, and Attractions
Visit Roanoke—www.visitroanokeva.com
Downtown Roanoke—www.downtownroanoke.org

Bike Shops
East Coasters Bike Shop—eastcoasters.com
UnderDog Bikes—www.underdogbikesva.com
Just the Right Gear—justtherightgear.com

Restaurants
Fork in the Alley—www.forkinthealley.rocks
Billy's Barn—www.facebook.com/Billys-Barn-220993324614802
Mac and Bobs—macandbobs.com
Wasena City Tap Room and Grill—www.wasenacitytaproom.com
Parkway Brewing Company—parkwaybrewing.com
Big Lick Brewing Company—biglickbrewingco.com

Restrooms
Not available as this book goes to press. An initiative is under way to build two bathrooms for public use, including one at the Bennet Springs parking area.

32 Pandapas Pond (Poverty Creek/Brush Mountain)

This is a great ride in the Jefferson National Forest right outside Blacksburg Virginia.

Start: Start from the parking area immediately to the left as you drive in onto the Pandapas Pond Recreation area. The trailhead will be directly across from it.
Length: Up to 21.8 miles
Ride time: Dependent on route
Difficulty: Novice to expert. The Basin Trails (Poverty Creek) are suitable for novice riders.
Trail surface: Smooth and technical single-track trails in mountainous terrain.

Lay of the land: Smooth and technical single-track trails with long climbs and equally long descents. Excellent creek side trails for novice riders.
Land status: Public
Nearest town: Blacksburg
Other trail users: Hikers, trail runners, and horseback riders
Trail contacts: GWNF, www.fs.usda.gov/gwj
Schedule: Open year-round
Fees: Free to public

Getting there: From Blacksburg: Head North on US 641 for approximately 6 miles and turn left into the Pandapas Pond Day use area. The parking area will be immediately to your left.
GPS coordinates: 37.285130, –80.461383.

The Ride

No matter what you call it, Pandapas Pond, Brush Mountain, Gap Mountain, or Poverty Creek, there is definitely something to satisfy your mountain biking needs along the trails within this section of the Jefferson National Forest, just north of Blacksburg, VA. Poverty Creek has been a popular destination for Blacksburg mountain bikers for a long time. Its proximity to the town and Virginia Tech's campus has made it a venerable haven for off-road cycling.

The trails can be broken up into three general sections. The spine of the system is the Poverty Creek trail, one of the more popular trails in the system. Poverty Creek offers cyclists of all levels a super fun and easy to follow path. Also known as the Basin trail, the Poverty Creek Trail is your access point to two hillsides that flank its course. Because of its proximity to the creek, the Poverty Creek trails have little elevation change and tend to remain wet after periods of heavy rain. A sign at the main trailhead adjacent to the parking/staging area will inform you of the trail's status.

To the northwest of Poverty Creek is Gap Mountain. Although higher than its eastern counterpart, Brush Mountain, the trails along Gap Mountain don't climb as drastically or nearly as high. What the trails lacks in elevation (there's still plenty of climbing by the way), they make up for in technical difficulty. Prickly Pear, Skullcap, and Trillium will definitely test your skills. You could feasibly spend a day crafting a loop on this side of the system alone.

To the southeast is Brush Mountain, the "steeper" of the two flanking hills. Brush Mountain is also easy (relatively speaking) to access from Heritage Park, a small community park along Glade Road (off of 460). From Heritage Park, you can climb up Gateway Trail to access the system; for our purposes, however, we will do so from within the Basin. Brush Mountain includes one of the coolest sections of trails in the Old Dominion, Joe Pye. Joe Pye meanders through a thick rhododendron forest that is spectacular when it blooms. The climbing along Brush Mountain is much more severe than that along Gap Mountain, and so is the descending. Jacobs' Ladder and Snakeroot, which are both documented on this ride, are two exhilarating descents. To enjoy them, you must climb! Like Gap Mountain, you could easily spend a day exploring the trails along this side of the creek.

It's no wonder that Pandapas Pond is such a popular destination in the Blacksburg Area. Its proximity to the city, the abundance of trails for all skill levels, along with the serene beauty of the hardwood forest that blankets the area will keep you coming back.

The trails at Pandapas Pond (Poverty Creek) are clearly marked and easy to follow. There's something for all ability levels.

Pandapas Pond

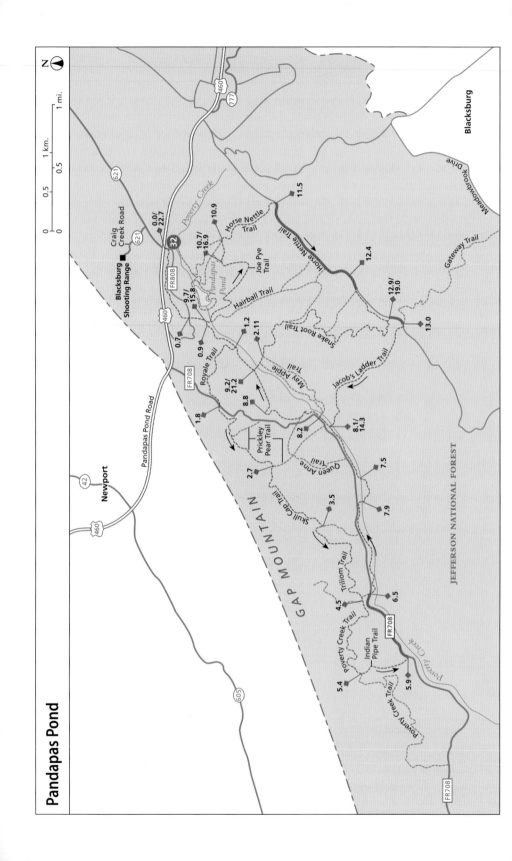

Note: The trails immediately around Pandapas Pond are off limits to bikes. The Basin trails tend to stay wet after periods of heavy rain, so please use common sense when visiting this popular destination. The trails are also extremely popular with hikers and equestrian enthusiasts, please observe the rules of the trail and yield to other users.

Miles and Directions

Every trail is clearly marked and the majority of intersections have some form of signage. This ride is actually three rides in one. You can choose to do the long loop, the medium loop, or the short loop. The long loop will have extensive climbs that will add up to a little over 3,400 feet of climbing. Every up pedal is worth the effort.

0.0 Start from the trail conditions sign and hop onto the Poverty Creek Trail. This is a "green trail" and it is blazed with orange markings. The Poverty Creek Trail is super fun, and you can easily do an out and back along it if you don't want to tackle the more technical and difficult trails. We'll hit all of those for this ride. Continue on Poverty Creek for approximately 1 mile until you reach the intersection with Royale.

0.3 Cross over the Forest Service Road.

0.7 Cross over the Forest Service Road.

0.8 Continue straight on Poverty Creek. The trails to the left are closed to bikes and clearly marked.

0.9 Continue straight on Poverty Creek, the trail to the left is Joe Pye. We will revisit this intersection three more times (depending on which loop you decide to complete.)

1.2 Turn right onto Royale, blazed with blue markings, and get ready to climb.

1.8 Immediately after crossing the road, hop onto the white blazed Prickly Pear Trail.

2.7 Turn right onto Skullcap, blazed with blue markings. A left turn will take you down toward Queen Anne and the Forest Road if you want to bail.

3.5 Turn right onto Trillium, blazed with white markings. If you continue on Skullcap to the left, you will end down on the forest road.

4.5 You reach the end of Trillium and the Poverty Creek Trail. A left turn will take you down to the forest road; continue to the right onto Poverty Creek.

5.4 Turn left onto Indian Pipe and get ready for a fast descent to the forest road. Indian Pipe contains several man-made features, including a log ride and at least three small drops/jumps. Watch your speed! If distance is what you want, continue following Poverty Creek to the right, it will circle back to the forest road.

5.9 Turn left onto the forest road.

6.5 Turn right onto the Poverty Creek Trail; a large boulder will mark the entrance to the trail. The trail will be blazed with orange markings. At this point, we'll stick to the Poverty Creek Trail all the way back to Joe Pye. Follow the orange blazes. This is area is known as "the basin" locally.

7.4 Reach the first of two creek crossings; continue following the orange blazes.

7.5 Reach the second creek crossing. Continue following Poverty Creek to the left. The trail to the right is the exit of "Beauty. We'll save that one for another time.

8.1 Jacobs Ladder will be to your right. Depending on what loop you choose, we will revisit this intersection again on the way down from Jacobs Ladder.

8.2 May Apple is to your right. Continue on Poverty Creek. May Apple parallels Poverty Creek along the other side of the Creek and ends at Snake Root.

8.8 Poverty Creek turns sharply right. The left fork is an entrance to the trail system and alternate (albeit smaller) parking spot.

9.2 Continue straight on Poverty Creek. The trail to the right is Snake Root. Depending on what loop you choose, we'll be coming down Snake Root to finish out the ride.

9.4 You're back at the intersection of Royale. Continue straight on Poverty Creek.

9.7 You're back at the intersection of Joe Pye (blazed with white markings), turn right and then follow the trail to the left past the next two intersections after the creek crossing. The next section of trail is a beautiful Rhododendron tunnel. This is your bailout point. If you don't want to climb 800 feet, continue straight and double back to the parking area to complete loop 1 (10.6). Get ready to climb!

10.7 Continue following Joe Pye to the right. The trail to the left (Lake Spur) is Hikers only.

10.9 You reach the intersection of Lady Slipper and Horse Nettle. This is another chance to bail out. Turning left on Horse Nettle will take you back down to the parking area. Continue to climb!

11.5 Turn right on the Forest Service Road; this continues to be Horse Nettle, blazed with blue markings. A left turn will take you down toward Pandapas Pond Road. Continue to climb!

12.4 You reach the fire circle and the top of the climb! The trail is clearly marked and continues to be blazed blue.

12.9 You reach the intersection of Horse Nettle and Snake Root. If you want to complete loop 2, turn right and get ready for a great downhill back to Poverty Creek (1.1 miles). We'll continue straight to descend along Jacob's Ladder.

13.0 Make a sharp right on the doubletrack. You'll begin to descend quickly, stay sharp because our next turn will come up quickly.

13.0 Horse Nettle will shoot right into the woods and quickly end at Jacob's Ladder. Follow Horse Nettle to the right and then make a right onto Jacob's Ladder. CHECK YOUR BRAKES! The first section of Jacobs consists of a series of tight and technical switchbacks; you'll have some nice stretches with long sight lines that will allow you to pick up some serious speed. USE CAUTION. The trail to the left is Gateway, another great downhill. Gateway will take you away from Pandapas Pond, no easy way to get back other than riding back up; if you have the legs, go for it!

14.3 You're back at the Poverty Creek Trail. Turn right and double back to the intersection with Joe Pye.

15.8 Turn right on Joe Pye to climb back up to the fire circle and Snake Root. Had enough? Continue straight along Poverty Creek for 0.9 miles to finish out the ride.

16.9 You're back at Lake Spur, continue following Joe Pye to the right.

17.1 You're back at the intersection of Lady Slipper and Horse Nettle. Had enough? Turn left on Horse Nettle to head back to the parking area. We'll continue right and keep climbing back to the fire circle and into the singletrack.

19.0 Turn right onto Snake Root. Once again, check your brakes and get ready for a phenomenal downhill.

21.1 Continue straight on Snake Root. May Apple Trail will be to the left. If you want to extend the ride a little more, turn left on May Apple and then right on Poverty Creek. We'll continue straight to Poverty Creek until we reach the starting point.

21.2 Turn right on Poverty Creek and double back to the starting point.

21.5 Continue on Poverty Creek to the right past Royale.

21.8 Continue on Poverty Creek past Joe Pye.

22.7 You're back at the starting point, the loop is complete.

Ride Information

Local Information

Step into Blacksburg—stepintoblacksburg.org

Bike Shop

East Coasters—eastcoasters.com
Bike Barn—www.bikebarnblacksburg.com
Hokie Spokes—www.hokiespokes.com

Local Events and Attractions

Virginia Tech—www.vt.edu
Do Blacksburg—www.doblacksburg.com

Restaurants

Gaucho Brazilian Grille—www.gauchogrille.com
The Rivermill—www.facebook.com/RivermillBarandGrill
Blacksburg Taphouse—www.blacksburg-taphouse.com/
Rising Silo Brewery—risingsilobrewery.com/

Restrooms

Along Pandapas Pond (no bikes allowed on those trails).

33 Peaks View Park

The trails at Peaks View Park in Lynchburg, VA, are a testament to what a community can do to avoid losing access to a valuable natural resource. In the late 1990s, shortly after the baseball fields and many of the facilities at Peaks View Park were completed, the City of Lynchburg began a study to build a golf course adjacent to the handful of fields located in the park.

Bill Foot, for whom the Mountain Bike and Hiking Preserve is named, immediately began to set the wheels in motion to prevent said golf course from ever taking shape. As a member of the local Natural Bridge Appalachian Trail Club (NBATC), and an avid cyclist, Bill did not want to see the forests where the trail system is now located lost to a golf course. He reached out to Tim Miles, a Lynchburg resident and fellow cyclist. Together they set out to plan and flag what would become the first of the trails detailed in this ride.

The trails at Peaks View Park are dedicated to Bill Foot, a "force of nature" that was responsible for the trail system's development.

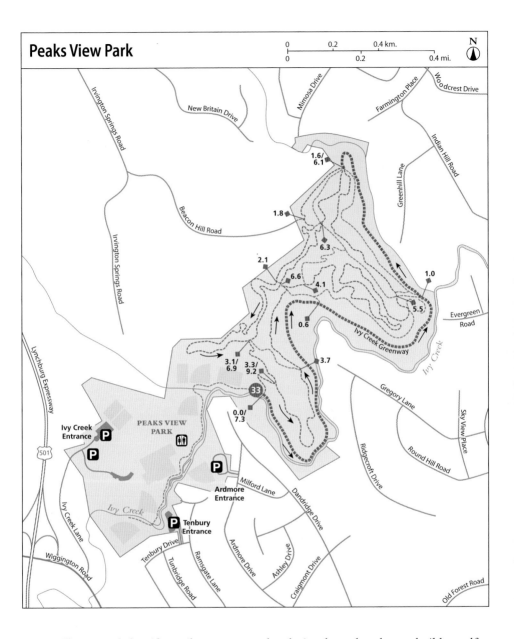

Bill reasoned that if a trail system was already in place, the plan to build a golf course would be less likely to come to fruition. Over the course of several months, Bill worked with local advocates and the regional Parks and Recreation Department to obtain the necessary approvals and permits to begin the project. By early 2000, nearly half of the system was completed, and within a year—in the spring of 2001— more than 90 percent of the present trail system was built and the plans for the golf course were abandoned.

During the process, Bill delegated planning and building of the trail system to several Lynchburg residents and members of the NBATC, making the process a truly efficient community effort. In recent years, the Greater Lynchburg Off Road Cyclists (GLOC) has taken over the responsibility of maintaining the trails, and holds regular volunteer trail maintenance events, including visits from IMBA's Trail Care Crew. As you ride through the system, you'll notice the efforts of the systems builders, including clear signage and several trail maintenance boxes along strategic points in the system. These boxes contain tools and materials necessary for the upkeep of the system.

It's worth noting that GLOC isn't quite finished with the trails at Peaks View Park. Future plans call for the addition of a pump track, as well as a skills area which will feature log jumps, skinnies, berms, and other TTFs to help riders improve their skills.

Miles and Directions

There are several entrances to Peaks View Park from which you can access the paved Ivy Creek Greenway. Whichever point you choose to access the park from, take the paved greenway trail to trailhead number 1, it is from there that our ride begins. The trails at Peaks View are clearly marked. At trailhead 1, you can grab a detailed and handy park map that includes all trails. The loop 1 present here has been crafted to hit pretty much all the trails in the system. I do urge you to explore this great park and enjoy the trails that Bill Foot helped make a reality.

0.0   Take the Ivy Creek Greenway to Trailhead #1. Continue following the Greenway to its terminus at trailhead #3.

0.6   Continue past trailhead #2.

1.0   You reach trailhead #3. Enter the trails and follow the signs toward Fire Road. You want to basically take the furthest right branch. You are now on Mimosa Trail.

1.6   Turn right at this intersection and continue a short climb to the next intersection. Almost immediately after you turn right, you'll reach the intersection of Mimosa with Upper Piney, Fire Road, and Outback. Follow the trail to the right to hop onto outback. We're basically going to ride the system's perimeter and eventually make our way back to this intersection.

Once you hop onto Outback, it will merge with Fire Road for a brief section, just stay to the right to remain riding the system's perimeter.

1.8   Continue following the trail straight and to the left. The right fork is an access point to the system from Beacon Hill Road. Immediately after this access point, you reach the intersection with Tom Cat, turn right on Tom Cat.

2.1   After a short technical descent, you reach a small bridge and access point to Steve's Bowl-a-Rama.

3.1   You reach a three-way intersection that includes Grape Vine, Ridge Cap, and Rock Pile. We'll continue following the system's perimeter and turn right to hop on Grape Vine.

3.3   Continue straight through this intersection to remain on Grape Vine and head toward Slick Rock. A right turn will take you back to trailhead #1.

3.7   Turn right to hop on Roller Coaster. The next section of trail has a fun series of whoops. Skilled riders will love getting a little air of the trails features.

4.0 You reach the end of Roller Coaster and a short connector to Cyclone. Make a left on the connector trail and then a right on Cyclone. The intersection is clearly marked.

4.1 Continue straight on Cyclone, the trail to the left is Tomb Stone. Tomb Stone is one of two trails we'll skip on this ride.

5.5 Continue straight through this intersection (Fire Road) and past the second one to the right (Slalom) to enter Lower Piney.

6.1 You're back at basically mile marker 1.6. To the left is Upper Piney and straight ahead is Ivy Ridge and Mimosa. Turn left, and then immediately left again to hop on Upper Piney.

6.3 You reach the intersection with Fire Road and the entrance point to Tom Cat and Squeeze. Continue across Fire Road and slightly left to enter Squeeze.

6.6 Continue straight through this intersection to access Rock Pile. The next section will be the most difficult climb in the system, it's "punchy," steep and technical; get ready!

6.9 You reach the intersection with Steve's Bowl-a-Rama, Grape Vine, and Ridge Gap. We were here before at mile marker 3.1. At this point, you can turn left on Ridge Cap and follow the trail past Roller Coaster toward the exit trail to trailhead head one or follow along as we head out along Grape Vine. If you want additional mileage, follow Steve's Bowl-a-Rama in the opposite direction and along the system's perimeter back toward Tom Cat, and Outback, basically backtracking what we rode initially.

7.2 Turn right at this intersection to finish out the loop.

7.3 After a short, but fun, switchback descent you're back at trailhead one. The loop is complete.

Ride Information

Local Information
Downtown Lynchburg—www.downtownlynchburg.com/

Bike Shops
Blackwater Bike Shop—www.blackwaterbikeshop.com
Bikes Unlimited—www.bikesunlimited.com

Local Events and Attractions
Liberty Mountain (See HM-X) Snowflex Centre—www.liberty.edu/snowflex/

Restaurants
El Jéfe Taquería Garaje—www.eljefetaqueriagaraje.com/
Water Stone Fire Roasted Pizza—www.waterstonepizza.com/
LoLa's Mexican Cuisine and Cantina—www.facebook.com/lolasmexicancuisine
Beer 88—www.beer88va.com

Restrooms
Available throughout the park.

34 Dragon's Back/North Mountain

Aptly named. If you visualize a dragon's back, you'll probably come up with something similar to the elevation profile of this ride. This ride is not for beginners, nor intermediate riders who have an aversion to climbing—steep climbing. Even seasoned riders have been pummeled by this trail's brutal climbs. But people keep coming back, because despite the harsh climbing, the resulting descents are worth the effort, and the classic Virginia Ridge riding, is one of the finest in the state.

Start: See ride description for starting point alternatives.
Length: Depends on route
Ride time: Depends on route, plan on several hours
Difficulty: Expert
Trail surface: Steep rocky and technical singletrack.
Lay of the land: Mountainous backcountry.

Land status: Public
Nearest town: Roanoke
Other trail users: Hikers
Trail contacts: Jefferson National Forest, www.fs.usda.gov/gwj/; Roanoke IMBA, www.roanokeimba.org/
Schedule: Open year-round
Fees: Free to public

Getting there: From Roanoke take 581 North to 81 South and then take exit 141 for VA-419 toward VA-311. Turn right onto Rte. 311, Catawba Valley Drive. Continue on Catawba Valley Road for approximately 9.5 miles to the Dragon's Tooth parking area to the left.

If you are starting along Wildlife Road, continue past the Dragon's Tooth parking area for approximately 2 more miles and turn right onto the gravel road and continue for 2 miles to the Deer Trail trailhead, or 3.8 to the Grouse Trail Trailhead. **GPS coordinates:** 37.37878, –80.15605.

The Ride

There's a good reason why this ride is called the Dragon's Back. Dragons, after all, are some of the fiercest creatures of lore. Dragons can be beaten, even tamed, but they should always be feared. There's a quote by JRR Tolkien that comes to mind when thinking of the Dragon's Back: "never laugh at live dragons," for obvious reasons. Surprisingly, the quote applies to this inanimate dragon, the one lying along the spine of the North Mountain in the New Castle Ranger District of the Jefferson National Forest. This Dragon should not be mocked; however, if taken seriously, the dragon can be tamed.

I'll be perfectly honest with you; the first time I took on this beast, it beat me to a pulp; I was unprepared for the adventure, and I suffered, badly. The ratio of pain to joy hovers a little toward the suffer side. But, if you can handle the "agony," you'll be rewarded with some phenomenal Blue Ridge "ridge" riding, and some descents that will "burn" an imprint in your memory; you'll be talking about them for a long time to come.

Once you get to the ridge, "Most Difficult" will be a welcome sign.

Rather than send you on a predetermined loop, I think it's best you tackle this beast on your own accord. I've presented several alternatives that will give you plenty to think about as you plan your trip to the North Mountain. Be aware, however, that no matter what route you choose, this IS back country Virginia mountain biking at its finest. Be prepared since the trails you will be riding are highly demanding and there is no cell connectivity. Pack right, be safe, have fun.

Dragon's Back

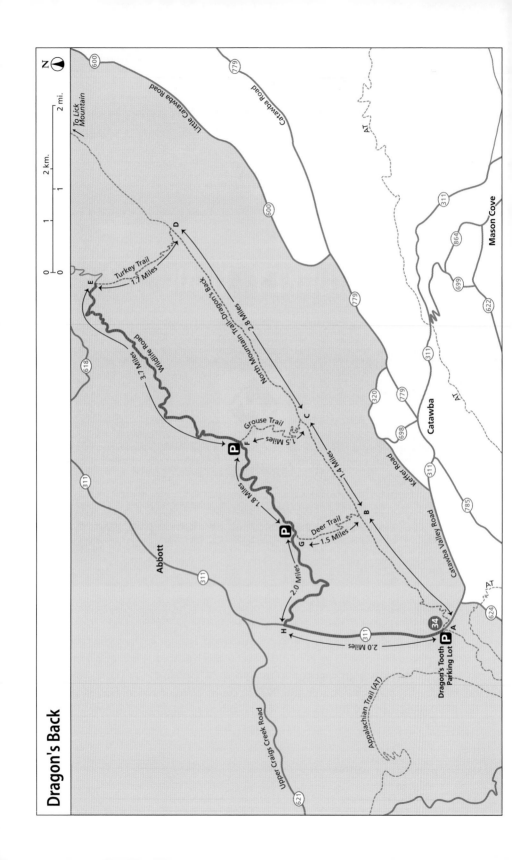

Miles and Directions

Below are several options on how to tackle this ride. All intersections are clearly marked, and since there all but three turn off points, I'll let you decide which to take.

The riding area is basically configured as a rectangle with three perpendicular trails connecting the "long" sides. Those "long edges" are the actual Dragon's Back (North Mountain) ridge trail on the high side, and Wildlife Road (gravel) on the low side. To the south, Rte. 311 (Catawba Drive) marks one of the "short" edges, and to the northwest is Turkey Trail closing things out. In between are Deer and Grouse.

Option #1

If you are a masochist, or looking to painfully punish yourself for some dirty deed, then park at the Dragon's Tooth trailhead along Rte. 311 and take the North Mountain Trail #263 up to the ridge. Simply exit the parking area, cross Rte. 311 and turn right to connect with the trailhead on the other side. Depending on the time of year, spotting the trailhead may be difficult. Tall grasses often obscure the entrance point in the summer; the trailhead is about 100 yards to the right as you come out of the parking area. Once you enter the trail, you'll have a 1.2-mile slog up to the ridge; please contact me if you are able to ride all the way up; I'll buy you a beer. Once on top, follow the Dragon's Back (North Mountain) ridge trail down to Grouse or Turkey.

You'll notice I skip Deer. I do so because if you are going to suffer the climb from Rte. 311 to the ridge, then you might as well enjoy one of the longer descents to Wildlife Road. If you choose to go down Deer, you'll only savor a little over a mile of downhill through some seriously technical and difficult to negotiate switchbacks, whereas Grouse and Turkey will offer you a little more gravity-assisted riding—with a few of those technical switchbacks to keep you honest. Plus, the fun part of this ride, other than the descents, is actually riding the Dragon's Back.

Once you reach Wildlife Road (regardless of descent), turn left and head back east toward Deer Trail. At this point, you can choose the relatively "easy" gravel road to Rte. 311, or turn left and head up the wall that is Deer back up to the ridge. If you chose the latter, you'll be treated to a white-knuckle descent back to Rte. 311 along the North Mountain Trail, remember that climb at the beginning? Yes, you'll go down that.

Option #2

The parking area along Rte. 311 tends to be very busy with people heading out to the Appalachian Trail and the Dragon's Tooth. For that reason, many cyclists opt to park along Wildlife Road at the Deer or Grouse trailheads.

This is my preferred route. Park your vehicle at the base of Deer Trail and make your way up to the ridge. There will be plenty of hike a bike, but it's only a "short" 1.2 miles before you reach (sort of) the summit. Once at the ridge, turn left and continue to Grouse (1.4 miles); if you still have the legs continue to Turkey (2.8 miles). Grouse and Turkey are both great downhill rides, so regardless of which one you choose, you'll be treated to some phenomenal descending. Once at Wildlife Road, turn left and head back to your vehicle.

Option #3

Park and start your ride at the Grouse trailhead. This is the furthest point to which you can drive along Wildlife road. Ride up Grouse to the ridge and turn left to ride along the ridge (2.8 miles) to Turkey. Descend along Turkey and then turn left onto Wildlife Road to finish the ride.

Other Options...

You can easily extend distances by parking at the Dragon's Tooth parking area and riding along Rte. 311 to Wildlife Road and then picking one of the three trails, Deer, Grouse, or Turkey to get to the ridge, and then descend along another. Or climbing up North Mountain, descending along any of the three trails and returning along wildlife road to Rte. 311, you get the idea...

Ride Information

Local Information, Events, and Attractions

Visit Roanoke—www.visitroanokeva.com/
Downtown Roanoke—www.downtownroanoke.org

Bike Shops

East Coasters Bike Shop—eastcoasters.com
UnderDog Bikes—www.underdogbikesva.com
Just the Right Gear—justtherightgear.com

Restaurants

Fork in the Alley—www.forkinthealley.rocks
Billy's Barn—www.facebook.com/Billys-Barn-220993324614802
Mac and Bobs—macandbobs.com
Wasena City Tap Room and Grill—www.wasenacitytaproom.com
Parkway Brewing Company—parkwaybrewing.com
Big Lick Brewing Company—biglickbrewingco.com

Restrooms

Available at the Dragon's Tooth parking area.

35 Spec Mines/Dody Ridge

Often overlooked, the Spec Mines and Dody Ridge trails are two of the best destinations in the Roanoke area. Ridden individually, or as part of a figure 8 loop (described here), these trails are bound to become two of your favorite go-to rides.

Start: Start form the Dry Creek parking area along Blackhorse Gap Road.
Length: 20.8 miles
Ride time: 3-4 hours
Difficulty: Advanced to expert. Difficult due to long climbs and technical singletrack descents.
Trail surface: Steep fire road climbs, fast and technical singletrack with two sections of pavement along the Blue Ridge Parkway.
Lay of the land: Mountainous roads and technical singletrack trails

Land status: Public
Nearest town: Roanoke
Other trail users: Hikers, trail runners, horseback riders
Trail contacts: Jefferson National Forest, www.fs.usda.gov/gwj/; Roanoke IMBA, www.roanokeimba.org
Schedule: Open year-round
Fees: Free to public

Getting there: From Roanoke, take Rte. 221 N/460 E for approximately 10 miles to Camp Jaycee Road. Turn left on Camp Jaycee Road and continue for approximately 0.75 miles to Blackhorse Gap Road. Turn left on Blackhorse Gap Road and then left again to enter the Dry Creek Recreation Area, park here. **GPS coordinates:** 37.40883, -79.74838.

The Ride

When most people mention Roanoke Mountain biking, the trails at Mill Mountain, Carvins Cove, and Dragon's Back are what generally come to mind. But there is so much more to this southwestern Virginia destination than meets the eye.

The folks at Roanoke IMBA have been cooking up plans to make Roanoke an IMBA designated ride center. In the future, family-friendly and beginner trails will likely grace the land of Explorer's Park. Add to them the Mill Mountain urban trails, a network of 40+ miles of singletrack at Carvins, and the challenging trails at North Mountain. All together, they make up the endless adventures you can have in the Roanoke area.

Not to be overlooked are a couple of other very tasty morsels just waiting for you. Spec Mines and Dody Ridge, two singletrack downhills along the Blue Ridge Parkway, are sure to satisfy the appetites of most mountain bikers.

I came across this ride after driving down to Roanoke shortly after a long rain. I sought the advice of local cyclists and was convinced to head out to ride this local favorite with one of the area's residents—Carter Shumaker. He gracefully offered to show me one of his preferred loops, and so off we went to ride Spec Mines and Dody Ridge.

The Spec Mines Trail gets its name from the town slightly to the north of our ride. The area is known for the iron ore crystals, specular hematite, that was once mined around its vicinity. Spec, a once thriving mining community, is today just a few homes and abandoned buildings. Shortly after the mines closed in the early part of the twentieth century, many of its mining residents left in search for other economic opportunities. A few families remained, and continue to call this small corner of Southwestern Virginia home.

The Specs Mine Trail could easily be renamed the "Spec-tacular trail." Hitting this ribbon after the long climb from Dry Creek, and the pavement spin along the Blue Ridge Parkway, will make any discomfort felt in the ascent disappear. The trail is simply a mountain biker's dream. Once you enter the trail, it will descend quickly as it hugs the contours. Its smooth shale surface, reminiscent of trails at Douthat State Park, will allow you to pick up speed quickly. Use caution though, because the trail is actually very narrow and can be intimidating in places. About two-thirds into the

The road section along this loop is worthwhile, the views from the Blue Ridge Parkway are spectacular.

Specs Mine & Dody Ridge

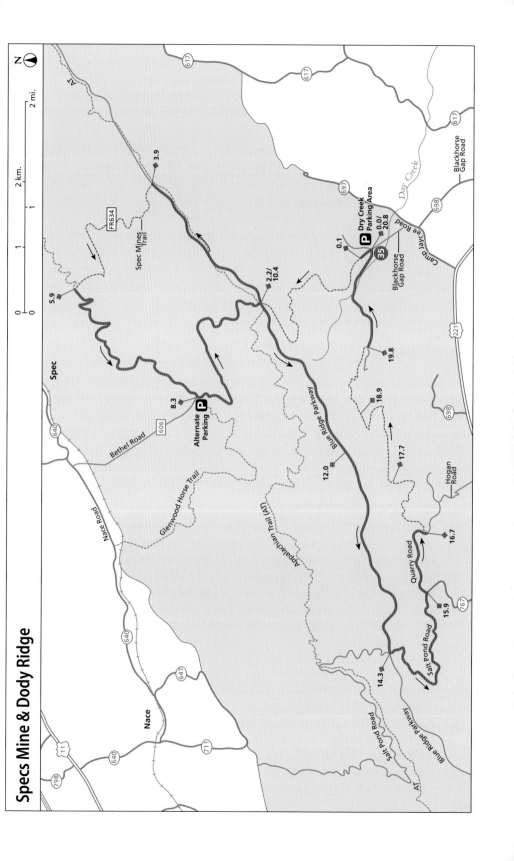

descent, the trail will turn loose a technical before turning sharply right. The final third will smooth out once again and deliver you to the Forest Service Road.

The next portion of the ride will give you ample time to think about what you just rode and prepare you for the next morsel, Dody Ridge.

To put it mildly, Dody is a somewhat different than Spec Mines. Once you hit the ridge, you'll have to negotiate the technical limestone surface of the trail. Riding will be considerably slower than it was at Spec Mines, but just as enjoyable and rewarding. The first portion of the ridge ride is generally flat and offers great views of the Roanoke Valley below. You'll have to stop to admire them, because concentrating on the trail will require all of your attention.

Before you know it, the trail will begin a maddening descent over some of the toughest, loose, and rocky trails in the region. Lots of Roanoke riders I spoke with told me that they come to Dody for the "Dragon's back feel" closer to home. The assessment is somewhat accurate; I still contend that very little comes close to the brutality that is North Mountain. Either way, you will be tested, and once you hit the Forest Road at the end of the ride, just like at Spec Mines, you'll be wanting to ride it again.

Miles and Directions

The ride below can be ridden as two separate loops or combined for a nice long day on the saddle. Regardless of option, you'll start your culinary adventure from the Day Creek parking area along Blackhorse Gap Road. Like much of the riding in Roanoke, you must pay your dues before collecting the rewards, and this ride is no different.

We'll begin measuring from the entrance point to the parking area, there is a large sign marking this point. From here, head straight toward the forest road gate (same direction as you were driving in along Blackhorse Gap Road) to begin the arduous climb to the Blue Ridge Parkway.

0.0 Start from the Dry Creek parking area along Blackhorse Gap Road. The ride actually begins a little beyond the parking area along Blackhorse Gap Road along the first Forest Service gate. Continue along the road toward and through the forest road gate.

0.0 We'll begin measuring from the intersection of Blackhorse Road and the entrance to the parking area. Turn left along Blackhorse Gap Road and head toward the gate.

0.1 Go through the gate and get ready for a 2.2-mile grinder—no way out of this climb. Right before the gate, you'll notice the Blackhorse Gap Trail (3004) trailhead. This is an optional out and back.

2.2 You reach the Blue Ridge Parkway. Turn right and enjoy the views; be careful though, there is plenty of traffic along this stretch of road, and chances are some drivers will be a little distracted by the views. **Note:** If you only want to do Dody Ridge, turn left and follow the directions after mile marker 14.3.

2.4 Glance to the right and you can see the Peaks of Otter in the distance, including Sharp Top and Flat Top. Stones from the Peaks of Otter were set to Washington for the construction of the Washington Monument.

3.9 Pay attention to the left side of the road. Immediately after a wood railing, you'll see the entrance to the Spec Mines Trail. Cross the road and get ready for a phenomenal descent.

5.9 Everything we climbed is now gone, but what a reward! Turn left on FR 634 and enjoy the rollers; another climb is in the horizon.

8.3 You reach Glenwood Horse Trail. This is a three-way intersection and an alternate starting point to the ride. Make a sharp left to follow the high road. We'll begin the second long climb of the day. This is an alternate starting point for this ride.

10.4 You're back at the Blue Ridge Parkway. If you're spent, you can cross the road and continue straight down along the road we climbed at the beginning of the ride and tackle Dody Ridge another day. Otherwise, turn right to continue with the route.

12.0 You reach the Great Valley Overlook. Take a minute to soak in the views before you continue on along the parkway. From here, you can see other regional mountain bike destinations to the west, including Dragon's Back, Potts Mountain, and Bald Mountain. Visit www.MTBDC.com for additional details about this overlook.

14.3 You reach the intersection of Salt Pond Road and a Forest Service Road gated on both sides. Turn left and get ready to descend!

15.9 Turn left on Quarry Road.

16.7 Turn left onto the steep wide trail to the left, it's shortly after a house along the right.

17.7 Continue following the trail to the right, the climbing is over.

18.9 Stay to the left, the trail to the right takes you along the creek, the left branch is way more fun.

19.8 You reach a gravel road, this is Blackhorse Gap Road. Turn left and coast back down to the starting point.

20.8 You're back at the starting point, the loop is complete.

Ride Information

Local Information, Events, and Attractions

Visit Roanoke—www.visitroanokeva.com/
Downtown Roanoke—www.downtownroanoke.org

Bike Shops

East Coasters Bike Shop—eastcoasters.com
UnderDog Bikes—www.underdogbikesva.com
Just the Right Gear—justtherightgear.com

Restaurants

Fork in the Alley—www.forkinthealley.rocks
Billy's Barn—www.facebook.com/Billys-Barn-220993324614802
Mac and Bobs—macandbobs.com
Wasena City Tap Room and Grill—www.wasenacitytaproom.com
Parkway Brewing Company—parkwaybrewing.com
Big Lick Brewing Company—biglickbrewingco.com

Restrooms

Available at the Dry Creek parking area.

Honorable Mentions

Compiled here is an index of great rides in Virginia's Mountain and Shenandoah Valley region that didn't make the A list this time around but deserve recognition. Check them out and let us know what you think. You may decide that one or more of these rides deserves higher status in future editions, or perhaps you may have a ride of your own that merits some attention. Some of these rides are documented on our website, www.mtbdc.com

R. The Southern Traverse: The Southern Traverse is one of IMBA's classic Epic rides. The loop is just shy of 40 miles and is one that requires your absolute commitment, since it will take you to what Burg locals call the "backcountry." The loop, best ridden in a counterclockwise direction, starts from Deerfield Valley along a 4-mile climb on FSR 173. Take VA Rte. 629 for approximately 6 miles south from the Hankey Mountain Highway, Rte. 250. Turn right on FR 173 (easy to miss!) and continue on for a little under a mile to the small parking area and gate on the left. Begin the ride by climbing up along the trail beyond the gate to the left. You'll climb for approximately 4 miles to the entrance of the Shenandoah Mountain Trail; turn left (south) and enjoy the ridge ride. Once you commit to the ridge, you will have ridden it for about 11 miles before you begin the grin-inducing descent back to VA Rte. 629. Once on VA 629, turn left to head back along the road to the starting point, approximately 13 miles. Around the 14th mile of the ride, you'll reach the Jerkemtight forest road. The Shenandoah Mountain Trail continues in a southerly direction and is haphazardly marked. I recommend you ride this trail in the fall or winter when the overgrowth is at a minimum.
GPS coordinates: 38.21838, −79.39101

S. Longdale Recreation Area—North Mountain: Until the early twentieth century, Longdale Furnace, just west of Lexington, was known for its iron ore, limestone, and charcoal furnaces. Today, it is known for its trails. North Mountain is a 15-mile loop that starts at a small parking area along Rte. 770, Collierstown Road. From I-64, take the exit for Longdale Road heading west; turn left on State Rte. 770 and the parking area will be approximately 1 mile to your right. The ride begins with a gravel climb along state Rte. 770 to the entrance to the North Mountain Trail. At around the 3-mile mark, you will need to make a sharp right and begin to look for the North Mountain Trailhead to your right. The trail will follow the ridge for about 5 miles at which point you'll make another sharp right to descend back toward Longdale Road along an off-camber ravine trail. Both the ridge and descent are typical GWNF riding. The ridge has the usual ups and downs (speed scrubbers), and the descent can be sketchy in places. The ride has some really cool rock formations along the highest points of the ride, including Pete's Cave.
GPS coordinates: 37.81148, −79.6659

T. Whetstone Ridge—Whetstone Ridge is full of what the guys in the Burg call "speed scrubbers." These are uphills along a ridge ride that eat up all the speed you've gained on a descent and force you to slog up a hill; that puts it mildly. Whetstone Ridge is pretty brutal, after all, it's near Vesuvius, VA. The climbs are steep; the descents are steep; but everything in between is glorious and worth the effort. The loop at Whetstone is best done in a counterclockwise direction from the trailhead just north of mile 29 of the Blue Ridge Parkway. The ride starts [deceptively] with a smooth singletrack climb that transitions into, as my buddy Mark Humbertson loves to call them— "a series of walls," before finishing off with a tight and fast singletrack downhill to Irish Creek Road. Mark's "walls" consist of six hike-a-bikes that run along the spine of the punishing backcountry ridge. Each of these brutal sections, however, has some fantastic views that make the effort worthwhile. Whetstone is a true backcountry ride, so be prepared if you do venture out to explore its trails. And don't head out alone, after all, misery loves company. The ride can be easily done as a shuttle if you want to avoid the punishing climb back to the starting point along Irish Creek Road.

GPS coordinates: 37.86908, −79.14861

U. Falling Creek Park—Less than an hour west of Roanoke, and only minutes off of Rte. 460 along Falling Creek Road, is Falling Creek Park in Bedford, VA. The park is known for having one of the best skate parks in the state, and is quickly making a name for itself in mountain bike circles. The addition of a little over 10 miles of natural surface trails, along with a bike park where riders can work on their skills, is helping put this regional park on the state's mountain biking map. The majority of the trails are smooth and suitable for all levels of riders and can be ridden in either direction. Several "expert" trails include jumps and berms that the more advanced riders will love to session over and over. If you are in the region, and are looking to kill a couple of hours on some super fun purpose-built mountain bike trails, then definitely put Falling Creek on your agenda.

GPS coordinates: 37.31108, −79.49864

V. Mountain Lake—The Mountain Lake Conservancy, just north west of Blacksburg, manages a little over 2,500 acres along a 400-feet mountain plateau in the Jefferson National Forest. The nearly 15 miles of trails within the conservancy's property are open to bikes and are suitable for all rider levels. In order to ride the trails, you will need to purchase/donate a daily entrance fee, or purchase an annual trail access pass from the Lake Conservancy office. Detailed trail maps are also available for purchase. If you happen to find yourself in the area without a bike, you can rent one from the Conservancy. Additional information about the trails and the Mountain Lake Conservancy's mission can be found at http://mtnlakeconservancy.com.

GPS coordinates: 37.3556, −80.53527

W. Explore Park—Located about 20 minutes from Downtown Roanoke, along milepost 115 of the Blue Ridge Parkway, and the banks of the Roanoke River, is a 1,100-acre county park with approximately 9 miles of IMBA-certified mountain bike trails for all levels of riders. As part of Roanoke IMBA's effort to become an IMBA Ride Center, Explore Park should be getting some new amenities, including a new skills area and a pump track. With the exception of an expert trail's descent to the Roanoke River, most of the trails in Explore Park follow the contours along a typical Blue Ridge hardwood forest. Explore Park offers an easier alternative to the otherwise rugged and difficult nearby trails in Jefferson National Forest. In addition, the mountain bike trails in Explore Park aren't the only things available; there are hiking trails, river frontage, historical buildings, and a visitor information center to help you plan your activities.

GPS coordinates: 37.23819, −79.85122

X. Mill Mountain—There are very few cities in the Old Dominion that can boast about public riding opportunities available to mountain bikers within its city limits. Residents of Harrisonburg and Richmond, along with those living in Roanoke, are really fortunate to have world-class trail systems readily available from their doorsteps. In Harrisonburg, there's the Rocktown trails at Hillandale Park (Ride 28); in Richmond, the vast network of trails along the James River (Ride 12), and in Roanoke—the Star of the South—Mill Mountain. Every rider I met when visiting this Southwestern Virginia destination raved about the trails on the mountain in the middle of the city. Mill Mountain has approximately 10 miles of intermediate to advanced trails virtually minutes away from the downtown Roanoke area. On average, riders can be enjoying the trails on Mill Mountain within a 15-minute ride from their doorstep. What's even more remarkable about this urban park is that the mountain offers riders high quality trails; you can bust out some serious climbs and get rewarded with an equally serious descent. Advanced riders love it because it provides them with a technically challenging ride they can hit without the need to hop in a car. The trails at Mill Mountain can be accessed from several locations in the city, but one of the most popular is along SE Riverland Road, just west of Garden City Boulevard. If you must drive, that's where you'll find a small parking area from which to access the trails. Once you reach the summit, at 1,703 feet, take a moment to enjoy the panoramic views of Roanoke from one of the available overlooks. Mill Mountain is also well known for the star perched atop its summit. The Roanoke Star is the world's largest free-standing illuminated man-made star and can be seen from as far as 60 miles away.

GPS coordinates: 37.249862, −79.935573 (Riverland Road Parking area: 37.249324, −79.921861)

Y. Candler Mountain—Located on the grounds of Liberty University in Lynchburg, the Candler Mountain Trial system includes over 50 miles of singletrack, doubletrack, and logging roads within 5,000 acres open to hiking, running, and mountain biking. Although the trails are on private property, they are open for individual use year-round during daylight hours. The trails generally run from the top of the ridge to the base of the mountain. The lower dam trails tend to be smoother and flatter than those closer to the ridge. Expect tough climbs as you make your way to the top, as well as fast and technical descents on the way down. Several of the trails include TTFs. The system can be accessed from several locations including along Candler Mountain Road from the Snowflex lot, and from Hydaway Lake along Camp Hydaway Road. For additional information, maps, and access information visit the Liberty University Website: www.liberty.edu/snowflex/trails-maps/.

GPS coordinates: 37.352887, −79.167884

Gravity-Assisted Mountain Biking

Ski resorts offer a great alternative to local trail riding. During the spring, summer, and fall, many resorts open their trails for mountain biking, and just like during ski season, sell lift tickets to take you and your bike to the top of the mountain. Lodging is also available for weekend mountain bike junkies, and rates are often discounted from the normal ski-season prices. Some resorts even rent bikes and lead guided mountain bike tours. Call ahead to find out just what each resort offers in the way of mountain bike riding, and pick the one that best suits your fancy.

The following is a list of many of the ski resorts near the Washington, D.C./Baltimore area that say yes! to mountain biking when the weather turns too warm for skiing.

Bryce

Basye, VA
www.bryceresort.com

Massanutten Mountain

Harrisonburg, VA
www.massresort.com

Wintergreen

Waynesboro, VA
www.wintergreenresort.com

The Homestead

Hot Springs, VA
www.thehomestead.com

Snowshoe

Marlinton, WV
www.snowshoemtn.com

Timberline

Davis, WV
www.timberlineresort.com/Summer14/

Canaan Valley

Davis, WV
canaanresort.com

Wisp

McHenry, MD
www.wispresort.com

Rails to Trails

The mission of the Rails-to-Trails Conservancy is to "enhance America's communities and country side by converting thousands of miles of abandoned rail corridors and connecting open spaces into a nationwide network of public trails."

Every large city and small town in America, by the early twentieth century, was connected by steel and railroad ties. By 1916, the United States had laid over 250,000 miles of track across the country, giving it the world's largest rail system. Since then, other forms of transportation, such as cars, trucks, and airplanes have diminished the importance of the railroad, and that impressive network of rail lines has shrunk to less than 150,000 miles. Railroad companies abandon more than 2,000 miles of track each year, leaving unused rail corridors overgrown and idle.

It wasn't until the 1960s that the idea to refurbish these abandoned rail corridors into usable footpaths and trails was introduced. In 1963, work began in Chicago and its suburbs on a 55-mile stretch of abandoned right-of-way to create the Illinois Prairie Path.

In 1986, the Rails-to-Trails Conservancy was founded, its mission specifically to help communities realize their dreams of having a usable rail corridor for recreation and non-motorized travel. At the time the Conservancy began operations, only 100 open rail-trails existed. Today, nearly 2,000 trails are open to the public, totaling more than 22,000 miles of converted pathways. The Rails-to-Trails Conservancy is currently working on more than 700 additional rails-to-trails projects with a potential of an additional 8,200 miles of potential trails.

Ultimately, its goal is to see a completely interconnected system of trails through-out the United States. If you are interested in learning more about rails-to-trails and wish to support the conservancy, please contact:

Rails-to-Trails Conservancy
1100 17th Street, NW
Washington, D.C. 20036
(202) 331-9696
www.railstrails.org
railstrails@transact.org

RTT—1: The VA Creeper Trail

The Virginia Creeper Trail, one of America's premier rail-to-trails, begins in Abing-don and stretches for 34 miles to the Virginia–North Carolina Border. The trail passes through striking scenery along some of Southwestern Virginia's most rugged lands. The VA Creeper Trail can be accessed at several locations along its length, but the most popular entry points are found along Abingdon and Damascus. From the VA Creeper Trail, you can access the Iron Mountain Trail within the Mount Rogers Recreation Area. Additional information about the VA Creeper Trail can be found at www.vacreepertrail.org.

GPS coordinates:

36.709201, –81.971487 (Abingdon Terminus)

36.591044, –81.619032 (Dolinger Road Terminus)

RTT—2: Guest River Gorge Trail

The gentle grades and gravel surfaces of the Guest River Gorge Trail make it an ideal place for beginner mountain bikers and families to spend an afternoon on the saddle. There are several benches along the trail's length that present riders with the perfect opportunity to enjoy the natural beauty of the Guest River Gorge. The trail was opened to the public in 1994 after the Norfolk and Southern Railroad donated the abandoned railway right-of-way to the Forest Service. The trail is only 5.8 miles out and back, and it meanders along the edge of the Jefferson National Forest with great views of the Guest River. Striking rock formations along the way, including a trip through the Swede Tunnel, have made the Guest River Gorge Trail a popular regional destination. Near the trail's end, at the confluence of the Guest and Clinch Rivers, you'll find an access point to the Heart of Appalachia Bike Route, which extends for 125 miles to Burke's Garden in Tazewell County. The trail has one access point along FR 2477 just south of Coeburn, Virginia and Alt. US 58. For additional information visit www.fs.usda.gov/gwj

GPS coordinates: 36.92332, –82.45171

RTT–3: Jackson River Scenic Trail

The Jackson River Scenic Trail, a crushed stone trail just north of Covington, meanders north along the banks of the Jackson River for nearly 14 miles through the beautiful Alleghany Highlands. The trail starts at Intervale and is easy to access from Hot Springs Road (Rte. 220). The trail, which runs along an old Chesapeake and Ohio Railway bed, travels through several wooded patches, small communities, and cultivated fields on its way toward Cedar Creek and the Lake Moomaw area. Highlights along the trail include rocky cliffs, waterfalls, mountain views, and plenty of wildlife. Like many other rail-to-trails, it is perfect for beginners and families looking for a mellow day on the bike. For additional information visit www.jacksonrivertrail.com

GPS coordinates:

37.8196, −79.98683 (Intervale trailhead)

37.84122, −79.98909 (Petticoat Junction)

RTT–4: New River Trail State Park

The New River Trail State Park is a 57-mile linear park in Southwestern Virginia. The trail follows the New River for nearly 40 miles and runs through the city of Galax and four Southwestern Virginia Counties, including Grayson, Carroll, Wythe, and Pulaski. Like other rail-to-trails in Virginia and around the country, the New River Trail's gentle slope is perfect for beginner cyclists and families looking to spend the day enjoying the outdoors. Along the trail's length, visitors can enjoy several historic landmarks, including two tunnels, three major bridges, nearly 30 smaller trestles and bridges, as well as a shot tower that was used to make ammunition for early settler firearms. The 75-foot tower, which was built over a seven-year period by a local miner, Thomas Jackson, was completed in 1807. Lead was melted at the tower's top room and fell nearly 150 feet to a cooling kettle deep underground. The fall, through different-sized sieves, produced shot of varying sizes that was sold to local settlers. The trail can be accessed from several locations along its length including the cities of Galax, Pulaski, and Fries. For additional information visit www.dcr.virginia .gov/state-parks/new-river-trail

GPS coordinates:

36.66828, −80.92504 (Galax)

37.04545, −80.74939 (Pulaski)

36.71523, −80.97696 (Fries)

36.87005, −80.8703 (Shot Tower)

RTT–5: Richmond and Danville Trail

The Richmond and Danville rail-to-trail, also known as the Ringgold Trail, follows a 5.5 mile east to west portion of the right-of-way of the old railroad of the same name. The Richmond Danville Railroad once served as a critical supply link between Danville and Richmond during the Civil War. The railroad was used by the retreating confederate leadership at the end of the Civil War (See Ride 16). The historic route between Ringgold and Sutherlin in southern Virginia just east of Danville passes through light woodlands and rural farmlands. It is an easy-to-ride flat path that is perfect for families and beginner cyclists. For additional information visit www .pittsylvaniacountyva.gov/479/Ringgold-Rail-Trail

GPS coordinates:

36.60763, −79.29735 (Ringgold)

36.62452, −79.19984 (Sutherlin)

RTT–6: Wilderness Rail Trail

In 1775, local legend and pioneer Daniel Boone blazed a Wilderness Road through the Appalachian Mountains across the Cumberland Gap from North Carolina and Tennessee into Kentucky. There he founded the village of Boonesborough, one of the first settlements west of the Appalachians. Before the end of the eighteenth century, over 200,000 Americans would follow the same route to migrate to the western fringes of Virginia. Later, that same route would become a part of the Louisville & Nashville Railroad, and today it has been transformed into a scenic rail-to-trail. Throughout its east to west path, the 8.5-mile trail parallels sections of US 58, often venturing far from the highway behind the treeline and through rural farmlands.

GPS coordinates:

36.60256, −83.6282 (Cumberland Gap)

36.63259, −83.48927 (Wilderness Road)

Fat-Tire Vacations

Virginia Touring Companies

There are literally dozens of off-road bicycling tour companies offering an incredible variety of guided tours for mountain bikers. On these pay-as-you-pedal fat-tire vacations, you will have a chance to go places around the globe that only an expert can take you. Your experiences will be much different than those you can have sitting in a tour bus.

From hut to hut in the Colorado Rockies or inn to inn through Vermont's Green Mountains, there is a tour company for you. Whether you want hard-core singletrack during the day and camping at night or scenic trails followed by a bottle of wine at night and a mint on each pillow, someone out there offers what you're looking for. The tours are well organized and fully supported with expert guides, bike mechanics, and "sag wagons" that carry gear, food, and tired bodies. Prices range from

$100 to $500 for a weekend to more than $2,000 for two-week-long trips to far-off lands such as New Zealand or Ireland. Each of these companies will gladly send you their free literature to whet your appetite with breathtaking photography and titillating stories of each tour.

Selected Touring Companies

Elk River Touring Center
Slatyfork, WV
ertc.com

Roanoke Mountain Adventures (RMA)
Roanoke, VA
www.roanokemountainadventures.com

Shenandoah Touring Company
Harrisonburg, VA
mtntouring.com

The Art of Mountain Biking

Everything you need to know about off-road bicycling in the Old Dominion can be found in this book. This section explores the fascinating history of the mountain bike itself and discusses everything from the health benefits of off-road cycling to tips and techniques for bicycling over logs and up hills. Also included are descriptions of the types of clothing that will keep you comfortable and riding in style; essential equipment ideas to keep your rides smooth and trouble-free; and explanations of off-road terrain, which will prepare you for the kinds of bumps and bounces you can expect to encounter.

The mountain bike, with its knobby tread and reinforced frame, takes cyclists to places once unheard of—down rugged mountain trails, through streams of rushing water, across the frozen Alaskan tundra, and even to work in the city. There are few limits on what this fat-tired beast can do and where it can take us. Few obstacles stand in its way, few boundaries slow its progress. Except for one—its own success. If trail closure means little to you now, read on and discover how a trail can be here today and gone tomorrow. With so many new off-road cyclists taking to the trails each year, it's no wonder trail access has become a contentious issue. A little education about the issue and some effort on your part can go a long way toward preserving trail access for future use. Nothing is more crucial to the survival of mountain biking itself than to read the examples set forth in this book and practice their message.

Without open trails, the maps in this book are virtually useless. Cyclists must learn to be responsible for the trails they use and to share these trails with others. This guidebook addresses why trail use has become so controversial and what can be done to improve the image of mountain biking. We also cover how to have fun and ride responsibly, how to do on-the-spot trail-repair techniques. And we provide trail maintenance hot lines for each trail and the worldwide-standard rules of the trail.

Mountain Bike Beginnings

It seems the mountain bike, originally designed for lunatic adventurists bored with straight lines, clean clothes, and smooth tires has become globally popular in the time it takes to race down a mountain trail.

Like many things of a revolutionary nature, the mountain bike was born on the West Coast. But unlike in-line skates, purple hair, and the peace sign, the concept of the off-road bike cannot be credited solely to imaginative Californians—they were just the first to make waves.

The design of the first off-road-specific bike was based on the geometry of the old Schwinn Excelsior, a one-speed, camel-back cruiser with balloon tires. Joe Breeze was the creator behind it, and in 1977, he built ten of these "Breezers" for himself and his Marin County, California, friends at $750 apiece—a bargain.

Breeze was a serious competitor in bicycle racing, placing thirteenth in the 1977 US Road Racing National Championships. After races, he and friends would scour local bike shops, hoping to find old bikes they could then restore.

It was the 1941 Schwinn Excelsior, for which Breeze paid just $5, that began to shape and change bicycling history forever. After taking the bike home, removing the fenders, oiling the chain, and pumping up the tires, Breeze hit the dirt. He loved it.

His inspiration, though prescient, was not altogether unique. On the opposite end of the country, nearly 2,500 miles from Marin County, East Coast bike bums were also growing restless. More and more old beat-up clunkers were being restored and modified. These behemoths often weighed as much as eighty pounds and were so reinforced they seemed virtually indestructible. But rides that take just 40 minutes on today's 25-pound featherweights took the steel-toed-boot and blue-jean-clad bikers of the late 1970s and early 1980s nearly 4 hours to complete.

Not until 1981 was it possible to purchase a production mountain bike, but local retailers found these ungainly bicycles difficult to sell and rarely kept them in stock. By 1983, however, mountain bikes were no longer such a fringe item, and large bike manufacturers quickly jumped into the action, producing their own versions of the off-road bike. By the 1990s, the mountain bike had firmly established its place with bicyclists of nearly all ages and abilities. Mountain bikes now command nearly 90 percent of the US bike market.

There are many reasons for the mountain bike's success in becoming the hottest two-wheeled vehicle in the nation. They are much friendlier to the cyclist than traditional road bikes because of their comfortable upright position and shock-absorbing fat tires. And because of the health-conscious, environmentalist movement of the late 1980s and 1990s, people are more activity minded and seek nature on a closer front than paved roads can allow. The mountain bike gives you these things and takes you far away from the daily grind—even if you're only minutes from the city.

Mountain Biking into Shape

If your objective is to get in shape and lose weight, then you're on the right track, because mountain biking is one of the best ways to get started.

One way many of us have lost weight in this sport is the crash-and-burn-it-off method. Picture this: You're speeding uncontrollably down a vertical drop that you realize you shouldn't be on—only after it is too late. Your front wheel lodges into a rut and launches you through endless weeds, trees, and pointy rocks before you come to an abrupt halt in a puddle of thick mud. Surveying the damage, you discover, with the layers of skin, body parts, and lost confidence littering the trail above, that those unwanted pounds have been shed—permanently. Instant weight loss.

There is, of course, a more conventional (and quite a bit less painful) approach to losing weight and gaining fitness on a mountain bike. It's called the workout, and bicycles provide an ideal way to get physical. Take a look at some of the benefits associated with cycling.

Cycling helps you shed pounds without gimmicky diet fads or weight-loss programs. You can explore the countryside and burn nearly 10–16 calories per minute or close to 600–1,000 calories per hour. Moreover, it's a great way to spend an afternoon.

No less significant than the external and cosmetic changes of your body from riding are the internal changes taking place. Over time, cycling regularly will strengthen your heart as your body grows vast networks of new capillaries to carry blood to all those working muscles. This will, in turn, give your skin a healthier glow. The capacity of your lungs may increase up to 20 percent, and your resting heart rate will drop significantly. The Stanford University School of Medicine reports to the American Heart Association that people can reduce their risk of heart attack by nearly 64 percent if they burn up to 2,000 calories per week. This is only 2–3 hours of bike riding!

Recommended for insomnia, hypertension, indigestion, anxiety, and even recuperation from major heart attacks, bicycling can be an excellent cure-all as well as a great preventive. Cycling just a few hours per week can improve your figure and sleeping habits, give you greater resistance to illness, increase your energy levels, and provide feelings of accomplishment and heightened self-esteem.

Be Safe—Know the Law

Occasionally, even hard-core off-road cyclists will find they have no choice but to ride the pavement. When you are forced to hit the road, it's important for you to know and understand the rules.

Outlined below are a few of the common laws found in Virginia, as well as some common-sense ideas.

- In Virginia, you can pedal on any paved public road except urban freeways.
- Follow the same driving rules as motorists. Be sure to obey all road signs and traffic lights.
- Wear a helmet and bright clothing so that you are more visible to motorists. Bright colors such as orange and lime green are highly visible at night.
- Equip your bike with lights and wear reflective clothing at night. When riding at night, the bicycle or rider must be equipped with a white light visible at least 500 feet to the front and a red light or reflector visible at least 600 feet to the rear.
- Pass motorists on the left, not the right. Motorists are not expecting you to pass on the right, and they may not see you.
- Ride single file on busy roads so motorists can pass you safely.
- Use hand signals to show motorists what you plan on doing next.
- Ride with the traffic, not against it.
- Follow painted lane markings.
- Make eye contact with drivers. Assume they don't see you until you are sure they do.

- Ride in the middle of the lane at busy intersections and whenever you are moving the same speed as traffic.
- Slow down and announce your presence when passing pedestrians, cyclists, and horses.
- Turn left by looking back, signaling, getting into the left lane, and turning. In urban situations, walk your bike across the crosswalk when the pedestrian walk sign is illuminated.
- Never ride while under the influence of alcohol or drugs. Remember that DUI laws apply when you're riding a bicycle.
- Avoid riding in extremely foggy, rainy, or windy conditions.
- Watch out for parallel-slat sewer grates, slippery manhole covers, oily pavement, gravel, wet leaves, and ice.
- Cross railroad tracks at a right angle. Be especially careful when it's wet out. For better control as you move across bumps and other hazards, stand up on your pedals.
- Don't ride too close to parked cars—a person opening a car door may hit you.
- Avoid riding on sidewalks. Instead, walk your bike. Pedestrians have the right-of-way on walkways. By law, you must give pedestrians audible warning when you pass. Use a bike bell or announce clearly "On your left/right."
- Slow down at street crossings and driveways.

The Mountain Bike Controversy

Are off-road bicyclists environmental outlaws? Do we have the right to use public trails?

Mountain bikers have long endured the animosity of folks in the backcountry who complain about the consequences of off-road bicycling. Many people believe that fat tires and knobby treads do unacceptable environmental damage and that our uncontrollable riding habits are a danger to animals and other trail users. To the contrary, mountain bikes have no more environmental impact than hiking boots or horseshoes. This does not mean, however, that mountain bikes leave no imprint at all. Wherever people tread, there is an impact. By riding responsibly, though, it is possible to leave only a minimum impact—something we all must take care to achieve.

Unfortunately, it is often people of great influence who view the mountain bike as the environment's worst enemy. Consequently, we as mountain bike riders and environmentally concerned citizens must be educators, impressing upon others that we also deserve the right to use these trails. Our responsibilities as bicyclists are no more and no less than any other trail user. We must all take the soft-cycling approach and show that mountain bicyclists are not environmental outlaws.

Etiquette of Mountain Biking

When discussing mountain biking etiquette, we are in essence discussing the soft-cycling approach. This term refers to the art of minimum-impact bicycling and should apply to both the physical and social dimensions of the sport. But make no mistake—it is possible to ride fast and furiously while maintaining the balance of soft-cycling. Here are a few ways to minimize the physical impact of mountain bike riding:

- Stay on the trail. Don't ride around fallen trees or mud holes that block your path. Stop and cross over them. When you come to a vista overlooking a deep valley, don't ride off the trail for a better vantage point. Instead, leave the bike and walk to see the view. Riding off the trail may seem inconsequential when done only once, but soon someone else will follow, then others, and the cumulative results can be catastrophic. Each time you wander from the trail, you begin creating a new path, adding one more scar to the earth's surface.

- Do not disturb the soil. Follow a line within the trail that will not disturb or damage the soil.

- Do not ride over soft or wet trails. After a rain shower or during the thawing season, trails will often resemble muddy, oozing swampland. The best thing to do is stay off the trails altogether. Realistically, however, we're all going to come across some muddy trails we cannot anticipate. Instead of blasting through each section of mud, which may seem both easier and more fun, lift the bike and walk past. Each time a cyclist rides through a soft or muddy section of trail, that part of the trail is permanently damaged. Regardless of the trail's conditions, though, remember always to go over the obstacles across the path, not around them. Stay on the trail. Keep the singletrack "single."

- Avoid trails that, for all but God, are considered impassable and impossible. Don't take a leap of faith down a kamikaze descent on which you will be forced to lock your brakes and skid to the bottom, ripping the ground apart as you go.

- The concept of soft-cycling should apply to the social dimensions of the sport as well, since mountain bikers are not the only folks who use the trails. Hikers, equestrians, cross-country skiers, and other outdoors people use many of the same trails and can be easily spooked by a marauding mountain biker tearing through the trees. Be friendly in the forest and give ample warning of your approach.

- Take out what you bring in. Don't leave broken bike pieces and banana peels scattered along the trail.

- Be aware of your surroundings. Don't use popular hiking trails for race training.

- Slow down! Rocketing around blind corners is a sure way to ruin an unsuspecting hiker's day. Consider this: If you fly down a quick singletrack descent at 20 miles per hour, then hit the brakes and slow down to only 6 miles per hour to pass someone, you're still moving twice as fast as the hiker!

Like the trails we ride on, the social dimension of mountain biking is very fragile and must be cared for responsibly. We should not want to destroy another person's enjoyment of the outdoors. By riding in the backcountry with caution, control, and responsibility, our presence should be felt positively by other trail users. By adhering to these rules, trail riding—a privilege that can quickly be taken away—will continue to be ours to share.

Trail Maintenance

Unfortunately, despite all the preventive measures taken to avoid trail damage, we're still going to run into many trails requiring attention. Simply put, a lot of hikers, equestrians, and cyclists use the same trails—some wear and tear is unavoidable. But like your bike, if you want to use these trails for a long time to come, you must also maintain them.

Trail maintenance and restoration can be accomplished in a variety of ways. One way is for mountain bike clubs to combine efforts with other trail users (hikers and equestrians) and work closely with land managers to cut new trails or repair existing ones. This work not only reinforces to others the commitment cyclists have in caring for and maintaining the land, but it also breaks the ice that often separates cyclists from their fellow trail mates. Another good way to help out is to show up on a Saturday morning with a few riding buddies, ready to work at your favorite off-road domain. With a good attitude, thick gloves, and the local land manager's supervision, trail repair is fun and very rewarding. It's important, of course, that you arrange a trail-repair outing with the local land manager before you start pounding shovels into the dirt. Managers can lead you to the neediest sections of trail and instruct you on what repairs should be done and how best to accomplish the task. Perhaps the most effective way to help maintain your local trails is to reach out and join your local mountain bike advocacy group. Organizations like The Mid Atlantic Off-Road Enthusiasts (MORE), The Frederick Area Mountain Bike Enthusiasts (FAMBE), the Fredericksburg Area Trail Users Group (FATMUG), Eastern Shore IMBA (ESIMBA), and Southern Maryland Mountain Bike (SMMB) have taken the lead to make sure our region's trails are maintained properly. These advocacy and social groups have packed calendars with rides and trail days in which you can easily participate. Check the Regional Clubs and organizations section of this guide for contact information for the area's most prominent and active clubs to see how you can help them help you keep riding.

Rules of the Trail

The International Mountain Bicycling Association (IMBA) has developed these guidelines to trail riding. These "rules of the trail" are accepted worldwide and will go a long way in keeping trails open. Please respect and follow these rules for everyone's sake.

1. Ride only on open trails. Respect trail and road closures (if you're not sure, ask a park or state official first), do not trespass on private property, and obtain permits or authorization if required. Federal and state wilderness areas are

off-limits to cycling. Parks and state forests may also have certain trails closed to cycling.

2. Leave no trace. Be sensitive to the dirt beneath you. Even on open trails, you should not ride under conditions by which you will leave evidence of your passing, such as on certain soils or shortly after a rainfall. Be sure to observe the different types of soils and trails you're riding on, practicing minimum-impact cycling. Never ride off the trail, don't skid your tires, and be sure to bring out at least as much as you bring in.

3. Control your bicycle! Inattention for even one second can cause disaster for yourself or for others. Excessive speed frightens and can injure people, gives mountain biking a bad name, and can result in trail closures.

4. Always yield. Let others know you're coming well in advance (a friendly greeting is always good and often appreciated). Show your respect when passing others by slowing to walking speed or stopping altogether, especially in the presence of horses. Horses can be unpredictable, so be very careful. Anticipate that other trail users may be around corners or in blind spots.

5. Never spook animals. All animals are spooked by sudden movements, unannounced approaches, or loud noises. Give the animals extra room and time so they can adjust to you. Move slowly or dismount around animals. Running cattle and disturbing wild animals are serious offenses. Leave gates as you find them, or as marked.

6. Plan ahead. Know your equipment, your ability, and the area in which you are riding, and plan your trip accordingly. Be self-sufficient at all times, keep your bike in good repair, and carry necessary supplies for changes in weather or other conditions. You can help keep trails open by setting an example of responsible, courteous, and controlled mountain bike riding.

7. Always wear a helmet when you ride. For your own safety and protection, a helmet should be worn whenever you are riding your bike. You never know when a tree root or small rock will throw you the wrong way and send you tumbling.

Thousands of miles of dirt trails have been closed to mountain bicycling because of the irresponsible riding habits of just a few riders. Don't follow the example of these offending riders. Don't take away trail privileges from thousands of others who work hard each year to keep backcountry avenues open to us all.

The Necessities of Cycling

When discussing the most important items to have on a bike ride, cyclists generally agree on the following four items.

Helmet. The reasons to wear a helmet should be obvious. Helmets are discussed in more detail in the "Be Safe—Wear Your Armor" section.

Water. Without it, cyclists may face dehydration, which may result in dizziness and fatigue. On a warm day, cyclists should drink at least one full bottle during every hour of riding. Remember, it's always good to drink before you feel thirsty—otherwise, it may be too late.

Cycling shorts. These are necessary if you plan to ride your bike for more than 30 minutes. Padded cycling shorts may be the only thing keeping your derriere from serious saddle soreness by ride's end. There are two types of cycling shorts. Touring shorts are good for people who don't want to look like they're wearing anatomically correct cellophane. They look like regular athletic shorts with pockets, but have built-in padding in the crotch area for protection from chafing and saddle sores. The more popular, traditional cycling shorts are made of skintight material, also with a padded crotch. Whichever style you find most comfortable, cycling shorts are necessity for long rides. If you plan on riding longer distances, or for extended periods of time, you will want to invest in some chamois cream. A quality cream will help reduce friction between the points where your body meets the chamois of your shorts and help reduce, or flat out eliminate saddle sores.

Food. This essential item will keep you rolling. Cycling burns up a lot of calories and is among the few sports in which no one is safe from the "bonk." Bonking feels like it sounds. Without food in your system, your blood sugar level collapses, and there is no longer any energy in your body. This instantly results in total fatigue and light-headedness. So, when you're filling your water bottle, remember to bring along some food. Fruit, energy bars, or some other forms of high-energy food are highly recommended. Candy bars are not, however, because they will deliver a sudden burst of high energy, then let you down soon after, causing you to feel worse than before. Energy bars are available at most bike stores and are similar to candy bars, but they provide complex carbohydrate energy and high nutrition rather than fast-burning simple sugars.

Be Prepared or Die

Essential equipment that will keep you from dying alone in the woods:
- Cell Phone
- Spare Tube
- Tire Irons
- Patch Kit
- Pump/CO2 Cartridges
- Money
- Spoke Wrench
- Spare Spokes: tape these to the chain stay
- Chain Tool
- Allen Keys: Bring appropriate sizes to fit your bike

- Compass/GPS
- Duct Tape
- First–aid Kit
- Rain Gear: for quick changes in weather
- Matches
- Guidebook: In case, all else fails and you must start a fire to survive, this guidebook will serve as an excellent fire starter.
- Food and Water
- Jacket

To carry these items, you may need a bike bag. A bag mounted in front of the handlebars provides quick access to your belongings, whereas a saddlebag fitted underneath the saddle keeps things out of your way. If you're carrying lots of equipment, you may want to consider a set of panniers. These large bags mount on either side of each wheel on a rack. Many cyclists, though, prefer not to use a bag at all. Some use large hydration backpacks or they just slip all they need into their jersey pockets and off they go.

Be Safe—Wear Your Armor

While on the subject of jerseys, it's crucial to discuss the clothing you must wear to be safe, practical, and—if you prefer—stylish. The following is a list of items that will save you from disaster, outfit you comfortably, and, most important, keep you looking cool.

Helmet. A helmet is an absolute necessity because it protects your head from complete annihilation. It is the only thing that will not disintegrate into a million pieces after a wicked crash on a descent you shouldn't have been on in the first place. A helmet with a solid exterior shell will also protect your head from sharp or protruding objects. And you can of course paste several stickers from your favorite bicycle manufacturers all over the helmet's outer shell, giving

companies even more free advertising for your dollar. If you are riding along one of the several downhill-specific locations listed in the book, you may want to also invest in a full-face helmet and neck protector to avoid serious injury.

Shorts. Padded cycle shorts provide cushioning between your body and the bicycle seat. Cycle shorts also wick moisture away from your body and prevent chafing. Form-fitting shorts are made from synthetic material and have smooth seams to prevent chafing. If you don't feel comfortable wearing form-fitted shorts, baggy padded shorts with pockets are available.

Gloves. You may find well-padded cycling gloves invaluable when traveling over rocky trails and gravelly roads for hours on end. When you fall off your bike and land on your palms, gloves are your best friend. Long-fingered gloves may also be useful, as branches, trees, assorted hard objects, and occasionally small animals will reach out and whack your knuckles. Insulated gloves are essential for winter riding.

Glasses. Not only do sunglasses give you an imposing presence and make you look cool (both are extremely important), they also protect your eyes from harmful ultraviolet rays, invisible branches, creepy bugs, and dirt. They also hide your glances at riders of the opposite sex wearing skintight, revealing Lycra.

Shoes. Mountain bike shoes have stiff soles that transfer more of the power from a pedal stroke to the drive train and provide a solid platform to stand on, thereby decreasing fatigue in your feet. You can use virtually any good light outdoor hiking footwear, but specific mountain bike shoes (especially those with inset cleats) are best. They are lighter and breathe well and are constructed to work with your pedal strokes instead of the natural walking cadence.

Other clothing. To prepare for Virginia's weather, it's best to dress in layers that can be added or removed as weather conditions change. In cold weather, wear a wicking layer made of a modern synthetic fiber next to your skin. Avoid wearing cotton of any type. It dries slowly and does not wick moisture away from your skin, thus chilling you directly as it evaporates. The next layer should be a wool or synthetic insulating layer that helps keep you warm but also is breathable. A fleece jacket or vest works well as an insulating layer. The outer layer should be a jacket and pants that are waterproof, windproof, and breathable. Your ears will also welcome a fleece headband when it's cold out.

Oh! Those Chilly Metropolitan Days

If the weather chooses not to cooperate on the day you've set aside for a bike ride, it's helpful to be prepared.

Tights or leg warmers. These are best in temperatures below fifty-five degrees. Knees are sensitive and can develop all kinds of problems if they get cold. Common problems include tendinitis, bursitis, and arthritis.

Plenty of layers on your upper body. When the air has a nip in it, layers of clothing will keep the chill away from your chest and help prevent bronchitis. If the air is cool, a polypropylene long-sleeved shirt is best to wear against the skin, beneath other layers of clothing. Polypropylene, like wool, wicks away moisture from your skin to keep your body dry. Try to avoid wearing cotton or baggy clothing when the temperature falls. Cotton holds moisture like a sponge, and baggy clothing catches cold air and swirls it around your body. Good cold-weather clothing should fit snugly against your body, but not be restrictive.

Wool socks. Don't pack too many layers under those shoes, though. You may restrict circulation, and your feet will get real cold, real fast.

Thinsulate or Goretex gloves. There is nothing worse than frozen feet—unless your hands are frozen. A good pair of Thinsulate or Goretex gloves should keep your hands toasty and warm.

Keeping your head warm. Sometimes, when the weather gets really cold and you still want to hit the trails, it's tough to stay warm. Ventilated helmets are designed to keep heads cool in the summer heat, but they do little to help keep heads warm during rides in subzero temperatures. Polypropylene and thin merino wool skullcaps are great head and ear warmers that snugly fit over your head beneath the helmet without compromising protection.

All of this clothing can be found at your local bike store, where the staff should be happy to help fit you into the seasons of the year.

To Have or Have Not—Other Very Useful Items

There is no shortage of items for you and your bike to make riding better, safer, and easier. We have rummaged through the unending lists and separated the gadgets from the good stuff, coming up with what we believe are items certain to make mountain bike riding easier and more enjoyable.

Tires. Buying a good pair of knobby tires is the quickest way to enhance the off-road handling capabilities of a bike. There are many types of mountain bike tires on the market. Some are made exclusively for very rugged off-road terrain. These big-knobbed, soft rubber tires virtually stick to the ground with magnetic-like traction, but they tend to deteriorate quickly on pavement. Other tires are made exclusively for the road. These are called "slicks," and they have no tread at all. For the average cyclist, though, a good tire somewhere in the middle of these two extremes should do the trick. Realize, however, that you get what you pay for. Do not skimp and buy cheap tires. As your primary point of contact with the trail, tires may be the most important piece of equipment on a bike. With inexpensive rubber, the tire's beads may unravel, or chunks of tread might actually rip off the tire. If you're lucky, all you'll suffer is a long walk back to the car. If you're unlucky, your tire could blow out in the middle of a rowdy downhill, causing a wicked crash.

Clipless pedals. Clipless pedals, like ski bindings, attach your shoe directly to the pedal. They allow you to exert pressure on the pedals during down- and upstrokes. They also help you maneuver the bike in the air or while climbing various obstacles. Toe clips may be less expensive, but they are also heavier and harder to use. Clipless pedals and toe clips both take a little getting used to, but they're definitely worth the trouble.

Hydration Backpack. These bags are ideal for carrying keys, extra food and water, guidebooks, foul-weather clothing, tools, spare tubes, and a cellular phone, in case you need to call for help.

Bike computers, GPS receivers. These fun gadgets are much less expensive than they were in years past. They have such features as speedometers, odometers, clocks, altimeter, alarms, and GPS systems. Bike computers will come in handy when you're following these maps or just want to know how far you've ridden in the wrong direction.

Types of Off-Road Terrain

Before roughing it off-road, you may first have to ride the pavement to get to your destination. Don't be dismayed. Some of the country's best rides are on the road. Once we get past these smooth-surfaced pathways, though, adventures in dirt await us.

Rails-to-Trails. Abandoned rail lines are converted into usable public resources for exercising, commuting, or just enjoying nature. Old rails and ties are torn up and a trail, paved or unpaved, is laid along the existing corridor. This completes the cycle, from ancient Indian trading routes to railroad corridors and back again to hiking and cycling trails.

Unpaved roads. These are typically found in rural areas and are most often public roads. Be careful when exploring, though, not to ride on someone's unpaved private drive.

Forest roads. These dirt and gravel roads are used primarily as access to forestland and are kept in good condition. They are almost always open to public use.

Singletrack. Singletrack can be the most fun on a mountain bike. These trails, with only one track to follow, are often narrow, challenging pathways through the woods. Remember to make sure these trails are open before zipping into the woods. (At the time of this printing, all trails and roads in this guidebook were open to mountain bikes.)

Open land. Unless there is a marked trail through a field or open space, you should not ride there. Once one person cuts his or her wheels through a field or meadow, many more are sure to follow, causing irreparable damage to the landscape.

Techniques to Sharpen Your Skills

Many of us see ourselves as pure athletes—blessed with power, strength, and endless endurance. However, it may be those with finesse, balance, agility, and grace that get around most quickly on a mountain bike. Although power, strength, and endurance do have their places in mountain biking, these elements don't necessarily form the framework for a champion mountain biker.

The bike should become an extension of your body. Slight shifts in your hips or knees (body English) can have remarkable results. Experienced bike handlers seem to flash down technical descents, dashing over obstacles in a smooth and graceful effort as if pirouetting in Swan Lake. Here are some tips and techniques to help you connect with your bike and float gracefully over the dirt.

Braking. Using your brakes requires using your head, especially when descending. This doesn't mean using your head as a stopping block, but rather to think intelligently. Use your best judgment in terms of how much or how little to squeeze those brake levers.

The more weight a tire is carrying, the more braking power it has. When you're going downhill, your front wheel carries more weight than the rear. Braking with the front brake will help keep you in control without going into a skid. Be careful, though, not to overdo it with the front brakes and accidentally toss yourself over the handlebars. And don't neglect your rear brake! When descending, shift your weight back over the rear wheel, thus increasing your rear braking power as well. This technique will balance the power of both brakes and give you maximum control.

Good riders learn just how much of their weight to shift over each wheel and how to apply just enough braking power to each brake so not to "endo" over the handlebars or skid down a trail.

Going Uphill—Climbing Those Treacherous Hills

Shift into a low gear. Before shifting, be sure to ease up on your pedaling to decrease pressure on the chain. Find the gear that best matches the terrain and steepness of each climb.

Stay seated. Standing out of the saddle is often helpful when climbing steep hills with a road bike, but you may find that on dirt, standing may cause your rear tire to lose its grip and spin out. Climbing requires traction. Stay seated as long as you can and keep the rear tire digging into the ground. Ascending skyward may prove to be much easier in the saddle.

Lean forward. On very steep hills, the front end may feel unweighted and suddenly pop up. Slide forward on the saddle and lean over the handlebars. This position will add more weight to the front wheel and should keep you grounded.

Keep pedaling. On rocky climbs, be sure to keep the pressure on, and don't let up on those pedals! The slower you go through rough trail sections, the harder you will work.

Going Downhill—The Real Reason We Get Up in the Morning

Shift into the big chain ring, if you have one! Most modern bikes now only sport one chain ring. Shifting into the big ring (if you have one) before a bumpy descent will help keep the chain from bouncing off. And should you crash or disengage your leg from the pedal, the chain will cover the teeth of the big ring so they don't bite into your leg.

Relax. Stay loose on the bike, and don't lock your elbows or clench your grip. Your elbows need to bend with the bumps and absorb the shock, while your hands should have a firm but controlled grip on the bars to keep things steady. Steer with your body, allowing your shoulders to guide you through each turn and around each obstacle.

Don't over steer or lose control. Mountain biking is much like downhill skiing, since you must shift your weight from side to side down narrow, bumpy descents. Your bike will have the tendency to track in the direction you look and follow the slight shifts and leans of your body. You should not think so much about steering but rather the direction you wish to go.

Rise above the saddle. When racing down bumpy, technical descents, you should not sit on the saddle but instead stand on the pedals, keeping them level, and allowing your legs and knees to absorb the rocky trail.

Drop your saddle. For steep, technical descents, you may want to drop your saddle 3 or 4 inches. This lowers your center of gravity, giving you much more room to bounce around. Several manufacturers make "dropper posts" that allow you to do this on the fly.

Keep your pedals parallel to the ground. The front pedal should be slightly higher so that it doesn't catch on small rocks or logs.

Stay focused. Many descents require your utmost concentration and focus just to reach the bottom. You must notice every groove, every root, every rock, every hole, and every bump. You, the bike, and the trail should all become one as you seek single-track nirvana on your way down the mountain. But if your thoughts wander, then so may your bike, and you may instead become one with the trees!

Watch Out!

Back-Road Obstacles

Logs. When you want to hop a log, throw your body back, yank up on the handlebars, and pedal forward in one swift motion. This technique clears the front end of the bike. Then quickly scoot forward and pedal the rear wheel up and over. Keep the forward momentum until you've cleared the log, and, by all means, don't hit the brakes, or you may do some interesting acrobatic maneuvers!

Rocks. Worse than highway potholes! Stay relaxed, let your elbows and knees absorb the shock, and always continue applying power to your pedals. Staying seated will keep the rear wheel weighted to prevent slipping, and a light front end will help you respond quickly to each new obstacle. The slower you go, the more time your tires will have to get caught between the grooves.

Water. Before crossing a stream or puddle, be sure to first check the depth and bottom surface. There may be an unseen hole or large rock hidden under the water that could wash you up if you're not careful. After you're sure all is safe, hit the water at a good speed, pedal steadily, and allow the bike to steer you through. Once you're across, tap the breaks to squeegee the water off the rims.

Leaves. Beware of wet leaves. These may look pretty, but a trail covered with leaves may cause your wheels to slip out from under you. Leaves are not nearly as unpredictable and dangerous as ice, but they do warrant your attention on a rainy day.

Mud. If you must ride through mud, hit it head on and keep pedaling. You want to part the ooze with your front wheel and get across before it swallows you up. Advanced riders will generally speed through mud by lifting their front tire (small wheelie) and letting the rear guide through it. Above all, don't leave the trail to go around the mud. This just widens the path even more and leads to increased trail erosion, keep singletrack "single."

Urban Obstacles

Curbs are fun to jump, but as with logs, be careful.

Curbside drains are typically not a problem for bikes. Just be careful not to get a wheel caught in the grate.

Dogs make great pets but seem to have it in for bicyclists. If you think you can't outride a dog that's chasing you, stop and walk your bike out of its territory. A loud yell to "Get!" or "Go home!" often works, as does a sharp squirt from your water bottle right between the eyes.

Cars are tremendously convenient when we're in them, but irate motorists in big automobiles can be a real hazard when you're riding a bike. As a cyclist, you must realize that most drivers aren't expecting you to be there and often wish you weren't. Stay alert and ride carefully, clearly signaling all your intentions.

Potholes, like grates and back-road canyons, should be avoided. Just because you're on an all-terrain bicycle doesn't mean you're indestructible. Potholes regularly damage rims, pop tires, and sometimes lift unsuspecting cyclists into spectacular swan dives over the handlebars.

Last-Minute Check

Before a ride, it's a good idea to give your bike a once-over to make sure everything is in working order. Begin by checking the air pressure in your tires to make sure they are properly inflated. Modern mountain bikes are sometimes equipped with tubeless tires so pressures vary from situation to situation. We've found that about 45–55 pounds of air pressure per square inch will do the trick for most situations. If your "tubed" tires are underinflated, there is greater likelihood that the tubes may get pinched on a bump or rock, causing the tire to flat.

Looking over your bike to make sure everything is secure and in its place is the next step. Go through the following checklist before each ride.

- Pinch the tires to feel for proper inflation. They should give just a little on the sides but feel very hard on the treads. If you have a pressure gauge, use it.
- Check your brakes. Squeeze the rear brake and roll your bike forward. The rear tire should skid. Next, squeeze the front brake and roll your bike forward. The rear wheel should lift into the air. If this doesn't happen, then your brakes are too loose. Make sure the brake levers don't touch the handlebars when squeezed with full force.
- Check all quick releases on your bike. Make sure they are all securely tightened.
- Lube up. If your chain squeaks, apply some lubricant.
- Check your nuts and bolts. Check the handlebars, saddle, cranks, and pedals to make sure that each is tight and securely fastened to your bike.
- Check your wheels. Spin each wheel to see that it spins through the frame and between brake pads freely.
- Have you got everything? Make sure you have your spare tube, tire irons, patch kit, frame pump, tools, food, water, and guidebook.

Appendix: Local Bicycle Clubs and Organizations

CAMBC: Charlottesville Area Mountain Bike Club, www.cambc.org

CAMBO: Culpepper Area Mountain Bike Operators, www.cambomtb.com

EVMA: Eastern Virginia Mountain, www.evma.org

FAMBE: Fredericksburg Area Mountain Bike Enthusiasts, fambe.org

FATMUG: Fredericksburg Area Trail Management User Group, www.fatmug.org

GLOC: Greater Lynchburg Off-Road Cyclists, www.ridewithgloc.com

MORE: Mid-Atlantic Off-Road Enthusiasts, www.more-mtb.org

MTB LoCo: Mountain Bike Loudoun County, www.mtbloco.org

QMTB: Quantico Mountain Bike Club, qmtb.org

Roanoke IMBA, www.roanokeimab.org

rvaMORE: Richmond Virginia MORE, www.rvamore.org

SVBC: Shenandoah Valley Bicycle Coalition, www.svbcoalition.com

SVMBA: Southern Virginia Mountain Bike Association, www.svmba.org

Virginia Bicycling Federation, www.vabike.org

National Organizations

IMBA International Mountain Bicycling Association, www.imba.com

USA Cycling, www.usacycling.org/mtb

Rails-to-Trails Conservancy, www.railtrails.org

Ride Index

About the Author

When not working with his local IMBA chapter, MORE, **Martín Fernández** is out riding the backcountry trails and roads around Northern Virginia and the DC region looking for routes for one of his guidebooks. A native of Lima, Perú, Martín has lived in the DC region for nearly three decades. For two of those, Martín has been actively involved with MORE to ensure we have quality places to ride. Shortly after leaving the Armed Forces, Martín settled in Virginia where he now lives with his wife Courtney and daughter Ari. You may run into Martin at one of his local rides at Fountainhead, Laure Hill, Meadowood or the gravel and paved roads of Prince William Forest Park. Martín would appreciate your comments. Correspond with him and follow his activities at www.bestridesdc.com; editorial@ bestridesdc.com.

MARTIN FERNANDEZ © *Ty Long* 2014